To Doug Hardy,

With warm regards
to a fellow soldier

JAPAN'S
FINANCIAL
REVOLUTION

in the trenches of
corporate life and political
correctness. Your generous help
and unique insights made this
a much better book.

Stephen Harner

2000. 7. 13

JAPAN'S FINANCIAL REVOLUTION

AND HOW AMERICAN FIRMS ARE PROFITING

STEPHEN M. HARNER

M.E.Sharpe
Armonk, New York
London, England

Library of Congress Cataloging-in-Publication Data

Harner, Stephen M.
    Japan's financial revolution and how American firms are profiting / Stephen M. Harner
      p. cm.
    Includes bibliographical references and index.
    ISBN 0-7656-0593-7 (hardcover : alk. paper)
      1. Finance—Japan. 2. Financial crises—Japan. 3. Financial institutions—Japan.
    4. Investments, American—Japan. I. Title.

HG187.J3 H375 2000
332´.0952—dc21   99-052783

Printed in the United States of America

The paper used in this publication meets the minimum requirements of
American National Standard for Information Sciences
Permanence of Paper for Printed Library Materials,
ANSI Z 39.48-1984.

BM (c)   10   9   8   7   6   5   4   3   2   1

Table of Contents

List of Illustrations

Acknowledgments

The inspiration for this book came gradually in the months of late 1998 and 1999, when I returned to Japan after an absence of five years. Meeting again with friends and colleagues in the financial services community in Tokyo, I was impressed by their optimism and sense that we were entering a new era. For those in companies like Merrill Lynch, Citibank, Goldman Sachs, Bankers Trust, and Fidelity, the excitement was not only about the future, but about the present. Compared with five years earlier, these firms were markedly bigger and more important players, often market leaders. This was true in absolute terms. It was even more dramatically the case in comparison with the humbled and weakened conditions of Japan's domestic financial institutions. Gradually it occurred to me that this was an historic development in international finance and a dramatic story of challenge and response that deserved to be told.

It is not possible to acknowledge all of the many colleagues and friends who contributed to this work through their encouragement and advice. I will mention only a few and hope others will not feel slighted. For much help in understanding the fascinating world of Japanese consumer finance, I thank one of the world's experts in this field and a good friend, Doug Hardy of AIC Corporation. Ron Strauss, president of Merrill Lynch Japan Securities, a great leader and an old friend, was very encouraging toward the project and generously shared his thoughts on financial industry trends in Japan. Mark Fouty of Goldman Sachs was most helpful in providing information on the company's mutual funds business. Bill Wilder and Leon Kumpe of Fidelity Investments provided useful details of their company's retail and institutional strategies. For their insights into various aspects of the financial services marketplace, I am grateful to Rike Wooten of ING Barings, Fumio Umemoto of American Express, Kai Sotorp of AIG, and Milton Isa, formerly of Merrill Lynch Japan.

For logistical support during the research and writing, I am grateful to the cheerful and patient staff of the library at the Foreign Correspondents Club of Japan, as well as to the anonymous but no less helpful workers at the National Diet Library. For use of his Tokyo flat for several weeks during August, I am greatly indebted to Hiromi Yoshida. Other logistical support was provided by the Yoshida family of Nagoya, our friends of twenty years. For his wise advice on what to do after this book, I thank Atsuhiko Tateuchi, one of Japan's deservedly successful entrepreneurs. At M.E. Sharpe, Sean M. Culhane was always encouraging and a pleasure to work with.

In this and every previous project, including the project of life itself, the one indispensable and steadfast partner has been my wife, Annie.

JAPAN'S FINANCIAL REVOLUTION

Introduction

In mid-August 1999 global financial markets were jolted when the presidents of three of Japan's largest banks—Industrial Bank of Japan, Fuji Bank, and Dai-Ichi Kangyo Bank—announced plans to combine operations to form the world's largest financial institution, a gargantuan $1 trillion megabank. Given that major banks in Japan not only stand at the head of huge financial groups, but also form the dynamic core of Japan's massive *keiretsu* industrial and commercial groups, it was clear to observers that this merger would accelerate and deepen the much needed restructuring of Japan's economy that was in its tentative early stages. The breathtaking news was consumed by the market like one of Japan's energy drinks, pushing the Nikkei stock index to heights not seen in years and pushing up the value of the Japanese yen. Suddenly, all eyes were on the future. Change was in the air. Everyone was speculating on which would be the next big Japanese bank or corporation to announce a strategic merger, acquisition, or divestiture.

The year 1999 is likely to be seen as the watershed for postwar Japan's economy, certainly for its financial system. In March, only a few months before their triumphant August announcement, the same three bank presidents had joined the presidents of all but one of Japan's major banks in prostrating themselves before the Japanese government and gratefully accepting quasinationalization in the form of $61 billion in public funds. The funds were necessary to recapitalize the banks, which had accumulated hundreds of billions of dollars in loan losses. The weakened banks' problems had ramified throughout the economy, causing Japan to sink into a deepening recession. Stock prices were touching lows not seen in over a decade. A financial system collapse, leading to world financial panic, was a credible scenario.

By mid-1999, following the collapse of the asset price "bubble" during the 1990s, the Japanese financial system had been devastated. Not just a few, but most of Japan's banking, insurance, and securities firms had faced insolvency and collapse. Repeated government bailouts had resulted in virtual nationalization of the entire banking sector. Insurance firms were in most cases technically insolvent and would have been forced to close if they were operating in the United States. Probably half of Japan's securities companies were not expected to survive deregulation of brokerage commissions in 1999.

But devastation and ruin were only part of the picture, and not the most interesting part. Picking up Japan's leading financial paper, the *Nihon Keizai Shimbun*, on any day in 1999, and especially on August 20, the day of the megabank merger announcement, one was likely to feel a giddy excitement at the scope and depth of changes sweeping the financial marketplace. The year 1998 had marked the beginning of a bold three-year "big bang" deregulation and liberalization program. In 1999 the imperatives of this program for Japan's formerly slow-moving financial institutions became apparent: change, restructure, innovate, or die. It was something to which veteran observers of Japan could draw only one parallel—the forced restructuring and reconstruction of Japan's financial system following World War II. This time, however, it was not General MacArthur writing the new rules. It was the Japanese themselves.

The big bang reforms were adopted by the Japanese government after it became inescapably clear that Japan—the world's second largest economy—and its financial firms had fallen hopelessly behind trends in global finance in the 1990s. Heavy-handed bureaucrats in Japan's Ministry of Finance and cosseted managements of Japan's financial institutions had allowed Japan and its marketplace to wither, while competitors abroad, particularly in the United States and Britain, had grown massively more robust. By the late 1990s the hubris seen in Japan in the late 1980s had dissipated. Even Japan's notoriously intransigent bureaucrats could not deny the contrast between the United States' relatively quick resolution of its S&L crisis and Japan's decade-long banking crisis, America's 1990s breathtaking bull market and Japan's 1990s punishing bear market, and America's thriving venture capital market and the absence in Japan of anything comparable.

Another factor driving change, and proving the point on relative competitiveness, was the unprecedented success in Japan of foreign financial firms, particularly those from the United States. By the mid-1990s Merrill Lynch, Goldman Sachs, and Morgan Stanley, among others, were often trading more in the Japanese securities markets than Japan's leading firms. And the U.S. firms were always more profitable. In consumer banking, Citibank was innovating and gaining market share even as its "home team" Japanese rivals were puzzling over how to make consumer banking profitable. In insurance, AIG and AFLAC were proving that the Japanese insurance market was potentially lucrative if products and services offered were actually designed to meet clients' needs. In the upscale card market, American Express was establishing an unbeatable brand. Associates First Capital was anonymously "banking the unbanked" at profit margins higher than anywhere else in the world. Better, more profit-oriented management; better strategies; aggressive stances toward regulators; product innovation leveraging knowhow gained in more advanced markets; better risk management; deep pockets—these are some of the factors that have helped foreign firms emerge as winners.

In the 1998–2001 period of the big bang, more segments of the financial services marketplace will be opened to new competitors. Regulations that have stifled competition and innovation will be further removed. The Japanese financial marketplace will increasingly come to resemble those of the United States and Europe. In this new marketplace—undoubtedly the most attractive outside the United States—aggressive and innovative foreign firms, as well as a group of new Japanese firms, will join, and often surpass, Japan's major firms to realize new and greater business growth opportunities.

This book is a survey of the exciting changes taking place in Japan's financial marketplace today and of far-sighted U.S. foreign financial firms like AIG, Citigroup, Merrill Lynch, Fidelity, American Express, and GE Capital that are seizing this opportunity to establish new businesses, acquire Japanese firms, form joint ventures, introduce services, and capture clients. **Part One** analyzes major trends in Japan's financial marketplace and the content and implications of Big Bang deregulation. **Part Two** surveys the dramatic changes occurring in Japan's banking, securities, insurance, asset management, mutual funds, and consumer finance industries. An overview of each sector, supported by illustrations, aids understanding. Major developments—such as the public bailout of banks, the emergence of new megabanks, new securities alliances between Daiwa and Sumitomo and between Nikko and Citigroup, the collapse of two life insurance companies, and acquisitions in consumer finance—are examined. The key players, both Japanese and foreign, are introduced. The main business challenges and trends in each industry are analyzed.

Part Three surveys and illustrates the new groupings and alliances, and the new strategies, extending across industry sectors in the context of Big Bang deregulation and industry restructuring. This section also presents the current status of realignments and the strategies of some dominant companies and groups—Mizuho Financial Group, Sumitomo Bank, Bank of Tokyo-Mitsubishi, Nomura Securities, Sanwa Bank, and Nippon Life—as well as those of upstarts like Orix Corporation and Softbank.

Part Four expands and deepens the analysis of the growing presence and success of leading U.S. financial firms in Japan and reviews the businesses and strategies of the major players noted above, plus some others. **Part Five** will draw upon the insights of the previous sections to offer a view of the future development of Japan's financial marketplace and the ways foreign financial firms can profit from it. An **Epilogue,** written in November 1999, provides an update of important market developments that were being announced almost daily in the late fall.

It is hoped that this book will prove valuable to students of Japan and international business and also to practitioners—staff and management of financial firms seeking to take advantage of the enormous growth and profit opportunities in the Japanese marketplace.

Part One

Japan's Changing Financial Marketplace

Chapter One

Major Features of Japan's Financial Marketplace

Financial Markets Since 1990

The Bubble Period

In the late 1980s, Japan appeared unstoppable. Its currency was the world's strongest, its exporters the most competitive, its technology in the hottest commercial areas like consumer electronics, semiconductors, automobiles, machine tools, telecommunications, even computers, apparently the most advanced. Together with its manufacturers, Japanese banks, insurers, and securities firms were among the strongest in the world; or so they seemed.

In reality, easy, cheap credit, a herd instinct, unfathomable credit risk policies, a "damn-the-customer-just-sell" culture in the securities industry, unsophisticated individual and institutional investors, antiquated and quirky accounting standards, and a perverse tax regime combined to fuel one of the most extreme asset bubbles in financial history.

In the late 1980s, the market value of financial assets in Japan, including the traditional store of value—land—soared. Japanese financial institutions played a key role in fueling the expanding bubble by underwriting equity issues of Japanese corporations at astronomical P/E ratios and flogging these stocks to a gullible institutional and individual investing public. In a market rising with dizzying momentum, equity warrants became another way for traders to get into the game. Japan's commercial banks were the leaders in issuing new equity, needed to meet capital requirements as their balance sheets expanded with fixed asset investment loans, often collateralized by land.

A combination of the strong yen and an ever rising market provided Japan's largest corporations and financial institutions with virtually free money. One mechanism was the Eurobond with equity warrants attached. Japanese corporations issued the bonds, which were underwritten abroad by Japanese banks and securities companies and sold to Japanese investors, particularly insurance companies. A swap of the foreign currency (usually U.S. dollars) back into yen often produced subzero cost for the Japanese borrowers. These funds were used for investments in fixed assets both domestically and abroad. This was the era when Japanese companies outbid all others to acquire trophy properties like Rockefeller Center in the United States. The equity warrants were sold separately, usually to foreign speculators who, for a few years, had a great ride.

After the imposition of Bank of International Settlements capital adequacy standards, Japanese commercial banks became a major contributor to the stock market frenzy through repeated issues of new stock in the period 1987 through 1989. Fuelled by these and other sources, the value of new shares offered in the market swelled to ¥3,466.8 billion in fiscal 1988 and to an all-time high of ¥6,257.1 billion in fiscal 1989.

After the Bubble Burst

It is always the same. After a bubble bursts, people cannot imagine how they could have thought and behaved as they did. By the early 1990s, the absurdity and imprudence of financial thinking at the height of the bubble were obvious. Wiser now, investors faced the problem of dealing with the aftermath. A whole financial system was now under stress. What followed was ten years of pain and adjustment. The malaise was evident in the anemic growth produced by the economy during most of the decade, finally becoming contraction in 1998 (Figure 1.1). Figure 1.2 shows how Japan's stock market deflated and remained weak and directionless during virtually the entire decade of the 1990s.

The government, aided by the Bank of Japan (BOJ), repeatedly sought to revive the economy. The BOJ steadily lowered interest rates (Figure 1.3). The government launched a succession of ever larger public spending programs. Spurred by a deepening sense of crisis in 1998, emergency economic recovery legislation, including massive fiscal and monetary stimulus, was passed by the Diet, Japan's parliament, in October 1998. The legislation allocated a mind-boggling $500 billion (¥60 trillion) in public funds for restructuring the country's devastated financial system, including $208 billion (¥25 trillion) for recapitalizing its tottering banks, two of which—Long Term Credit Bank and Nippon Credit Bank—were nationalized in late 1998. In the first half of 1999 the government injected $62.5 billion in new capital into its major banks (see Chapter Three), implemented the largest ever public works supplemental budget, and provided a much-needed tax cut. On its part, the BOJ adopted a "zero interest rate" policy that essentially lowered money market borrowing rates to the cost of processing the transactions (some two basis points).

Figure 1.1 Japan's Post-Bubble Economic Slowdown

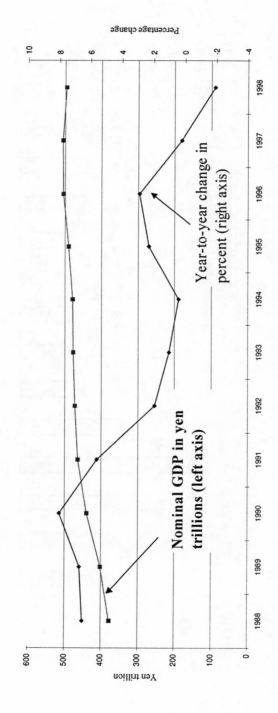

Source: Bank of Japan, *Financial and Economic Statistics Monthly.*

Figure 1.2 **Total Value of Traded Stocks and Nikkei Index by Year**

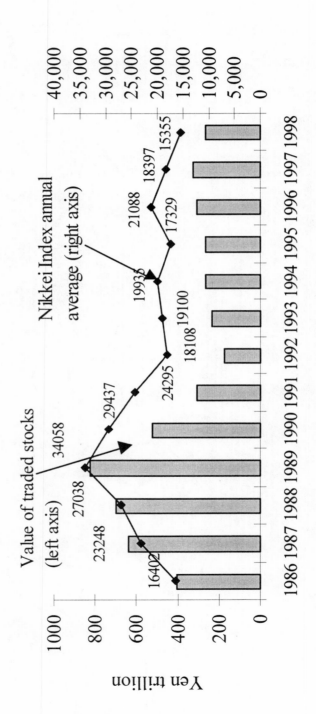

Source: Tokyo Stock Exchange, *Annual Securities Statistics, 1998.*

Figure 1.3 **BOJ Discount Rate and Money Market Rates**

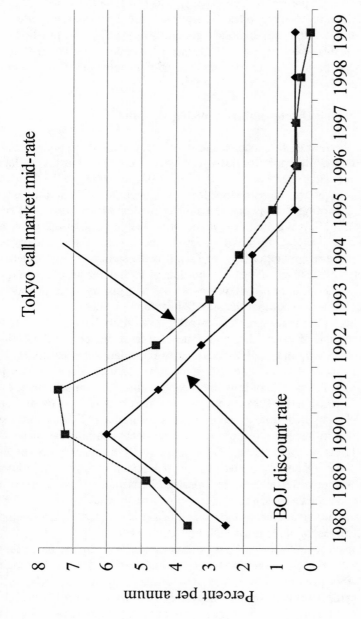

Tokyo call market mid-rate

BOJ discount rate

Percent per annum

8 7 6 5 4 3 2 1 0

1988 1989 1990 1991 1992 1993 1994 1995 1996 1997 1998 1999

Source: Bank of Japan, *Financial and Economics Statistics Monthly.*
Note: First half of 1999.

All this monetary and fiscal stimulus, and the real restructuring plan put in place for the financial system, began to take effect in 1999. By fall 1999 the stock market, in particular, recovered from its late 1998 lows to the 17,000–18,000 level on the Nikkei Index. The market's recovery had the effect of restoring some cautious optimism to a generally demoralized population. No one, however, was expecting a quick return to economic growth and rising incomes. Also, there were fundamental societal concerns that cast a shadow of doubt over the future for most Japanese.

Japan's Graying Demographics Causing Disquiet

Looking to the future, the Japanese are worried. At the core of their disquiet is their nation's demographic outlook. The average number of births per Japanese woman posted a record low of 1.38 in 1998, according to the Ministry of Health and Welfare. Japan's labor force will peak in 2005 and then begin to decline, according to Ministry of Labor estimates. More worrisome still, in the year 2007 Japan's total population will stop growing and start to decline. In twenty-five years there will be fewer Japanese than today, and, worse, they will on average be older (Figure 1.4). It is the same vexing problem as in the United States—an increasing burden of caring for an older, retired population, even as the ratio of wage earners and taxpayers to dependent oldsters declines—except that the situation in Japan is much worse.

The reality of getting older, the slowest growth since World War II, prospects for the kind of wrenching corporate restructuring seen in the United States in the 1980s, and the hard lessons of speculative losses during the 1980s have caused the Japanese to hunker down, reduce spending, and increase savings. The profile of how the Japanese allocate their savings shows that they are risk-averse, seeking the stable—if very low—yields on bank deposits and guaranteed-rate dividend-paying insurance policies rather than more volatile returns on securities. The contrast between how Japanese and U.S. households save and invest is interesting. In 1998 Japanese households were holding only 8 percent of their financial assets in securities and mutual funds, against some 32 percent for American households. Savings-type insurance products accounted for 25 percent of investments, versus 2 percent for U.S. households, and bank deposits and cash accounted for a whopping 61 percent versus 14 percent for U.S. households (Figure 1.5).

Many Japanese and foreign financial institutions—including all of those surveyed in this book—are betting that this situation will change. It undoubtedly will—the question is how fast. It is a matter of time until Japanese people's inherent risk-aversion becomes focused not on, the volatility in higher risk, higher return investments such as mutual funds, but on the fact that "sav-

Figure 1.4 **Projection for Population Growth and Aging of Japanese Society**

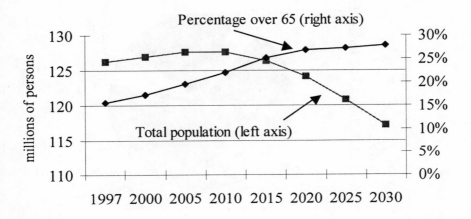

Source: Ministry of Health and Welfare.

ing" at current and expected future rates in low-risk bank deposits and insurance savings plans will not provide them the financial security they need in old age. Part of the optimism of financial service providers is based, as in the United States, on the weaknesses and credibility problems of Japan's government pension system.

A Pension System Headed for Trouble

All Japanese, and their employers, contribute to the national pension system (more detail on the system will be provided in Chapter Six). Like Social Security in the United States, retirees draw monthly pension payments until they die. As in the United States, but more so, the pension system can operate effectively only if the working population is far larger than the population drawing pensions.

In May of 1999 the Ministry of Health and Welfare made the shocking admission that government-managed corporate-employee pension schemes in Japan would likely encounter a first-ever funding shortfall, with contributions falling short of projected benefit obligation by some US$12.4 billion (¥ 1.5 trillion). It would be the first time receipts would not fully cover payouts since the program was established in 1942 (*Nikkei Weekly*, May 31, 1999). The system had roughly $1.12 trillion (¥134 trillion) in reserves as

Figure 1.5 **Allocation of Financial Assets by Households in Japan and the United States**

Japan
Total: $10,448 billion (end-1998)

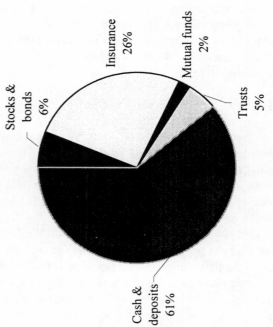

Source: Bank of Japan.

United States
Total : $26,969 billion (end-1997)

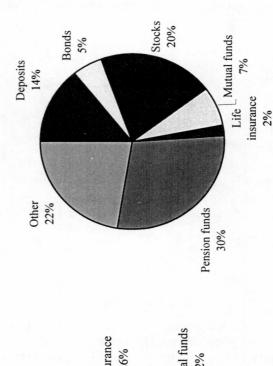

Source: U.S. Federal Reserve Board.

of March 31, 1999, and, even at low prevailing interest rates, investment income of $40 billion (¥4.8 trillion) was enough to fill the funding gap.

Japan's recession and rising unemployment accounted for much of the deterioration in the national pension accounts in fiscal 1998. However, going forward, the deficits will increasingly be structural: a declining number of contributors supporting ever more dependents. This is close to an inevitability, and the Japanese public is keenly apprehensive about the burden (in terms of higher taxes or lower benefits) that will attend any fix.

One key characteristic of Japan's pension system in 1999 is that it is entirely a "defined benefit" (DB) system—meaning that benefits are mandated and paid at certain levels. This is similar to Social Security in the United States, but it also extends to "private" pension schemes offered by most corporations. This means that Japanese corporations must plan to provide a specified benefit—annual payment or lump sum—to retirees. In the United States this corporate DB system has virtually disappeared, replaced by 401(k) plans. The 401(k) is a "defined contribution" (DC) system, meaning that benefits will change depending upon the investment performance of the individual plans. For corporations, 401(k) plans remove a huge burden of paying a predetermined benefit to retirees. It is the employee—the plan holder—who bears the downside risk of poor investment performance.

For Japan's struggling and restructuring corporations, the DB system is a luxury they can no longer afford. Moreover, most corporations have drastically underfunded their liabilities under existing DB plan programs. Kathy Matsui, a managing director and analyst at Goldman Sachs in Tokyo, was quoted in the *Financial Times* as estimating that the underfunding would be as much as US$670 billion (¥80 trillion) (*Financial Times*, May 21, 1999).

One definite response by the government to Japan's building pension crisis will be to legalize and, no doubt subtly, encourage adoption of 401(k)-type defined contribution corporate employee pension plans in 2000. Given the huge amount of money in pension plans in Japan, the introduction of 401(k) plans will constitute an epical event for financial institutions providing related services. The massive growth of the mutual fund industry in the United States over the past twenty years is often attributed to the advent of 401(k) and IRA plans for individuals. A similar impetus to mutual funds companies and asset managers can be expected as 401(k)s become a reality in Japan (please refer to Chapter Six for details).

Government Competition: The Postal Savings System

To an extent almost unimaginable to most Americans, whose domestic economic and financial system is relatively free of direct government competi-

Figure 1.6 **Personal Savings in Japan by Financial Institution**

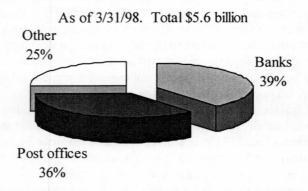

As of 3/31/98. Total $5.6 billion

Other
25%

Banks
39%

Post offices
36%

Source: Bank of Japan, *Financial and Economic Statistics Monthly.*

tion, Japan's economy and its private financial institutions have for decades been hugely influenced, often even dominated, by public institutions and public policy decisions. A useful guide to this pervasive influence is provided by a book, *Japan's Public Sector: How the Government Is Financed*, edited by Tokue Shibata. In surveying the Japanese marketplace, we cannot fail to mention the postal savings system.

Japan's post office collects deposits and lends these funds to various government agencies through the Fiscal Investment and Loan Program (FILP) to support government programs (see Chapter Six). Thus, it functions like a state-run bank, but without the need to make a profit and with an explicit state guarantee against failure. For many years the post office was able to offer rates and products that were more attractive than those of private commercial banks. Even today, the post office—with some 25,000 offices throughout the country, more than all private bank branches combined, subsidized staff and premises, no reserve requirements, and its state guarantee—competes unfairly with commercial and savings banks, and reduces the overall system's profitability and efficiency.

In the early postwar period, when Japan's banks were smaller and less able to meet the developing nation's need for intermediation between saving and investment, particularly public investment, the postal savings system served a useful purpose. Today, few would argue that its presence and role are justified from an economic policy point of view. The same doubt exists with respect to the FILP as a whole, and this system is slated for massive restructuring, possibly leading to its termination in the years ahead. Justified or not, the postal savings system enjoys great public support and patronage, as we see from Figure 1.6.

In the fiscal year ending March 1998, according to BOJ, individual savings in the postal system totaled $2,004 billion (¥240,524 billion), which was approximately 36 percent of all personal savings in all financial institutions in Japan. Clearly, as we will see in later chapters, this massive patronage exerts influence on the competitive marketplace. Some such influence is sure to be felt in 2000 and 2001 when some $880 billion in ten-year term deposits, established a decade earlier at high rates of interest, will mature. The Postal and Communications Ministry estimates that perhaps half the amount maturing will be withdrawn. The promise of attracting these funds is an important element in the Japanese financial market and a reason for cautious optimism and fierce competition among providers of such products as mutual funds.

Chapter Two

The Big Bang — Now and Tomorrow

Origins and Objectives of the Big Bang

What is the purpose of Japan's big bang financial system reforms? In any program so sweeping, it is to be expected that the sponsors would have numerous objectives. One way to begin to answer the question is to consider the context in which the program was conceived and adopted, looking at both the sponsors and those most affected.

One of the most exhaustive and instructive studies of Japanese financial reform and the big bang is Maximilian J. B. Hall's *Financial Reform in Japan: Causes and Consequences* (1998). Hall makes the point that deregulation in Japan's financial markets had been making slow progress since the 1970s. In the late 1970s Japan's financial institutions and markets were rigidly regulated and segmented—the three principal segments being securities, banking, and insurance—and Japan's system was largely insulated and protected from international competition and influences by strict foreign exchange controls. Interest rates were virtually completely determined by the decision of Ministry of Finance (MOF) and Bank of Japan (BOJ) officials, not by market forces, and every product idea and innovation required bureaucratic review and approval, which was not readily forthcoming.

Deregulation Begins in the 1980s

The 1980s saw the market become more internationalized with the venturing of Japanese banks and securities companies abroad and an even greater influx of foreign banks and securities companies to Japan. Deregulation of interest rates and relaxation on foreign exchange transactions began. New domestic markets and instruments successively appeared. Feeling powerful as Japan's wealth and liquidity expanded and, after the Plaza Accord of 1985, with the yen the world's strongest currency, conservative bureaucrats in the MOF and BOJ began to accept that deregulation was not only desirable, but possible. Indeed, some liberalization of investment mechanisms and capital flows became inevitable as Japan needed to recycle its huge payments surpluses with the rest of the world. The 1986 Securities Investment Advisory law broadens investment channels by allowing specialized investment management companies, including foreign companies, to compete with trust banks and life insurance companies in managing institutional customers' pension funds.

The MOF and the "Convoy System"

Many practices and attitudes did not change so easily, however, because they were rooted in bureaucratic and financial self-interest. The banking, securities, and insurance industries were regulated by specific, dedicated bureaus in the MOF. "Clientitis" ensured that each bureau fought to protect and advance the interests of its particular industry segment, usually at the expense of other segments. Banks wanted to enter the securities business; securities companies wanted to offer banking-type products, like Cash Management Accounts; insurance companies wanted change regulations that kept life and nonlife insurance sectors separate and noncompetitive. During the 1980s and most of the 1990s, unending turf conflicts were a prominent feature of any deregulation movement.

A second distinguishing characteristic of regulation was the so-called "convoy system." The bureaus supervising and regulating the securities, banking, and insurance industries saw their first duty as ensuring that each industry segment remained healthy, with no failures or shocks that might undermine public confidence in the financial system. No financial institution would be allowed to fail. As noted previously, this objective protected the industry from encroachments from outside. It also meant, in practice, ensuring that when firms grew weak the MOF would arrange a merger or tie-up with a stronger firm in the same industry. It also led to regulators stifling competitive products or strategies that one firm might wish to use to gain advantage over others in its industry. The industry segment was expected to move together in convoy fashion, slowing to the pace of the slowest member, not allowing any member to get too far out in front, and protecting all members from outside attacks.

Tentative Steps in Cross-Sectoral Entry in 1993

As Japan entered the 1990s and the depressing effect of post-bubble deflation began to take its toll, even the conservative MOF bureaucrats agreed to further loosen the financial system. The result was the Financial System Reform Act of 1993. This was an important, but still limited step to allow firms to do business across sectoral boundaries through wholly owned, separately capitalized subsidiaries (except insurance). Progress was slow, however, as MOF officials sought to shape the result by allowing certain players to diversify first: long-term credit banks and trust banks were generally favored at the expense of ordinary banks (Hall 1998, p. 127). The institutions themselves—evincing a complacent management mentality presumably nurtured by years of protection and subservience to the MOF—often made only halfhearted efforts to build the new businesses.

In many cases, the 1993 measures restricted the wholly owned subsidiaries in ways that crippled their competitiveness and their profit potential. For example, securities subsidiaries of banks were not allowed to engage in brokerage operations—that is, to trade stocks—but were restricted to underwriting bonds. They were really not in a position to compete with full securities firms, but rather functioned as adjuncts to the debt-raising activities of the banks. Notwithstanding these difficulties, by the end of 1997, some twenty banks had securities subsidiaries, and eighteen financial concerns operated trust banks. In September 1996, life insurance and nonlife insurance companies were allowed to enter each other's businesses through wholly owned subsidiaries.

Prime Minister Hashimoto Announces the Big Bang

By 1996 pressures for fuller liberalization had grown irresistible. The context was the growing awareness of the weakness and relative backwardness of Japan's financial system and of the system's pernicious effects on Japan's overall economic strength and social stability. By the mid-1990s, Japan's financial and economic system was locked in a structural crisis that only profound structural change could hope to resolve.

In November 1996 Prime Minister Hashimoto announced plans to accelerate reform with the aim of restructuring Japan's financial market so that it would be truly on a par with those of New York and London. He officially instructed the MOF and the Ministry of Justice to work out measures for a deregulation program to begin in 1998. The government set up five government-industry councils that, over the next year, diligently and meticulously drafted plans for changes across the entire financial and regulatory system. The results were incorporated in the government's "Three Year Deregulation Plan," released in March 1998, and in an omnibus Financial System Reform Bill, which was passed by the Diet on December 1, 1998. The program was labeled the "big bang," but it was vastly more sweeping and profound than the similarly named securities-related reforms introduced in London in 1986 (Hall 1998, p. 139).

"Free, Fair, Global"

"Free, fair, global"—these are the watchwords offered for the spirit and objectives of Japan's big bang reform.

Free means the liberalization of many highly restricted financial activities, such as foreign exchange transactions and the operation of expatriation of assets (e.g., opening accounts abroad) by Japanese residents; greater freedom—registration versus approval—to begin financial businesses; and lowering of barriers to entry between financial sectors.

Fair means greater transparency and standardization of rules and regulations, and measures to ensure equal treatment of all participants. Fairness also entails withdrawing administrative intervention and placing the burden of risk management on the individual investor.

Global means adopting practices and procedures common in global (read: U.S.) financial markets and discarding practices that have often made Japan the odd man out. These include quirky and inadequate accounting and disclosure standards, certain taxation rules, and other regulatory practices and conventions. Subtly but importantly, *global* means that Japanese enterprises should introduce a Western way of thinking. Companies should begin to give priority to the interests of their owners, government should withdraw from most commercial, economic and financial activities, and individuals should begin to take responsibility for their own financial decisions.

Key Elements of the 1998 Big Bang Legislation

The reform measures of the omnibus Financial System Reform Bill—revising twenty-two laws—were divided by their sponsors into five groupings:

1. those designed to expand *user choice*
2. those designed to improve the *quality of service* and to *promote competition* among intermediaries
3. those designed to ensure the development of an *"easy-to-use"* market
4. those designed to ensure the establishment of a *"fair"* market
5. those designed to preserve *financial stability* in the face of financial reform and structural upheaval (Hall 1998, p. 139).

Table 2.1 provides details of the measures and their scheduled implementation. In a departure from normal Japanese bureaucratic style, implementation of most of the reform was "front loaded" to begin December 1, 1998, or early in 1999. Among the reforms that were implemented on December 1

Table 2.1

Key Elements of Japan's Big Bang Financial System Reform

Measures designed to expand user choice
- Lifting of restrictions on derivative transactions
- Money management funds to be allowed to introduce asset management accounts
- Banks to be allowed to sell securities investment trusts (mutual funds) and
- Insurance
- Legislation to facilitate securitization; e.g., providing legal framework for "special purpose companies"
- Liberalization of cross-border transactions

Measures designed to improve the quality of service and to promote competition
- Holding company system to be allowed
- Securities companies to be licensed via registration, rather than approval Approval system only for special activities, such as OTC derivatives and underwriting
- Liberalization of control on business scope of subsidiaries
  - ✓ Restrictions on business scope of banks' securities subsidiaries to be lifted in latter half of FY99
  - ✓ Insurance companies and other financial institutions allowed to enter each other's business by area-specific subsidiaries by April 2001 at the latest. Insurance companies allowed to enter banking, trust and securities business via separate subsidiaries; and securities companies allowed to enter insurance business through separate subsidiaries.
- Ordinary banks allowed to issue corporate bonds.
- Restriction of FX services to authorized foreign exchange banks abolished.
- System of obligatory specialization abolished, allowing securities companies to elect which securities-related activities to pursue and to engage in non-securities-related activities.
- Total deregulation of brokerage commissions by October 1999
- Promoting development of electronic money and electronic payment systems
- Diversifying non-banks' funding sources—nonbanks allowed to issue corporate bonds and commercial paper
- Compulsory use by members of a (nonlife) insurance industry rating system for setting premium rates abolished
- Liberalization of foreign exchange business

Measures to ensure development of an "easy-to-use" market
- Measures to promote use of financial futures
- Improvement of short-term money market trading and settlement practices and systems
- Liberalization of cross-border capital transactions: approval requirements for external settlements and capital transactions to be abolished
- Opening of off-exchange trading of listed securities
- Liquidity of registered OTC JASDAQ (Japanese Securities Dealers' Automated Quotation) market to be improved
- Trading and intermediating of unlisted and unregistered securities by securities companies to be allowed

Measures to ensure a "fair" market
- Strengthening of disclosure requirements
  - ✓ Financial disclosure to be primarily on a consolidated accounting and business basis
  - ✓ Accounting of financial instruments to include mark-to-market valuation
- External audit practice to conform to international standards
- Definition of "securities" to be updated so new products are covered in regulations for investor protection
- Securities and Exchange Law to be updated and expanded with rules to cover conflicts of interest, market manipulation, and insider trading
- Systems of inspection, surveillance, and enforcement enhanced; penalties violations to be increased
- System for dealing with civil disputes to be enhanced, including legal basis for mediation by self-regulating organization (e.g., Japan Securities Dealers' Association)
- * User protection to be enhanced in regard to confidentiality, consumer credit protection, etc
- Investor protection to be enhanced. Segregation of customers' assets mandated by April 1, 1999, and Securities Deposit Compensation Fund scheme to be strengthened

Measures to help preserve financial stability
- "Prompt corrective action" introduced, based on capital adequacy ratios, whereby authorities can take administrative action in advance of financial institution insolvency
- Reduction of settlement risk, e.g., BOJ-NET to be moved to an RTFS basis

Source: Hall, *Financial Reform in Japan*, pp. 140-146

---

were: (1) the change from approval to registration for setting up new securities companies; (2) legalization of a holding company structure; (3) permission for securities companies to sell life and nonlife insurance as agents; (4) permission for life insurance companies to set up investment trust (mutual funds) companies; (5) permission of banks and life insurance companies to sell mutual funds through their branch networks; and (6) permission for nonbanks to raise funds through issuance of bonds.

Essence of the Big Bang: Cross-Sectoral Entry and New Market Entrants

The epochal changes sweeping the Japanese financial marketplace are essentially the positioning moves of old and new players striving under new rules to approach customers with attractive products. The previous regulated segmentation of product and market sectors, as well as of prices, denied customers choice and inhibited competition and innovation.

Table 2.2

What Can a Financial Institution Do Ultimately as a Group?

	Bank	Trust Bank	Securities Company	Insurance Company
Banking business	Separation of short- and long-term finance weakens. (Long-term deposits. issuance of bonds.)	Normal banking services and medium-term lending.	CMA allowed. Access thru ATM *Bank subsidiary	*Bank subsidiary
Trust business	Trust bank subsidiary. Pension trust, etc. Full trust products and services by FY02.		Trust bank subsidiary. Pension trust, etc.	*Trust bank subsidiary
Securities business	Securities subsidiary. Stock & its derivatives: personal & secondary. Investment trusts: sales. *Investment trust management company.	Securities subsidiary. Stock & its derivatives: personal & secondary. Investment trusts: sales. *Investment trust management company.	Commission freed. Securities transaction tax abolished. Discretionary account (wrap account) allowed.	*Securities subsidiary *Investment trust management subsidiary. Sales agency for investment trusts.
Insurance business	Insurance sales *Insurance subsidiary (underwriting)	Insurance sales* Insurance subsidiary (underwriting)	Insurance sales *Insurance subsidiary (underwriting)	Mutual entry between life and casualty insurances through subsidiaries. Casualty insurance premium freed.

Sources: Author and industry sources.

Notes: 1. Underlined: allowed before the Big Bang. 2. *subsidiary probably under financial holding company. 3. Investment advisory companies not included; are allowed for all types of financial institutions and can also manage investment trusts.

Table 2.2 presents an outline of the ultimate scope of cross-sectoral entry offered by the big bang. In most instances, the ultimate reality was already present in 1999. And while a few of the reforms—for example, the, entry of banks and securities companies into insurance—are scheduled for the end of the three-year process, that is, in 2001, it appears that ways are being found to advance the process and regulators are doing little to slow things down.

Institutional Changes: Fall of the MOF Empire

The meltdown in Japan's financial system during the 1990s put paid to the conceit, widely held among Japanese in the late 1980s, that their unique system of government-by-bureaucracy was without serious flaws. The bubble and its abrupt deflation were widely attributed to the policies of the BOJ (which had been too willing to accommodate the requests of the United States). But the greatest public wrath and disillusionment were directed toward the MOF. The criticism was justified and inevitable because of the extent to which the MOF controlled economic and financial policies and practice.

No ministry elsewhere in the world had such wide-ranging powers over, *inter alia*, national and local budgets, taxation, financial supervision, and management of state-owned assets (Hall 1998, p. 181). The MOF's supervision and management of the financial sector was a particular focus of criticism. As Japan's banks, securities companies, and insurance companies sank further toward insolvency and, in many cases, like the *jusen* housing loan companies, Hyogo Sogo Bank, and Hokkaido Takushoku Bank, required massive bailouts using taxpayer funds, it was correctly concluded that the MOF had failed in its prudential management role.

Scandals focused attention on the conflicts of interest inherent in the MOF's functions as supervisory agency, regulator, inspector, and manager of problem cases of financial institutions, many of whose executives were retired MOF officials. Such conflicts either clearly explained or were suspected to explain why the MOF had so consistently failed to discover, disclose, and deal with the problems of failing institutions.

Also, a key element of the big bang reforms was bringing Japan into conformity with Western market practice. This required a change from the kind of "discretionary" bureaucratic guidance that had been the hallmark of MOF practice over the years. What was needed was clearly codified financial laws (provided by the Financial System Reform Law) and regulation based on such "transparent" rules by dedicated professional administrators. The discredited MOF was the wrong agency to administer Japan's new financial system in the twenty-first century.

Birth of the Financial Supervisory Agency and the Financial Reconstruction Commission

In March 1997 the Cabinet approved a bill to establish a new supervisory agency, the Financial Supervisory Agency (FSA). Legislation was passed by the Diet in June 1997. The agency was officially inaugurated on June 22, 1998. When conceived in 1997, the FSA was intended to assume the licensing, inspection, supervision and problem resolution responsibilities of the MOF, with respect to banks, securities firms, and insurance companies. Prior to its establishment, however, it was apparent that the work of cleaning up and restructuring weak and failed institutions was going to be so great as to overwhelm any organization that was not dedicated to the task. It was therefore decided to establish another agency for the specific purpose of resolving the issues of weak or failed institutions. This new agency was called the Financial Reconstruction Commission (FRC). Unlike the FSA, which was a new government agency whose existence was open-ended, the FRC was mandated to complete its work in a three-year period ending in March 2002.

The parallel existence of the FSA and the FRC caused much confusion at the outset, requiring time before the division of labor between the two agencies was clear. While there is still overlap, the clear division is between inspection and licensing, which is the preserve of the FSA, and management of problem cases, which belongs to the FRC. The first and most important accomplishment of the FRC was recapitalization and the approval of restructuring plans for Japan's major banks in March 1999 (see Chapter Three for details).

The FSA and FRC are staffed by former officials of the MOF. MOF remains charged with planning and drafting regulations for the financial sector. But its new, narrower role must be humiliating to many of the remaining bureaucrats. As of this writing, a further humiliation is planned for the formerly omnipotent and august MOF, whose name in Japanese—*Okurasho*—is held in great reverence by all MOF employees and many other people in the country. It is to change the ministry's name to Ministry of the Treasury (*Zaimusho*), which would be an appellation in both Japanese and English similar to the bureaucratic counterparts of the MOF in the United States and elsewhere. In effect, the MOF will become, in name as well as in fact, just another government ministry.

Part Two

The Playing Fields

Chapter Three

Banking Sector Imbroglio

It was a spectacle unlike anything seen before, an event the like of which no one could remember. In March 1999, fifteen of the largest private commercial banking institutions in the world, banks with names like Industrial Bank of Japan (IBJ), Dai-Ichi Kangyo Bank (DKB), Sumitomo, and Fuji—virtually the entire banking sector in the world's second largest economy—humbly and ashamedly approached their government for capital funds. This being Japan, the funds—$60.5 billion (¥7,259 billion)—were duly provided. (A year earlier, most of the same banks—and others—had received government aid amounting to some $17 billion.) There was hardly any choice, either for the banks or for the government. Japan's banking system was essentially insolvent and on the verge of collapse. Two of the three specialized long-term lending banks, Long Term Credit Bank (LTCB) and Nippon Credit Bank (NCB), had already collapsed and been nationalized in October and November of 1998.

Overview of the Banking Sector in 1999

By the late 1980s, Japan's commercial banks had become among the most powerful financial institutions in the world. Compared with banks anywhere else, their balance sheets were huge, so that in rankings of global banks by assets, usually eight or nine of the top ten banks were Japanese. A number of factors accounted for the banks' prominence. The strong yen had the effect of inflating the relative value of the banks' predominantly yen assets. More fundamentally, Japan's system allowed nationwide banking, so that the largest banks—called *city banks*—had nationwide networks. In the decades after World War II, these banks played the essential—if traditional—role of channeling consumer savings to industry for investment. For decades, these banks have been the primary source of capital for Japan's largest and most powerful corporate enterprises (see Table 3.1 for a list of Japan's major banks).

Most of today's city banks have their origins as the financial nuclei of Japan's large enterprising groupings (*keiretsu*). A number of bank mergers have reduced the city banks from thirteen in the 1980s to ten in 1999. The

Table 3.1

Japan's Largest Banks by Assets (March 31, 1999)

City Banks plus IBJ	Total assets in Yen (billions)	Total assets in US$ (billions)	
→ *Mizuho Financial Group*	*141,008*	*1,175*	→ from fall 2000
Bank of Tokyo Mitsubishi	69,807	582	
— DKB*	52,534	438	
Sumitomo Bank	51,531	429	
Sanwa Bank	47,593	397	
Sakura Bank	47,209	393	
— Fuji Bank*	46,385	387	
— Industrial Bank of Japan*	42,089	351	
Tokai Bank	30,363	253	
Asahi Bank	28,637	239	
Daiwa Bank	15,515	129	

Trust banks	Total assets in Yen (billions)	Total assets in US$ (billions)	Assets in trust in Yen (billions)
Mitsubishi Trust	16,999	142	31,860
→ *Combined Chuo-Mitsui***	*12,648*	*122*	*44,794*
Sumitomo Trust	14,619	122	36,094
— Mitsui Trust**	9,438	79	29,555
Toyo Trust	7,910	66	28,311
Yasuda Trust	6,957	58	22,160
— Chuo Trust**	5,210	43	15,239
Nippon Trust	1,497	12	5,900

Sources: Company reports.
Note: *IBJ, Fuji Bank, and DKB to come under joint holding company from fall 2000.
**Chuo Trust and Mitsui Trust will merge on April 1, 2000.

combination of IBJ, Fuji Bank, and DKB in 2002 will further reduce their numbers, as will additional expected mergers (see below). In some cases, as with Sakura Bank, formerly Mitsui Bank and the nucleus of the Mitsui Group, the names have also changed, but the *keiretsu* affiliations are still strong. (The future of these bank-*keiretsu* relationships will be covered in Chapter Nine.)

As previously mentioned, regulations after World War II segmented financial markets and intermediates, creating barriers to cross-entry. Within sectors, such as banking, subsegments were created. Thus, in addition to the city banks, there were three *long-term credit banks* set up after World War II to provide long-term credit to industry. They were the LTCB, IBJ, and NCB. IBJ over the years graduated from being a specialized long-term credit bank to be included among the city banks.

The provision of corporate and individual trust services, including pension fund asset management, was another subsegment, for which specialized institutions were licensed. These *trust banks* were in the privileged position of providing both trust services and ordinary banking services. Trust banks have been permitted to offer attractive special trust deposit products with names like "Big" and "Hit" that provided them with intermediate-term funds, used to make intermediate-term fixed asset and real estate development loans. Until the early 1990s there were only eight domestic trust banks, usually affiliated with one of the *keiretsu* groups, and nine foreign ones. By 1999, after new regulations allowed securities companies and commercial banks to enter trust banking through separate subsidiaries, the number had swollen to close to forty. In terms of size and relationships, the older trust banks continue to dominate this business. Given competition and consolidation of banks, the number of trust banks in 1999 is likely to peak.

A tier below the city banks are the *regional banks*, about sixty in number, that originate in Japan's diverse prefectures and cities and tend to serve narrow geographic regions; and "second association" regional banks, like the former but smaller. There are a number of specialized banks providing finance for small- and medium-sized corporations and serving agriculture and fisheries. Public sector (nondepository) banks include the Japan Development Bank and the Export-Import Bank of Japan.

A final category is *foreign banks,* of which there are over ninety. At the top of the system is the Bank of Japan (BOJ), the Central Bank.

The 1999 Recapitalization of City Banks

Given their proud and *keiretsu* origins, one can only imagine the humiliation of the fifteen banks that received public recapitalization in March 1999. These were nine of the ten city banks (Bank of Tokyo-Mitsubishi [BOTM] was able to decline, although it had accepted ¥10 billion in public funds in 1998), IBJ, and five trust banks. Several points may be made about this historic public bailout.

1) The recapitalization was vital to allow the banks to establish provisions for their massive bad loan portfolios and, at the same time, to maintain capital ratios sufficient to meet prudential and international capital adequacy ratios.

At the fiscal year 1998 financial reporting date of March 31, 1999, Japan's seventeen major banks (including BOTM) took bad-loan write-offs and built loan loss provisions totaling $87 billion (¥10.4 trillion). The nine city banks that received public money wrote-off or established bad debt provisions for $61 billion (¥7.3 trillion) in loans.

This dramatic action was proof that the banks' (and the Ministry of Finance's [MOF]) previous strategy—that of underestimating bad debts and hoping for economic recovery to help them "grow out" of the problem—was untenable. Under the weight of these mammoth nonperforming assets and gradually increasing write-offs, Japanese banks had encountered liquidity and capital adequacy problems. They had been forced to reduce credit extensions and call in loans, which had contributed to the contractionary pressures in the economy and a sinking stock market. These factors, in turn, were causing the banks' portfolios and capital ratios to deteriorate further. By 1998 Japan's banking system meltdown seemed (and was in fact) capable of plunging the economy into deep recession.

As a consequence of making provisions and write-offs, all seventeen of the largest banks except BOTM posted losses for the year, the largest that of Sakura Bank, which lost $6.3 billion (¥754 billion). Notwithstanding these losses, the banks' capital ratios after the recapitalization were bolstered to well above international standard levels.

The big question is whether the write-offs and provisions were such as to dispose of all or most of the bad debts in the banks' portfolios. If so, then the industry—and the economy—may be said to have weathered this storm.

2) The Japanese banking system was nearly nationalized, if temporarily. Of the total $60.5 billion (¥7,259 billion) injected into the fifteen banks, $45.5 billion (¥5,459 billion) was in exchange for convertible preferred shares, ¥600 billion in redeemable (bond type) preferred stock, and ¥1,200 in subordinated loans. Table 3.2 presents a summary of the recapitalization program for all the banks except Bank of Yokohama. The Financial Reconstruction Commission (FRC), in charge of the recapitalization and restructuring process, assigned different conditions to the provision of public capital, depending upon its assessment of the bank's restructuring plan. More severe conditions were ascribed to banks considered to be weaker, which seemed generally to be the trust banks.

Key among the conditions were the timing and price at which the state could convert its nonvoting preferred shares to common, actually taking a voting interest in the banks. Figure 3.2 shows the degree of nationalization that would occur if the FRC converted its shares at the floor price (set at some 70 percent of the initial conversion prices) and the time frame after which conversion was allowed. Conversion prices will be reviewed every year and adjusted either upward or downward in a complicated process of evaluating the banks' restructuring progress.

Suffice it to conclude here that the massive injection of state funds and at least the potential for the Japanese government to take a controlling position in the banks have temporarily placed the banks under effective state control. As long as significant public ownership of their shares continues, the banks

Table 3.2

Potential Degree of Nationalization of Fourteen Large Banks Receiving Public Funds

	Public funds received (Yen billions)	Provisions for NPL in 2H FY98 (Yen billions)	Capital ratio at 3/99 (%)	Period to start of preferred share conversion	Degree of nationalization (%)
IBJ	600	900	11.2	4 yrs 3 mos	25.1
DKB	900	970	10.2	5 yrs 4 mos	14.7
Sakura	800	994	11.7	3 yrs 6 mos	45.4
Fuji	1,000	700	10.9	5 yrs 6 mos	29.4
Sumitomo	501	1,050	10.2	3 yrs 1 mo	22.0
Daiwa	408	363	12.4	3 mos	35.6
Sanwa	700	900	10.7	2 yrs 3 mos	18.4
Tokai	600	560	12.1	3 yrs 3 mos	34.2
Asahi	500	634	11.2	3 yrs 3 mos	23.5
Mitsui Trust	400	418	12.8	3 mos	46.7
Mitsubishi Trust	300	501	10.6	4 yrs 4 mos	21.0
Sumitomo Trust	200	395	12.6	2 yrs	18.9
Toyo Trust	200	365	13.2	3 mos	33.9
Chuo Trust	150	104	13.5	3 mos	34.9

Sources: Company reports. *Weekly Toyo Keizoi*, April 17, 1999.

receiving state funds will be obliged to accept any guidance offered by the FRC. This is why it is widely believed that the banks will do their best to redeem the state-held shares, using either profits or new private equity funds, or both, as soon as possible and long before conversion is possible.

3) The recapitalization was inevitably political, but it could have been worse. Like other smaller efforts in the past, the recapitalization was rightly criticized as indiscriminate, meaning that money was offered to essentially everybody—relatively weak and poorly managed banks as well as relatively good ones. But this perception is not entirely accurate. Differential conditions applied suggest that the government was rendering some judgment. More importantly, the FRC stipulated that any further assistance would be forthcoming only if the banks were fulfilling the commitments of their restructuring programs.

Bank Restructuring Programs

All the banks receiving public funds were required to submit multi-year restructuring plans to the FRC, and the FRC was required to approve these plans before money was offered. Even banks not receiving money at this time, like BOTM, offered restructuring plans as a follow-up to assistance received previously. We are thus offered an amazing panorama of plans for essentially all Japan's major private banks (the merger initiative of IBJ, Fuji Bank, and DKB announced on August 20, 1999 [see below] largely altered their plans). Table 3.3 summarizes these plans.

For every bank that received public funds, restructuring means downsizing: cutting assets, expenses, and people (in the case of the IBJ, Fuji Bank, and DKB merger, the whole entity will be smaller than the sum of its parts—see below). According to the plans, the total number of employees of fourteen banks is to decline 13.6 percent, or 18,625, from 136,933 in March 1999 to 118,308 in March 2003. Nonpersonnel expenses (excluding computer system investment) are to decline from ¥1,343 billion to ¥1,268 billion. Restructuring also means increasing profitability, though the degree of improvement in every case seems modest. It is doubtless true that both the banks' managements and the FRC felt it prudent to set conservative and achievable targets. Of the banks receiving public funds, the aggregate net business profit is projected to expand ¥760 billion, or 30 percent, from FY99 to FY02, which may be considered modest.

The reason that restructuring banks will be getting smaller (and as banks merge, the whole will be smaller than the sum of the original parts), rather than bigger, is that the FRC has insisted that they cut money-losing activities and businesses. Such rationalization will encompass many activities, but clear and easy targets are overseas offices and most overseas lending, and domestic lending to large corporations. The lending that will be increased is to medium-sized enterprises and consumers, both because this is desired by the FRC and because it does provide the best chance for the banks to improve profit margins.

The Japanese banks' retreat from foreign business began after the Asian financial crisis in fall 1997 and accelerated during 1998. The process will continue, so that, in a few years, only BOTM will be a significant international player.

What is Wrong with Japanese Banks?

The fall from glory of the Japanese banks is one of the major global financial events of the 1990s. What caused this fall? Of course, the issue is complex, but it is not a great over-simplification to identify two main problems: (1) inability to manage profitability and (2) inability to manage risk.

The Problem of Profitability

Compared with American banks, Japanese banks are bizarrely unbalanced. They have huge assets, but surprisingly few employees (to become even fewer). Given that financial services companies are people-intensive business, there appears to be a mismatch here. The image of a dinosaur—great, distended body and egg-sized brain—comes to mind. Notwithstanding the banks' extensive branch networks, other operating expenses are also low. *The clear problem is that Japanese banks have not been able to earn reasonable gross returns on their huge asset bases.*

The disparity in profitability between U.S. commercial banks and Japanese commercial banks is evident in Table 3.4. It shows that in FY97, although operating expenses for Japanese banks were far lower than for U.S. banks, the operating profit ratio was less than one-fourth that of U.S. banks. Besides expenses, the big disparities occur in net interest income as a percent of assets and, most dramatically, in noninterest income. In the simplest terms, Japanese banks have earned only a fraction of both the interest and fees on their assets that U.S. banks have been able to earn.

There are, of course, many reasons for this discrepancy, but they probably can be summarized as the fault of Japanese bank managements and, inevitably, government. Japanese managements have fairly consistently displayed styles and behavior that could be generalized as conservative, risk-averse, unimaginative, passive, and overly deferential to bureaucratic leadership and direction. Habits nurtured in the "convoy system" of MOF regulation seem to have engendered or encouraged lock-step mind-sets and behavior. Certainly, a herd mentality is not unknown in U.S. or European banking circles, but the tendency in Japan seems extreme. Moreover, both Japanese bank management and staff seem particularly inclined to view their role as collecting deposits from individual customers and lending the funds to cherished corporate relationships.

One of the main reasons for the disparity in profitability is that, while banks in the United States quickly reoriented themselves to the consumer finance market when corporate lending spreads narrowed, Japanese banks never made the transition. A large part of the highly lucrative consumer lending market is in the hands of consumer finance companies (we shall study these in Chapter Eight). Japanese banks have never seriously tried to make money in their credit card businesses. Rather, they have treated these businesses as loss-leader services, designed to engender depositor loyalty. Indeed, while continuing to fawn over and indulge their corporate banking relationships, Japanese banks have usually ignored or declined to pursue aggressively the profit potential of providing differentiated services to consumers.

MOF regulation guidance was partly responsible for this dismal performance. The MOF's predilection for sector-wide stability led to "guidance" discouraging any particular bank from innovating and competing for consumer deposits and other business at the expense of other banks. New products and services would be approved only when the MOF was certain that all

Table 3.3

Restructuring Plans of Major Banks

	Total assets (yen billions)		Gross operating profit		Net operating profit		Ordinary profit	
	3/98	3/2003	3/98	3/2003	3/98	3/2003	3/98	3/2003
IBJ	45,593	44,175	418	371	231	216	-358	186
DKB	56,587	51,330	717	739	323	387	-155	279
Sakura Bank	53,788	50,270		790	294	403	-417	237
Bank of Tokyo-Mitsubishi			963	1,014	343	552		
Fuji Bank	53,418	48,190	670	795	320	440	-576	340
Sumitomo Bank	58,695	52,700	711	700	308	360	-617	250
Sanwa Bank	58,063	55,350	696	740	352	400	-413	280
Asahi Bank	29,857	29,117	407	442	156	180	-190	96
Tokai Bank	31,835	30,300	441	453	173	230	-44	180
Mitsubishi Trust	18,309	17,689	384	269	223	120	6	115
Sumitomo Trust	15,837	14,870	310	287	131	154	-93	149

	Expense ratio (%)		Funds profit margin (%)		ROA (%)		Employees	
	3/98	3/2003	3/98	3/2003	3/98	3/2003	3/98	3/2003
IBJ	0.52	0.48	0.11	0.14	0.50	0.48	4,776	4,482
DKB	1.02	1.04	0.23	0.34	0.57	0.75	16,130	13,200
Sakura Bank	1.12	1.14	0.26	0.48	0.54	0.80	16,700	13,200
Bank of Tokyo-Mitsubishi								
Fuji Bank	0.99	1.03	0.17	0.64	0.54	0.91	14,250	13,000
Sumitomo Bank	0.91	0.90	0.23	0.43	0.52	0.68	15,000	13,000
Sanwa Bank	0.86	0.92	0.35	0.50	0.61	0.72	13,600	11,400
Asahi Bank	1.13	1.12	0.27	0.46	0.52	0.61	12,800	11,800
Tokai Bank	1.09	0.96	0.08	0.44	0.54	0.76	11,125	9,731
Mitsubishi Trust	1.42	0.94	1.11	0.88	1.21	0.68	4,932	4,695
Sumitomo Trust	2.43	1.04	0.09	0.01	0.83	1.03	5,900	5,200

Sources: Company plans. Also, Yukiko Ohara, "Japan Banks: Limited Effect on Earnings from Restructuring Plans." *Morgan Stanley Dean Witter Japan Investment Research*, March 26, 1999.

Notes:
Ordinary profit = after provision to general reserves
Expense ratio = expenses divided by gross operating profit
Funds profit margin = yield on funds minus funding cost
ROA = business profit divided by total assets

Table 3.4

Profit Structure of Commercial Banks—Japan vs. the United States

		Japanese city banks (FY97 consolidated)		Total U.S. commercial (FY97)
		Yen billion	$ billion	$billion
Operating assets	A	435,107	3,626	4,702
Shareholders' equity	B	13,681	114	418
Equity ratio (Tier 1) (%)	B/A	3		9
Interest income	C	15,025	125	340
Interest expense	D	−10,299	−86	−166
Net interest income	E=C−D	4,726	39	175
% of net operating assets	E/A	1		4
Net non-interest operating income	F	1,594	13	105
% of operating assets	F/A	0		2
General and administrative expenses	G	−3,892	−32	−170
% of operating assets	G/A	−1		−4
Operating profit	H=E+F+G	2,428	20	109
% of operating assets	H/A	1		2
% of shareholders' equity	H/B	18		26

Source: Daiwa Institute of Research, *Strategy for the Financial Industry*, p. 38.

banks would be offering the same menu at the same prices, so as not to disrupt the competitive equilibrium. When the MOF was still supreme in the 1980s and 1990s, foreign banks commonly complained that seeking MOF approval for product innovations would only result in the MOF declining to approve the innovation until Japanese banks had acquired the knowhow (often believed to be through leaks from MOF staff) to be able to compete with the foreign banks. When the approval was granted, all banks offered the same products.

Happily, in the months following the receipt of public funds in 1999, the banks began to take action to fix the problem of their generally unprofitable consumer funds services. For the first time in eighteen years, the city banks began in the fall of 1999 to raise commission fees for funds transfers and to differentiate between transfers initiated over the telephone or through an ATM and transfers initiated by a visit to the banks' counters. In September, Fuji

Bank raised transfer fees as high as ¥420 for counter service and lowered them to ¥210 for internet service. The objective of all the banks was to increase revenues, but also to lower costs through promoting use of technology where variable, volume-driven costs are minimal (*Nihon Keizai Shimbun*, August 5, 1999).

The Problem with Managing Risk

The second issue is risk management. While failing to make a reasonable ongoing profit on earning assets, Japanese banks continue to write off trillions of yen in bad loan losses. This phenomenon derives from the same conservative traits of management described above. Viewed by foreign bank competitors (of which the writer was one for some fifteen years), the apparently irrational compulsion of Japanese banks to cut lending rates, competing among themselves, and to underprice risk acted for years like a toxic pollutant, killing lending markets in Asia and elsewhere. In their domestic market, the behavior resulted in a total lack of risk-differentiated pricing and absurdly thin spreads.

Very likely, there was simply not a clear understanding or recognition of risk. The history of *keiretsu* and personal relationships made critical, objective risk assessment and pricing impossible. Add to this, through at least the 1980s, the undisputed belief that land could never depreciate in value. Japanese banks have traditionally been relationship lenders and, secondly, balance sheet lenders. Both these tendencies have led to disastrous results. Weak accounting conventions have also been a problem.

And again, the MOF is partly to blame. For years the Taxation Bureau of MOF refused to allow Japanese banks to deduct bad debt provisions (as opposed to write-offs) as an expense against current income, thereby achieving a tax savings. Naturally, then, the banks were reluctant to recognize losses in advance of actual borrower bankruptcy. Weak accounting conventions, sanctioned by MOF, allowed banks to defer bad debt recognition by transferring losses to unconsolidated subsidiaries. Such a corruption of professional and prudential regulatory standards inevitably led to gross mismanagement and a mountain of disguised losses.

LTCB's Instructive Implosion

To get a sense of the result, we can look at the final audit of the bankrupt LTCB. In September 1998 the FRC conducted an audit of LTCB and determined that the bank had net liabilities (i.e., negative net worth) of $1.5 billion (¥182 billion), being the difference between net assets on the books of $1.3 billion (¥157 billion) and unrealized losses of $2.8 billion

(¥340 billion). Since the bank was insolvent, the FRC set in motion the process of temporarily nationalizing it, as a first step to a public funds bailout equivalent to the amount of the recognized net liabilities.

But something amazing happened on the way to the final injection of public bailout funds from a U.S. Resolution Trust Corporation (RTC)-like "bridge bank." On March 31, 1999, the FRC announced that the actual amount of LTCB's net liabilities—and the amount of public funds required for the bailout—would be $22 billion (¥2,654 billion). This was a massive $20.6 billion (¥2,472 billion) more than the net liabilities calculated just six months earlier! What had happened was that the FRC acknowledged that, on a liquidation basis, LTCB would have to recognize as losses the huge investments of debt and equity it had made in its affiliated companies.

The case was chilling because it was fairly representative of widespread practices in Japan's banking industry. LTCB had made many bad loans. Wanting to move the loans off its books (and being allowed to do so under Japanese accounting standards), LTCB "sold" the loans at face value to companies (often nonbanks) in which it had invested and provided purchase funds in the form of loans. Of course, this left the affiliates with damaged, often worthless assets. When the FRC finally closely examined LTCB's operations, it concluded that virtually all the bank's loans to affiliates were substandard and should be written off. Without LTCB's continued support, the affiliates were not viable. All the borrowers were virtually or actually bankrupt. It was this finding that caused the FRC to adjust its September 1998 valuation. The adjustment was to further write down loan assets by $17.1 billion (¥2,056 billion) and to write down investment securities by $4.6 billion (¥557 billion). The final calculation was unrealized liabilities of $23.4 billion (¥2,810 billion) against book net assets of $1.3 billion (¥157 billion), for a net adjusted assets of negative $22.1 billion (¥2,654 billion) (*Nihon Keizai Shimbun*, March 31, 1999).

As though to prove that the LTCB implosion was no anomaly, the FRC announced on June 14, 1999, that the net liabilities of NCB, LTCB's sister long-term credit bank, nationalized in December 1998, were determined to be some $25 billion (¥3 trillion) (*Asahi Shimbun*, June 15, 1999). In July NCB's former chairman and president were arrested and charged with violating securities laws by underreporting some $670 million in defaulted loans and falsifying financial statements. Given our understanding of the system, we can easily conclude that the extent of management malfeasance and coverup was much greater, at both LTCB and NCB, than these figures would indicate.

The Impact and Opportunities of Deregulation

Prior to the big bang and to the 1999 bailout, it was hard to distinguish among the Japanese city banks in terms of their strategies and structures. From Tokai Bank to Daiwa Bank to BOTM, all appeared to be pursuing the same universal all-things-to-all-people strategies. After the passage of the Financial System Reform Act of 1993, all the banks established securities and trust banking subsidiaries. All pursued the same strategies against their consumer depositor bases, offering the same products directly or through subsidiaries like credit card companies. All sought to provide the gamut of "wholesale" services to corporate customers, often through nonbank subsidiaries like leasing and finance companies.

This situation was in no small measure a cause of the general weakening of the Japanese banking system. So was the "convoy system" of MOF regulation, which militated to underwrite and support a pernicious tendency toward overcapacity.

What was clear in 1999, in the context of the big bang, was that the old system in Japan was really changing. One critical element of the change was the altered mind-set of government authority, most particularly in the FRC. Throughout 1999 it became clearer that, in contrast to the past, the government would play an accommodative and supporting role in the process of change and rationalization in the financial system. The financial system reform measures of 1998 established the "safety net" that politicians and regulators had insisted was a necessary precondition for undertaking or allowing wholesale restructuring of the banking system. This precondition met, an official like Hakuo Yanagizawa, head of the FRC, could state in spring 1999 that Japan's market was vastly overbanked and that the number of city and regional banks should decline by roughly one-third over the long term. (In this claim he was prescient, as we shall see below.)

The big bang reforms will complete the process of deregulation that in 1998 and 1999 had already begun to facilitate specialization and differentiation across sector/product boundaries. For example, in the spring of 1999 most of the major banks strengthened their securities subsidiaries or tied up with major securities houses in order to position themselves with customers. But the positioning was clearly differentiated. Sanwa was effectively building a retail securities capability to compete against the major retailer brokers. IBJ and Sumitomo, on the other hand, were forming alliances and investing to build wholesale securities and investment banking franchises. Tokai and Asahi banks, were cooperating to provide services to consumers and medium-sized business, and had pledged to consolidate and share resources in ways that would be hard to imagine outside the context of the big bang reforms.

Big Bang, Bigger Banks—The IBJ, Fuji, DKB Megabank Merger

In the context of Japan's systematic problems in the late 1990s, and the general weakness of its financial institutions, the announcement on August 20, 1999, of the proposed combination of IBJ, Fuji Bank, and DKB into Mizuho Financial Group was exceptionally important. Indeed, for a banking system looking ahead to the slow and fairly passive rationalization envisaged in the restructuring plans described above, the boldness of the IBJ, Fuji, DKB merger had an energizing, mind-expanding effect. It showed that there were solutions to the problems. By effectively reducing the number of city banks by two, the merger was at minimum a major step toward dealing with the problem of overcapacity. Also, as in the United States in the 1980s when major banking mergers became common, it created a dynamic in the marketplace that effectively required other market participants at least to consider merging in order to compete.

Moreover, to a Japanese and foreign public accustomed to unimaginative, risk-averse, passive management in Japanese banks, the massive scale and implications of the proposed merger were evidence that Japanese executives were possessed of a new mentality. When the executives of the prospective new bank met the press on August 20 and expressed the goal of being among the top five banks in the world, it was almost possible to believe them.

Two-Phase Process Toward Universal Megabank

The process of creating the megabank is described in Figure 3.1. It involves two steps. The first step, to be completed by fall 2000, is to form a joint holding company which will hold the shares of the three banks. Shareholders of the three banks would exchange their shares for shares of the new holding company. The bank entities would be delisted, and the holding company itself listed on the Tokyo Stock Exchange. In the period leading to the establishment of the holding company, each of the banks will undertake to organize its business operations into five distinct and manageable business groups: retail banking, small corporate banking, large corporate banking, securities and investment banking, and asset management. This reorganization is a precondition for the combination of the business groups of the three banks by spring 2002, which is step two. Another part of step one—to be completed by fall 2000—is the merger of the 100 percent owned wholesale securities subsidiaries of the three banks (this is further discussed in Chapters Four and Nine).

Figure 3.1 **Evolution of Japan's New Megabank—Mizuho Financial Group**

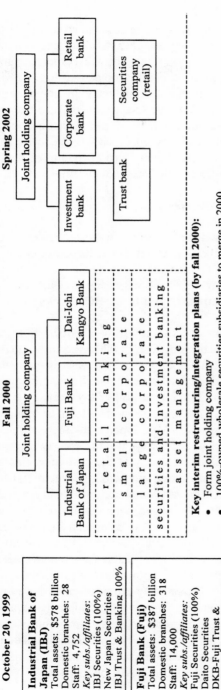

October 20, 1999

Industrial Bank of Japan (IBJ)
Total assets: $578 billion
Domestic branches: 28
Staff: 4,752
Key subs./affiliates:
IBJ Securities (100%)
New Japan Securities
IBJ Trust & Banking 100%

Fuji Bank (Fuji)
Total assets: $387 billion
Domestic branches: 318
Staff: 14,000
Key subs./affiliates:
Fuji Securities (100%)
Daito Securities
DKB-Fuji Trust &
Banking (50%). Yasuda
Trust & Banking (56.3%)

Dai-Ichi Kangyo Bank (DKB)
Total assets: $438 billion
Domestic branches: 360
Staff: 16,000
Key subs./affiliates:
DKB Securities (100%)
Kankaku Securities (54%)
DKB-Fuji Trust &
Banking 50%

Fall 2000

Joint holding company

Industrial Bank of Japan | Fuji Bank | Dai-Ichi Kangyo Bank

retail banking

small corporate

large corporate

securities and investment banking

asset management

Spring 2002

Joint holding company

Investment bank | Corporate bank | Retail bank

Trust bank

Securities company (retail)

Key interim restructuring/integration plans (by fall 2000):
- Form joint holding company
- 100%-owned wholesale securities subsidiaries to merge in 2000
- Each bank to organize business operations under retail, small corporate, large corporate, securities and investment banking, and asset management

Final restructuring/integration plans (by spring and fall 2002):
- Business divisions to be consolidated in five entities (spring): customer and consumer bank (retail), corporate bank (wholesale), investment bank, trust bank, and securities company (retail)
- Trust banking subsidiaries/affiliates to merge
- Retail securities affiliates to merge (fall)
- Branch network to be reduced by 150; total staff by 6000 (within five years)

Probable additional strategic initiatives (by fall 2002):
- Dai-Ichi Life to take equity position in holding company. Holding company to take equity positions in newly corporatized group insurance companies: Dai-Ichi Life (formerly IBJ Group); Asahi Life and Fukoku Life (DKB Group); and Yasuda Life (Fuyo [Fuji Bank] Group)
- Asset management and mutual funds operations to be rationalized, partially merged

Sources: Author. Press reports.

In step two, to be completed by spring 2002, the business groups of the three banks will be combined in five separately managed, market- and product-focused banks and corporations. These will be a retail bank, a corporate bank, an investment bank, a trust bank, and a retail securities company. The latter will be constituted from the merger of the four retail-oriented securities company affiliates of the three banks. These are New Japan Securities and Waco Securities, affiliate of IBJ; Kankaku Securities, affiliate of DKB; and Daito Securities, affiliate of Fuji Bank. This combined securities company will be the fourth largest securities company in Japan (see Chapter Four). Trust operations of the three banks, including Yasuda Trust and DKB-Fuji Trust, will be combined.

Number One in Japan (But Not Overseas)

On the basis of assets, the combined banking entity will be the biggest in the world, with $1.2 trillion (¥141 trillion) in March 1999, ahead of number two Deutsche Bank with $866 billion (December 1998). The largest U.S. bank, Citigroup, had assets in December 1998 of $668 billion. In Japan the new megabank will far outpace the current largest bank, BOTM, with assets of $582 billion (¥69.8 trillion).

The dominant position of the prospective company is evident from Table 3.5, which compares the combined company with BOTM and Sumitomo Bank. The combined company will be extending 27.3 percent of loans by major banks and collecting 22.2 percent of deposits. Its domestic branch network and staff, even after planned reductions, will place it far ahead of any rivals.

Notwithstanding the combined bank's adoption of a global benchmark, it seems unlikely that it will challenge BOTM as Japan's leading international bank for many years. During the initial few years, the bank will need to focus on internal operations and domestic markets and customers first. One possible exception is in the area of investment banking, where IBJ has a defensible international franchise, which the combination should strengthen.

One surprising finding from Table 3.5 is that, even with more than double the assets of BOTM, the operating profits of the combined IBJ, Fuji, DKB are roughly equal to BOTM. This bespeaks the problem of profitability, examined above. Increasing earnings will be an urgent requirement for the new bank, which—along with its dominant loan portfolio—also has the largest portfolio of nonperforming assets. Provisions have been taken for some of these assets, but substantial additional provision will undoubtedly be needed.

The massive scale of the merger gives us hope that profitability can be improved—first through cost savings, particularly in such high-ticket areas as systems development, and second, through more efficient and focused business operations. Management capability will be key.

Table 3.5

Comparison of Mizuho Financial Group with BOTM and Sumitomo Bank
(figures for year ended March 31, 1999)

	Mizuho Financial Group	Bank of Tokyo- Mitsubishi	Sumitomo Bank
(Yen billions)			
Capital	2,569	786	753
Public funds received	2,799	100	601
Loans	90,040	38,868	36,209
Operating profit	583	559	220
Net income	−965	45	−374
Non-performing assets	5,515	2,161	2,014
(Absolute values)			
Domestic branches	672	332	338
Staff	34,000	17,000	14,000
Shares of domestic market (in percent)			
Loans by major banks	27.3	12.4	10.7
Deposits of major banks	22.2	10.0	7.7
Non-performing assets of major banks	27.7	10.8	10.1

Sources: Nihon Keizai Shimbun, August 21, 1999. *The Nikkei Financial Daily*, August 20, 1999.

Implications for the Overall Financial Sector

As suggested above, the announcement of the new IBJ, Fuji, DKB megabank created in fall 1999 something like a Copernican revolution in the mind-set of the entire domestic financial industry. Suddenly, everything was different. Not only was the banking marketplace radically altered, so too was the securities sector, where there would again emerge a "Big Four" (see Chapter Four). With the likelihood of tie-ups with Dai-Ichi Life and Yasuda Life using the mechanism of a holding company, the future development of the insurance industry took on a new dimension. Likewise, massive change— like a new marketplace—appeared on the horizon for asset management, trust banking, and mutual funds.

And the turmoil was not limited to finance. The Japanese press was filled with speculation about how the union of major banking groups would affect the major industrial and commercial corporations for which the banks are the main financiers. (It is likely that mergers and acquisitions among industrial and commercial entities served by the combined banks will become easier and more frequent.)

For players in the financial services marketplace—foreign companies as well as Japanese—the Mizuho Financial Group represents a major change in the competitive environment, against which most companies will need to develop a strategic response. For the three companies involved, there will be massive restructuring and rationalization requirements relating to the many duplicate and overlapping companies and businesses developed over years of piecemeal deregulation. We examine the relationships and affiliations of Japanese financial groups and focus on the rationalization issues of IBJ, Fuji, and DKB in Chapter Nine and profile strategies of key players in Chapter Ten.

Certainly the changed competitive landscape created by the IBJ, Fuji, DKB combination will compel some other Japanese banks to respond. They may sense a need to defend customers and market franchises by strengthening product and service offerings or lowering delivery costs. Or they may realize that an often contemplated expansion, alliance, or merger can no longer be delayed, since the number of potential partners is rapidly declining. With systems development so important in banking, bigness—breadth and scope—seems to be a necessity to both justify and recover the costs of massive systems investments. This is true whether the bank's strategy is retail, wholesale, regional, supraregional, national or global.

Figure 3.2 suggests some probable, as well as planned, regroupings of banks by 2003 (more details and discussions of bank groups are provided in Chapters Nine and Ten). We see the full appearance of the holding company and combined operations of the former IBJ, Fuji Bank, and DKB. We posit that BOTM will remain independent, focused on serving as Japan's leading (and perhaps still only) global megabank. Sumitomo is another megabank, possibly made bigger through acquisition of Daiwa Bank. Sanwa, a domestically focused player, could very well merge or tie up with Sakura Bank. The Tokai/Asahi alliance is expected to become a full merger, possibly incorporating Bank of Yokohama and/or Daiwa Bank. This combination would be a powerful supraregional bank, focused on the retail and small corporate sector.

Trust Banking and Banks

Japan's major trust banks have shared with ordinary banks the weaknesses of low profitability and lax risk control—thereby accumulating huge loan losses—but have seemed unable to turn their special trust banking niche to advantage. For the year ended in March 31, 1999, the major trust banks raked up aggregated losses of $9.9 billion (¥1.2 trillion). Given Japan's aging demographics, the need for trust banking-type services should only in-

Figure 3.2 **Probable and Planned Future Bank Regroupings**

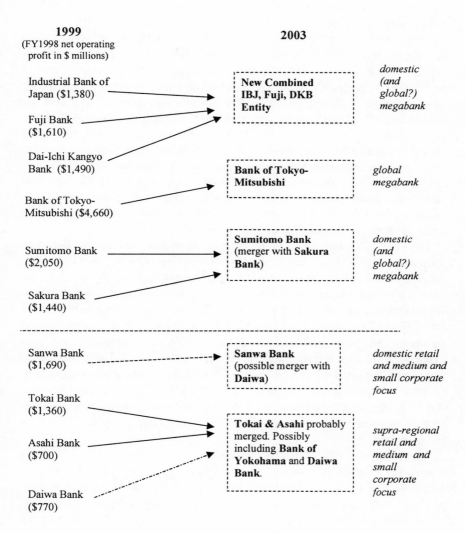

1999
(FY1998 net operating profit in $ millions)

2003

Industrial Bank of Japan ($1,380)

Fuji Bank ($1,610)

Dai-Ichi Kangyo Bank ($1,490)

New Combined IBJ, Fuji, DKB Entity

domestic (and global?) megabank

Bank of Tokyo-Mitsubishi ($4,660)

Bank of Tokyo-Mitsubishi

global megabank

Sumitomo Bank ($2,050)

Sakura Bank ($1,440)

Sumitomo Bank (merger with **Sakura Bank**)

domestic (and global?) megabank

Sanwa Bank ($1,690)

Sanwa Bank (possible merger with **Daiwa**)

domestic retail and medium and small corporate focus

Tokai Bank ($1,360)

Asahi Bank ($700)

Daiwa Bank ($770)

Tokai & Asahi probably merged. Possibly including **Bank of Yokohama** and **Daiwa Bank**.

supra-regional retail and medium and small corporate focus

Sources: Author. *Weekly Toyo Keizai*, August 7, 1999.

crease. Whether the old trust banks will be providing the services in the future is a question, however. In the post-big bang reality of Japan, the trust banking marketplace is likely to be subject to particularly severe competition. As with the rest of industry, but more so, trust banks will need to differentiate services to survive.

Loan losses have so weakened some of the banks that they are being forced to drastically restructure. Mitsui and Chuo Trust were obliged to merge on April 1, 1999, after receiving an injection of public funds. Toyo Trust, in addition to receiving public funds, received an equity injection from Sanwa Bank, bringing it closely under Sanwa. Toyo is scheduled to take over the Sanwa Trust Bank in the second half of FY99. Nippon Trust is restructuring as a subsidiary of BOTM. Yasuda Trust is under restructuring directed by its majority shareholder, Fuji Bank. The two strongest trust banks, Sumitomo Trust and Mitsubishi Trust, are strengthening group alliances. Sumitomo Trust is expected to take over Sumitomo Bank's Sumigin Trust Bank. The four main financial institutions of the Mitsubishi group, including Mitsubishi Trust, announced in fall 1998 a new cooperative alliance (these alliances and strategies are further discussed in Chapters Six, Nine, and Ten).

Between 1993 and 1997, under provisions of the Financial System Reform Act of 1993, over thirty new trust and banking subsidiaries were established by commercial banks and securities companies. Virtually every major bank and securities company established a trust bank during this period. Since then, however, a number of the new banks have closed or have been restructured. One of the newest trust banks is DKB-Fuji Trust Bank, a joint venture set up by DKB and Fuji Bank on April 1, 1999, to begin operations from twenty-four branches nationwide in October 1999. The JV was formed by combining the specialized businesses of both parents and took over the pension and securities agency business of Yasuda Trust (*Nihon Keizai Shimbun*, April 14, 1999). In the pension fund management business, investment advisory companies are increasingly successful at taking away business (see Chapter Six).

In August 1999 the MOF announced its intention to lift by March 2002 its twenty-five-year-old ban on the conduct of trust business by city banks (*Nihon Keizai Shimbun*, August 10, 1999). Thus all city banks would be able to offer products like loan trusts ("Big") and money trusts ("Hit"), pension trusts, securitized lease receivables, and securities and real estate trusts, formerly prohibited to commercial banks because of their investment risk characteristics. This eventuality will only aggravate already great competitive pressures in the trust banking field and accelerate the pace of the consolidation that has already begun.

Foreign Banks and Banking

Through the 1970s, foreign banks were Japan's main source of foreign currency "impact" loan funding for banks and corporations. In the 1980s and 1990s, as foreign exchange and other regulatory barriers were gradually removed and new instruments approved and markets opened, foreign banks often introduced state-of-the-art knowhow facilitating the modernization and internationalization of Japan's financial marketplace. But of course the main objective of the foreign banks has been to make money. For most of them, this has been difficult.

With few, if any, exceptions, the "main bank" system and *keiretsu* relationships of Japanese corporations always placed foreign banks in the position of a marginal provider of funds. In a marketplace where the price leaders were Japanese relationship banks with low return hurdles and priority claims on borrowers' collateral business (like foreign exchange and trade transactions), what foreign banks could earn by lending to Japanese banks and corporations almost always failed to reach return on assets (ROA) standards. (The exemption to the rule was lending to independent nonbank leasing, finance, and consumer credit companies that paid high interest rates because they were relatively high risk and because major city and regional banks often regarded them with disdain and would not lend to them.)

A few of the most innovative and aggressive foreign banks, like Citibank, Chase, Bank of America, and Hong Kong and Shanghai Bank, managed to make reasonable money through the 1980s by creating new products and services and finding customer need "niches," quickly capitalizing on these niches before the local and foreign competition drove returns down. The Citi, Chase and others also leveraged their strong foreign exchange and derivatives trading strengths to earn good money in the open FX and money markets. Chase—the successor to Chase, Manufacturers Hanover, and Chemical Bank—continues to be a dominant player in the FX and derivatives markets, along with J.P. Morgan, Citi, BoA, Deutsche Bank, and a few others.

Apart from these key players, most foreign banks have operated small and passive branch operations, often providing only trade finance and transaction services for overseas customers and for the Japanese operations of their overseas corporate relationships. In the 1980s, foreign banks seemed to capture a consistently puny 3 percent of the lending market year after year. In 1998 the total assets of foreign banks licensed in Japan were $491.8 billion (¥en 59,019 billion), or 7.7 percent of total banks' assets, which shows an improvement. In terms of lending, the 1998 foreign bank figure was $100.2 billion (¥12,025 billion), 5.6 percent of the figure for Japanese city banks,

Table 3.6

Ranking of Top Ten Foreign Banks by Assets, Loans, and Profits
(for year ended March 31, 1998. US$ millions)

Assets	Amount	Loans	Amount	Ordinary profit (pretax)	Amount
ING Bank	49,996	West LB	6,572	Citibank	133.3
Deutsche Bank	38,894	Citibank	4,830	Credit Suisse	99.8
Citibank	36,452	ING Bank	4,787	J.P. Morgan	62.7
Paribas	35,920	Credit Lyonnais	4,245	Deutsche Bank	36.8
Barclays Bank	28,981	BNP	4,199	Chase Manhattan	35.7
Swiss Bank Corp.	22,566	Paribas	3,760	Bank of China	34.6
West LB	22,513	Societe Generale	3,584	ING Bank	29.7
Credit Suisse	20,573	Commerzbank	3,436	Morgan Stanley Bank	28.2
BNP	19,929	Bayerische LB	3,192	Swiss Union Bank	25.6
Credit Lyonnais	18,567	Bayern Bank	2,955	Credit Lyonnais	22.1

Source: Japan Bankers Association.

but only 2.5 percent of the figure for all banks, fairly close to the traditional level (BOJ, *Financial and Economic Statistics Monthly*, April 1999).

American banks, with high ROA and return on equity (ROE) return targets, have largely withdrawn from the commodity lending market in Japan. As we will see in Chapter Twelve, Citibank has downsized its corporate business generally, to concentrate on structured finance, corporate finance, private banking, and, particularly, consumer banking. With the big bang, Citi is aggressively mining its consumer customer base to sell mutual funds. Chase makes most of its money from, and concentrates most of its assets in, FX, bonds and derivatives dealing. Table 3.6 provides rankings of some foreign banks in Japan.

For foreign banks, as for all banks, the way to profits in the Japanese market lies in differentiation and value-added. In the chapters ahead, we will examine how individual players are cutting their own paths.

Chapter Four

Securities Industry Shakeout

If the condition of Japan's banks appeared precarious in early 1999, that of its securities companies could only be described as catastrophic. It was an industry on the verge of collapse, leaderless, directionless, unprofitable, and fearful that the near-term future would be more perilous than the past. By August, a stock market recovery underpinned by the Bank of Japan's (BOJ) "zero interest rate" policy was generating commission income streams not seen for many months. But the strength and duration of the market's recovery were in doubt, and deregulation of brokerage commissions continued to cast a dark shadow over the industry's future.

FY1998: Record Losses for Japanese Firms; Record Profits for Foreigners

On March 31, 1999, Japan's three largest securities companies, Nomura, Daiwa, and Nikko, reported net record losses of some US$5.6 billion (¥ 700 billion) for the previous year, based upon consolidated accounts. On an unconsolidated basis, the loss was $4.5 billion (¥542 billion). In 1998 a raft of disasters—trading losses, especially in overseas offices, huge expenses to bail out affiliated companies awash in bad debts, restructuring costs—hit the companies, casting further doubt on the abilities of already discredited managements to cope with change.

And the problems of the securities industry were not confined to the Big Three. The Tokyo Stock Exchange reported that Japan's small and medium-sized brokerages cumulatively lost $275 million (¥33 billion) in 1998. This was the fifth year that the sector as a whole lost money.

The dismal performance of Japanese securities companies stood in stark contrast to the relatively brilliant performance in the same market of several American firms, and to the overall profitability of all foreign securities firms. The Tokyo Stock Exchange recorded record pretax profits of $736 million (¥88.3 billion) for all foreign firms trading in the exchange, up 18 percent from a year earlier and four times the level two years earlier (*Financial Times*, May 25, 1999).

In 1999, with brokerage commissions soon to be fully deregulated and the big bang ushering in a host of new competitors, Japan's securities industry was facing its most serious challenge ever. This chapter surveys the tumultuously changing scene in the securities industry and shows how a totally new industry and marketplace—with much greater foreign participation—will soon emerge.

Overview of the Securities Industry

In March 1998 there were 294 licensed securities companies in Japan, including about sixty foreign companies. In September 1998, the total number of companies actually operating as members of the Japan Securities Dealers Association (JSDA) was 271. As of mid-1999, the number is still around 280. The small number of net new additions tends to obscure the underlying reality of a host of new companies being established and begining operations during this period, while an almost equal number closed business operations.

First and Second Brokers—Continuing Consolidation

The Japanese securities industry can usefully be divided into (1) the Big Three, (2) the second tier firms, (3) small firms, (4) subsidiaries of banks, (5) foreign securities companies, and (6) new big bang entrants. Mutual fund companies, called investment trusts, are another category of securities firm (these companies and this market sub-sector will be presented in detail in Chapter Seven). Broadening the definition slightly, we are able to include investment advisors, who are specially licensed in Japan (see Chapter Six for details). We shall see below that, in the maelstrom of today's Japanese market, these categories and their constituents are in constant motion. Table 4.1 presents the Big Three and listed second tier firms by assets, revenues, and net income.

What is immediately clear about the Big Three is that they tower over the second tier companies, and that Nomura is by far the first among the Big Three. Its asset size is comparable to that of Merrill Lynch in the United States. Assets are a key differentiator among firms, as they are one important basis for generating earnings. Asset levels of the Big Three far exceed those of the second tier. This is largely because the Big Three, possessing greater capital resources and better knowhow, carry large proprietary trading positions in securities, while most of the second tier cannot compete in this area. A second key differentiator is operating revenues.

We define the second tier firms as those listed firms with assets over $666 million (¥80 billion). There are also about ten unlisted firms that are of this size. As in most of the rest of the Japanese business world, there are few

Table 4.1

Overview of First and Listed Second Tier Japanese Securities Companies

	Total assets (Yen billions)	Revenues (Yen billions)	Net income (Yen millions)
Big three			
Nomura	12,056	359	−241,841
Daiwa	4,671	257	−116,922
Nikko	3,812	209	−183,337
Second tier (top)			
Kokusai	2,255	92	1,516
Waco	1,037	61	−34,439
New Japan	792	75	−3,290
Kankaku	529	44	−20,170
Okusan	280	40	3,045
Universal	244	27	−8,986
Second tier (bottom)			
Tokai Maruman	188	19	1,036
Tokyo	153	22	−1,070
Marusan	146	16	306
Cosmo	137	18	−6,246
Dai-Ichi	129	18	−11,089
Mito	128	12	−1,933
Meiko National	112	11	−8,322
Toyo	90	11	−1,713
Taiheiyo	85	13	−3,214
Yamatane	83	17	1,389

Sources: Company reports for period ended March 31, 1999.

companies that are both relatively big and really independent. Affiliations and groupings are the rule. Thus, many second tier brokers are affiliates of Big Three brokers, banks, or insurance companies. We shall see below that, in the context of both the Big Bang reforms and financial stress, many of these affiliations are being strengthened by outright acquisition and merger.

There is significant disparity in the second tier, allowing a division into top second tier and bottom second tier. The top is occupied by Kokusai, New Japan, Kankaku, Waco, Okusan, and Universal. The bottom second tier comprises ten listed firms and about ten unlisted firms. The latter include Towa, Izumi, Tachibana, Koei Ishino, World Nichiei, Daito, Kyokuto, Chiyoda, Chuo, Hinode, Nihon, Century, Dainana, Naito, Hiraoka. As of the end of 1998, the first and first and second tiers of Japanese securities firms totaled some forty-four companies. However, given the changes in the industry, this number will quickly change.

Table 4.2

The Big Four—Again
Retail securities affiliates within IBJ, Fuji, DKB holding company

	Total assets	(Yen billions) Customer assets	Business revenues	Trading profits
Nomura	12,056	49,490	359	98
Daiwa	4,671	31,159	257	46
Nikko	3,812	30,400	209	40
Merged Four	**2,395**	**14,065**	**185**	**46**
New Japan	792	5,904	76	22
Waco	1,037	3,949	61	20
Kankaku	529	3,961	44	3
Daito	37	251	4	1

Source: Kinyu Business, September 15, 1999, pp. 129–133.
Note: Figures are for fiscal year ended March 31, 1999.

The Big Four Again—by 2002

One major expected change in the securities industry landscape, to be realized by the end of 2002, will be the merger of the retail securities affiliates of the Industrial Bank of Japan (IBJ), Fuji Bank, Dai-Ichi Kargyo Bank (DKB) megabank holding company. These are New Japan Securities and Waco Securities for IBJ, Daito Securities for Fuji Bank, and Kankaku Securities for DKB. Table 4.2 presents calculations of the relative prospective position in the industry of the combined operations of these securities companies. What is evident is that the new merged entity will clearly be the fourth-ranking securities company in Japan, below the Big Three. Given its broad reach and diversified customer base, we can expect the company to gain market share and to draw closer to the Big Three over time. Indeed, with the addition of this new company, it will be necessary again (as when Yamaichi Securities was extant) to refer to the Big Four of the Japanese securities industry.

Other Categories: Small Companies, Bank Subsidiaries, Foreign Companies and New Niche Players

The small securities companies, numbering some one hundred, are generally "mom and pop" companies serving a small locality or companies that are appendages of other financial and nonfinancial companies. In terms of business volume and presence, their importance is negligible. Like the second tier brokers, the small brokers are usually struggling to make a profit, and many, if not most, will find it difficult to survive the full deregulation of brokerage commissions in 1999.

Securities subsidiaries of banks make up an important category that will only increase in importance as banks further integrate securities into their business strategies. Nineteen banks established 100 percent-owned securities subsidiaries in 1993–1996 under provisions of the 1993 reform legislation (see Chapter Two). Until 1999 these subsidiaries were restricted to nonequity business, able to conduct significant bond underwriting and trading business for the corporate customers of their parent banks, but not permitted to underwrite or trade equity securities. There continues to be consolidation in this segment. And the pace is accelerating: By spring 2000 the three subsidiaries of IBJ, Fuji Bank, and DBK will be merged and brought under the joint holding company of the new megabank group. The combined capital of the new company will be $2.7 billion. In FY98 twelve active bank securities subsidiaries, led by IBJ Securities and Tokyo-Mitsubishi Securities, were able to report operating profits (*Nihon Keizai Shimbun*, April 24, 1999). Notwithstanding this success, by 1999 banks without strong corporate franchises and capital resources found it difficult to generate profits from securities subsidiaries. In 1999 all the trust banks and Asahi Bank appeared to have given up maintaining their low-profit securities subsidiaries. On the other hand, six city banks were increasing capital and preparing to enter equity brokerage (see below).

As we noted above, there are some sixty foreign securities companies operating in Japan. These range from huge investment banking firms like Merrill Lynch, Goldman Sachs, Morgan Stanley Dean Witter, Deutsche Securities, ING Barings, and Jardine Fleming, engaging in equity and fixed income underwriting and trading for institutional customers and proprietary accounts, to small firms like American Express Financial Advisors (Japan), essentially selling one product—mutual funds—by mail. Most major U.S. and foreign banks, like Citibank and Chase, have securities subsidiaries or affiliates operating in Tokyo. As we shall see in Chapter Thirteen, Merrill Lynch is pursuing both wholesale and retail business strategies in Japan.

Finally, after the big bang opened the sector to nonfinancial company entrants in December 1998 and changed licensing from approval to registration, we began to see a significant number of securities licenses being obtained by companies such as Hitachi, Toyota, and C. Itoh. Even before this, however, consumer credit companies like Credit Saison and finance companies like Orix had formed securities companies to complement comprehensive financial service strategies. The advent of deregulation of commissions and the financial stress of the second tier and, particularly, small securities companies have spawned a number of new entrants offering discount brokerage services. Companies like DLJ Direct, Charles Schwab, and E-Trade have tied up with Japanese firms to offer internet and discount trading (this is discussed further below).

How Securities Firms in Japan Make (and Lose) Money

Throughout the decade of the 1990s, to an extent not seen in the United States for twenty years, securities companies in Japan made their money from brokerage commissions—buying and selling stocks and, to a lesser extent, bonds—for clients' accounts and at clients' risk. Brokerage commissions constituted the largest category of revenue for all securities companies. For the second tier companies it regularly contributed about 50 percent of revenues, while small companies relied on commissions for nearly 70 percent of revenues.

Reliance on equity brokerage commissions meant reliance on active equity trading in clients' accounts. This reliance engendered a mentality and style of hard-selling new issues and "churning" of customer portfolios by the brokerage houses and their salesmen. Without a long-term investment approach and with the need to generate commissions—often to achieve head office sales quotas—the typical Japanese broker and brokerage encouraged speculation and overtraded customer accounts. Brokerage commissions were a fixed percentage of the value of trades. As share prices declined, the tendency of brokers was to encourage more client trading, so as to maintain income. Inevitably, clients lost money and became demoralized, and, during the early 1990s, most withdrew from the market.

Dropping Volume and Prices Choke Revenues

It has been the decline of brokerage commissions, brought about by the decline in both trading volume and value, that has caused the majority of Japanese securities companies to become unprofitable. Figure 1.2 showed how the value of traded stocks declined along with the Nikkei Index over the 1990s. It was simple arithmetic to calculate the revenues that could be generated from a certain level of stock trading at fixed commissions, and it was clear that this was not enough to cover the costs of the firms operating in the industry. Consolidation was inevitable. And this was in the period of fixed commissions. With commissions deregulated in late 1999, the outlook was for industry meltdown.

With some important exceptions, only the Big Three (until Yamaichi's collapse in November 1997, the Big Four) have been able to achieve meaningful diversification of revenues. They have done so because of their near monopoly on underwriting of primary issue stocks issued by corporate customers at market prices. This position has allowed them to earn underwriting fees and to profit from position-taking in equity offerings. Subunderwriter positions have often been offered to the second tier affiliates of the Big Three, but small firms have had to subsist on strict trading in the secondary market.

Second and Third Tier Brokers Most Vulnerable

Second tier firms like New Japan have been able to break into the primarily underwriting business on initial public offerings (IPOs) of shares of new companies on Japan's over-the-counter market. Also, several second tier firms, like Kokusai, have tied up with foreign mutual funds companies, like Alliance Capital and Fidelity, to sell mutual funds. From such mutual funds sales they earn a commission, usually 3 percent for equity funds and 1 to 2 percent for bond funds.

A second, though lesser, source of revenues has been bond underwriting and trading. The volume of government bonds, utility bonds, and corporate bonds issued has increased steadily through the 1990s. In 1998 some US$738 billion (¥94 trillion) in bonds were issued. Securities companies, particularly the well-capitalized and connected Big Three and bank subsidiaries, and foreign players, were the most active players in this business. Again, Japan's small securities companies played little or no role.

Notwithstanding their relatively diversified revenue, Japan's Big Three securities companies are still more commission-dependent than leading foreign securities companies. Figure 4.1 shows a composite picture of revenue sources for the Big Three compared with Merrill Lynch in the United States. The substantial gap between them is a key factor driving a huge restructuring of the entire securities sector.

Dramatic Change and Restructuring Sweeping the Industry

Restructuring to Remain Among the Big Three: Nikko and Daiwa

The dramatic restructuring of Japan's securities industry is well illustrated by the bold strategic changes happening at two of the Big Three leaders, Nikko and Daiwa. In March 1998, Nikko Securities reported a 25 percent drop in revenues, to ¥168 billion. In consequence, it was the only one of the four largest firms—including Nomura, Daiwa, and Kokusai—to record

Figure 4.1 **Comparative Revenue Sources of the Japanese Big Three and Merrill Lynch (in percent)**

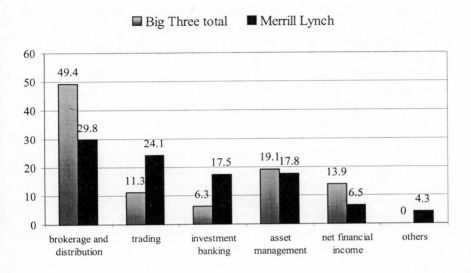

Source: Daiwa Institute of Research, *Strategy for the Financial Industry*, p. 66. Data for FY97 (Big Three) and CY97 (Merrill Lynch)

an operating loss, a large ¥39 billion. The company was evidencing weakness in all areas, particularly the critical areas of sales and trading, and seemed to be in danger of following the previous number four company, Yamaichi, which had collapsed the previous November. It was at this point that the Travelers Group's chairman and CEO, Sanford Weill, approached the president of Nikko, Masaki Kaneko, with a proposal to enter an equity partnership with Salomon Smith Barney, the securities and investment banking parts of the Travelers Group. (At the same time, Weill was talking to Citicorp's chairman and CEO John Reed about merging the two companies. Citigroup emerged.)

By summer, an unprecedented deal was announced. Nikko securities would issue to Travelers Group equity equivalent to 9.5 percent of total outstanding equity (making Travelers the largest shareholder) and convertible bonds equivalent (assuming conversion) to 15.5 percent of outstanding equity. The proceeds of this equity issue for Nikko would be about $1.83 billion

(¥220 billion). Nikko Securities would, in turn, purchase shares in Travelers Group equivalent to $80 to 420 million (¥10 to 50 billion).

Thus did Nikko achieve a much-needed capital infusion, essentially becoming a subsidiary of Travelers Group. But the tie-up was much bolder still. It was announced that the two firms would, on January 1, 1999, form a joint venture wholesale investment bank, to be owned 51 percent by Nikko and 49 percent by Salomon Smith Barney. Nikko would transfer its entire wholesale securities operations, investment banking operations, and Nikko Research Center, involving a total of 500 persons, to the JV. Salomon Smith Barney would commit 600 employees. The new company would be named Nikko Salomon Smith Barney. Also, the overseas operations of Nikko would be absorbed by Salomon Smith Barney. The retail business of Nikko would continue to operate in the domestic market with a staff of approximately 7,500 persons. The new configuration is illustrated in Figure 4.2.

Daiwa Securities, under its dynamic CEO, Yoshinari Hara, took an innovative but in some ways parallel approach, also looking for a financially strong partner. It tied up with Sumitomo Bank for the development of a wholesale investment banking business and the creation of a separate, wholly owned retail securities company. Thanks to the big bang, Daiwa has been able to use a holding company structure, officially named Daiwa Securities Group, Inc., which was formally launched on April 26, 1999. The JV wholesale company, Daiwa Securities SB Capital Markets, 60 percent owned by Daiwa and 40 percent by Sumitomo Bank, was created by combining wholesale securities operations of the two parents, including some 1,200 employees from Daiwa and 100 from Sumitomo. Daiwa could intially transfer some 6,200 staff to the wholly owned retail company, called Daiwa Securities, but staff reductions of 500 to 600 were planned immediately. The focus of management will be on group ROE (*The Nikkei Financial Daily*, April 27, 1999).

Daiwa will continue to rationalize its other financial businesses. In the assets management business, it has obtained capital investment not only from Sumitomo Bank, but also from Sumitomo Marine and Sumitomo Life. This evidences Daiwa's strategy of closely integrating its operations with the Sumitomo Group as a whole (Shimano 1998, pp. 160–161).

Mergers, Acquisitions, and Tie-Ups in 1999 and 2000

If two out of three of the Big Three have undertaken such dramatic strategic restructurings, what of the second tier brokers? The answer is, the same, but more so. But the restructuring of the second tier brokers differs from that of the first tier in the fundamental sense that for the most part these companies

Figure 4.2 **New Alliance and Business Structures Launched by Nikko and Daiwa Securities**

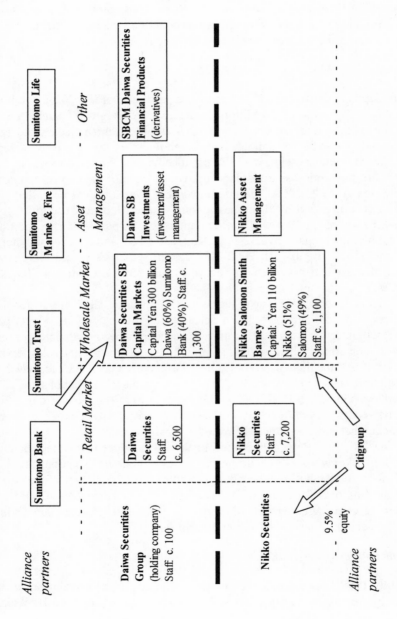

Source: Author.

cannot decide their own fates. They must seek and obey the direction provided by their key relationships, particularly banks. In the new competitive, post-big bang context, both banks and securities firms are seeking to strengthen their competitiveness, consolidate and marshal their resources, and, in many cases, focus on specific product and customer niches. Below we review some key relationships and changes.

New Japan and Waco Securities—IBJ

New Japan Securities and Waco Securities, affiliates of IBJ, lost a combined total of $700 million (¥84 billion) in the three years ended March 1999. In Japan, as elsewhere, when a company is in trouble, it must discuss and agree on strategy with its key bankers and shareholders. In the case of New Japan and Waco, the discussion with IBJ produced a bold strategic move. In June 1999 the companies' shareholders approved a plan for the two companies to merge on April 1, 2000. The combined new company will be called New Japan Securities and will become the fourth largest Japanese securities company. In August 1999 it was further announced, as part of the creation of a joint holding company by IBJ, Fuji Bank, and DKB, and the eventual merger of operations, that by fall 2002 New Japan Securities would merge with Kankaku Securities and Daito Securities, the retail securities affiliates of DKB and Fuji Bank, respectively.

With the financial backing of the new IBJ, Fuji Bank, DKB megabank holding company, the new New Japan Securities (and eventually its merger partners) will integrate itself into the megabank group to become the group's retail distribution arm. It will also focus on providing underwriting and sales services for small- and medium-sized companies. It is planned that in 2000 the new New Japan Securities will have some 5,000 employees, meaning a cut of some 2,200 from levels in March 1999. Offices will number 90 to 100, down from 127 for the two companies in March 1999. The new company will be purely domestic, meaning that overseas offices of New Japan will be closed.

The IBJ, Fuji Bank, DKB megabank will conduct investment banking and big-ticket wholesale securities strategies through its investment banking divisions and the entity to be created in 2000 from the merger of the securities subsidiaries of the banks, IBJ Securities, Fuji Securities, and DKB Securities. Asset management operations of New Japan will be consolidated within the megabank group (see Chapter Ten for details).

Kankaku Securities—DKB

In July 1999 DKB completed an equity injection into Kankaku Securities, thereby raising its equity share to over 50 percent and making Kankaku a full subsidiary. At the same time, it increased the capital of its existing securities subsidiary, DKB Securities. In total, DKB injected $667 million (¥80 billion) into the two companies. Like other banks, DKB was trying to strengthen its securities capabilities in advance of the full deregulation of securities commissions and the opening of full equity brokerage business to bank securities subsidiaries in fall 1999.

Kankaku Securities had lost an amazing $633 million (¥76 billion) on revenues of $1.65 billion (¥198 billion) in the four years ended March 1999. The DKB equity injection was needed to finance liquidation of liabilities and to restructure operations. Kankaku was forecasting a profit of $15 million (¥1.8 billion) on revenues of $375 billion (¥45 billion) in FY99. DKB planned to direct Kankaku's activities toward the retail market, while providing wholesale corporate services through DKB Securities (*Nihon Keizai Shimbun*, June 11, 1999).

As with New Japan Securities and Waco, all plans were subject to drastic change following the August 1999 decision of DKB to join IBJ and Fuji Bank in a joint holding company structure by fall 2000, to be followed by a combination of business operations by spring 2002. In this new context, it was decided that by fall 2002 Kankaku Securities would be merged with the retail securities affiliates of IBJ and Fuji Bank to form a new retail securities company under the megabank holding company (Table 4.2).

Yamatane, Koei Ishino, Kyokuto—Sakura

Yamatane had accepted directors and a new president from its main bank, Sakura. A Sakura-supervised restructuring yielded results in FY98 with the first profitable year in four years. Yamatane recovery may allow it to absorb two other, weaker, Sakura affiliates, Koei Ishino and Kyokuto.

Tokyo Mitsubishi Personal Securities—BOTM

In April 1999 two Bank of Tokyo–Mitsubishi (BOTM) affiliates, Ryoko Securities and Daishichi Securities, merged to form Tokyo Mitsubishi Personal Securities. This company will provide the retail securities services in BOTM's strategy, while it pursues corporate business through its subsidiary, Tokyo Mitsubishi Securities. In June 1999 Tokyo Mitsubishi Securities absorbed Mitsubishi Shin Securities, the securities subsidiary of Mitsubishi Trust Bank.

Meiko National Securities—Sumitomo Bank

Meiko National was formed on April 1, 1999, through a merger of two Sumitomo Bank affiliates, Meiko and National. Sumitomo Group ownership is 40 percent. This company can be expected to complement the wholesale securities activities pursued by Daiwa Securities SB Capital Markets and to compete with Daiwa Securities in providing retail services, particularly mutual funds.

(Universal, Taiheiyo, Towa)+Dai-Ichi—Sanwa

It was announced on May 13, 1999, that three second tier securities firms—Universal, Taiheiyo, and Towa—would merge in April 2000 to form Japan's seventh largest securities company. The three are Sanwa Bank affiliates and the surviving company, Universal, was expected to play a key role in Sanwa Bank's retail securities strategy, which is emphasizing offering mutual funds.

Sanwa acquired 30 percent of the issued shares of Universal from Daiwa Securities group. Taiheiyo is the largest shareholder of an investment trust (mutual funds) company, Partners Investment Trust, which is also an affiliate of Sanwa. Combining Taiheiyo with also-affiliated Towa will create a strong retail securities company through which to roll out a mutual fund sales strategy. Sales offices will be consolidated (there were 120 in May 1999). Staff will be reduced (the combined total staff in May 1999 was 3,700).

In June 1999 Sanwa took a further bold step and purchased from the nationalized Long Term Credit Bank (LTCB) for about $83 million (¥10 billion) the equity of second tier broker Dai-Ichi, giving Sanwa a controlling 29 percent interest (*Nihon Keizai Shimbun*, June 19, 1999). It was decided that Dai-Ichi would be a fourth component of the merger to take place in April 2000, forming the new Universal Securities. The new company would have customer assets under management of some $37.5 billion (¥4,500 billion), making it the sixth largest securities company, ranking above DKB's Kankaku and below Kokusai.

Sanwa will pursue corporate business through its securities subsidiary, Sanwa Securities, but emphasis will be on the retail market, particularly mutual funds. Plans were to consolidate all mutual funds development in Partners Investment Trust. At the end of March, Universal had $2.8 billion (¥339 billion) in investment trust assets. Partners had $9.2 billion (¥1,098 billion). The combined amount would be $12 billion (¥1,438 billion), giving Partners a ranking of seventh in the industry by assets volume (*Nihon Keizai Shimbun*, May 14, 1999).

Tokai Maruman—Tokai

Tokai Maruman is the surviving company following a merger of Tokai Maruman and Naigai, a former affiliate of Yamaichi, in April 1999. Tokai

Maruman is the only comprehensive securities company in the Chukyo region and a key component in the retail and small business strategy of Tokai Bank. Tokai is the largest bank shareholder and key backer of the company.

Cosmo—Daiwa

Cosmo Securities is a 59.6 percent-owned subsidiary of Daiwa Bank. It had lost ¥24 billion on revenues of ¥113 billion in the five years ended March 1999. The company has been restructured and should earn money in FY99. It has a strong franchise in retail and small corporate markets in the Kansai area. The viability of Cosmo depends on the viability of Daiwa Bank itself, which is in serious question. Very likely the latter will be merged, perhaps with Sumitomo Bank, and the former will be absorbed.

Opportunities of Deregulation: Equity Brokerage by Bank Securities Subsidiaries and Insurance Sales

Opening of equity brokerage to bank securities subsidiaries was an important big bang deregulation. In early 1999 six city banks, led by BOTM and IBJ, were increasing capital and staff of securities subsidiaries to prepare for entry. In March 1999 BOTM increased capital of Tokyo Mitsubishi Securities to $1.25 billion (¥150 billion). IBJ increased capital of IBJ Securities by $1.42 billion (¥170 billion). It was announced that the two companies would further increase their subsidiaries' capital in March 2001 by $791.7 million (¥95 billion) and $541.7 million (¥65 billion), respectively, bringing capitalization to the level of second tier securities companies. Fuji Bank announced that it would increase capital of Fuji Securities to $580 million (¥70 billion), from $330 million, in the first half of FY99, placing Fuji Securities just behind BOTM and IBJ subsidiaries (*Nihon Keizai Shimbun*, April 28, 1999).

An even more interesting development is the opening to securities firms of sales of life and nonlife insurance products. From December 1998 it became possible for securities companies to become agencies for sales of insurance products. In April Orix Securities and Japan Global Securities convened special shareholders' meetings to amend their articles of associations to include insurance agency and insurance product sales within their business scope. It was reported that over half of listed securities companies would take this step (*Nihon Keizai Shimbun*, April 16, 1999).

A necessary second step is to have sales staff pass exams required for registration as an insurance sales agent. This deregulation presents broad opportunities for multiproduct sales to customers and creates for securities a potentially important offset to falling commission revenue after deregulation in October 1999. Securities companies as agents present an interesting new distribution channel for insurance companies, including foreign insurance companies.

Foreign Securities Companies' Growing Power

The generally desperate condition of Japanese securities companies stands in stark contrast to the usually profitable operations of foreign firms in Japan. In Part Four we will view individual strategies and performance of some of the major American players. Here we will look more broadly at the subsector.

In 1998, the JSDA conducted a survey of the September 1998 half-year term financial results of its 271 members with the intention of trying to increase the transparency of the securities marketplace. The JSDA released the results on November 18, 1998. The report listed the earnings of eighty of the ninety-three companies with capital over ¥3 billion. Reporting was voluntary. The thirteen firms declining to respond included some important foreign companies, like Goldman Sachs (we present Goldman's numbers in Chapter Fifteen), ING Barings, Bear Stearns, Lehman Brothers, Jardine Fleming, and Societe Generale. But other major foreign firms did respond. The results are presented in Figure 4.3.

Figure 4.3 shows that by 1998 foreign firms were earning from the market revenues fully one-third as large as those of all Japanese companies. If the results of the thirteen nonparticipating firms were added, it is likely that foreign earnings would have approached 50 percent in this period. This is an amazing performance, showing a huge market presence and vastly superior capabilities man-for-man of the foreign securities firms. It contrasts also with the relatively negligible market presence of foreign banks versus domestic banks in Japan. Figure 4.4 presents the operating revenues of some of the reporting foreign firms, ranked against the second tier Japanese firms. It shows that foreign securities firms occupied positions in the marketplace equivalent to or stronger than most of the second tier Japanese brokers.

Operating in Profitable Institutional Markets

Foreign securities companies have generally sought to build franchises buying and selling securities with domestic and offshore institutional customers and, also, to profit from their sophisticated skills in proprietary trading, as well as superior research capabilities. Over the years, this strategy has been successful. Foreign securities houses operate large fixed income trading and equity desks,

Figure 4.3 **Total Operating Revenues of Domestic vs. Foreign Securities Firms** (for six months ended September 1998)

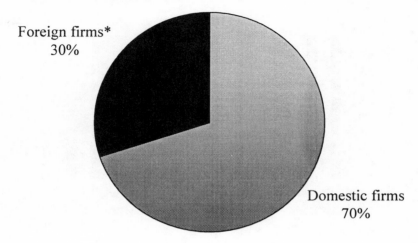

Foreign firms*
30%

Domestic firms
70%

Source: JSDA Member Survey, November 1ठ, 1998.
Note: *Foreign firms exclude Goldman Sachs, ING Barings, Bear Stearns, Lehman Brothers, ABN-Amro, Jardine Fleming, and IBJ Warburg.

selling foreign bonds and equities to domestic customers, and domestic bonds and equities to foreign customers, as well as trading and taking positions in futures, options, and swaps markets. In recent years, foreign, particularly American, houses, like Merrill Lynch, Goldman Sachs, Morgan Stanley, and J.P. Morgan, have become more successful at competing directly with the Big Three Japanese houses for business with Japanese institutional investors, by virtue of the foreigners' more professional approach and performance. Research capabilities and asset management skills have been instrumental in this success.

The prowess and strength of foreign brokers were demonstrated in March 1999 when Nikko Salomon Smith Barney began its operations. The firm seized an 8 percent share of trading on the Tokyo stock exchange in its first two weeks of operation, only slightly behind Nomura and Daiwa securities. Previously, Nikko and Salomon had separately maintained market shares of 2 percent and 3 percent respectively. The JV structure—which had implemented U.S.-style management—had clearly achieved synergy (*Financial Times*, May 18, 1999).

Winning More Corporate Finance Mandates

Another source of foreign, particularly American, firms' strong earnings has been their success in acquiring advisory roles in Japan's increasingly active

Figure 4.4 **Operating Revenues of Foreign and Second Tier Firms for Six Months Ending September 1998**

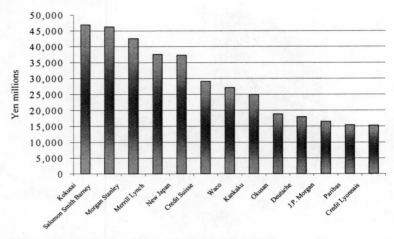

Source: JSDA Member Survey, November 18, 1998.
Note: *Survey did not include Goldman Sachs, ING Barings, Bear Stearns, Lehman Brothers, ABN-Amro, Jardine Fleming, and IBJ Warburg.

M&A market (see Chapter Fifteen). Also recently, in a development causing great consternation to Japanese houses, major U.S. securities houses have begun to win mandates as lead underwriters of primarily corporate bond issues by such issuers as Nippon Telephone and Telegraph (NTT) and Tokyo Electric Power. This success speaks well of these houses' high reputations for expertise and for their market placing power. This power will only increase.

Only one foreign firm, Merrill Lynch, has made a serious effort to develop the Japanese retail securities market through a branch office and retail sales force strategy. We will study Merrill's strategy, as well as those of other major U.S. firms, in Part Four. Fidelity has targeted the mutual funds market and adopted both direct and indirect approaches (Chapter Seven). The combination of the big bang and technology is facilitating other U.S. brokerages to challenge the Japanese domestic market, but with a new model. Morgan Stanley Dean Witter is reported to be studying entry. Citibank and others are seeking to enter the market by selling mutual funds.

New Market Entrants and Approaches

The year 1999 witnessed a host of new arrivals in the securities marketplace. These can be usefully placed into four categories: nontraditional nonfinancial and cross-sector financial entrants, foreign firms or JVs with new approaches, "new wave" players, and discounters. Some entrants cross categories.

Nontraditional Nonfinancial and Cross-Sector Financial Entrants

Here the list is long. It includes companies mentioned above like Hitachi, C. Itoh, and Toyota, entering the securities business for the first time on a small scale. It includes life insurance companies like Tokio Fire and Marine and Sony Life, obtaining securities or mutual fund licenses. In this group we also can include the securities subsidiary of the Hydra-headed Orix Group (see Chapter Eleven), which also operates a life insurance company and a bank, and the securities company of the Saison Group.

Foreign Firms or JVs with New Approaches

Here we can point to Charles Schwab and DLJ Direct (see Chapter Seventeen), each tying up with a domestic player—Tokio Fire and Marine and Sumitomo Group, respectively—to establish companies and provide products, in both cases via the internet. In this group as well is American Express Financial Advisors (Japan), which was licensed in January 1999 and began in March to sell mutual funds by direct mail, mainly to American Express card holders. Another example is a JV securities company formed in May 1999 between Cigna and Yasuda Fire and Marine for the purpose of entering the defined contribution pension business. The entrance of foreign banks and insurance companies through mutual funds sales since December 1, 1998, could be included this category.

"New Wave" Players

These companies are technology- and market niche-driven. They frequently target a young, hip customer base, offering more than simply stock trading. Representative of this group is E-Trade, an online broker established by the Softbank Group, which commenced operations in May 1999 (see Chapter Eleven). We also place the new 100 percent-owned subsidiary of Nomura Securities, Nomura Fundnet, in this category. Fundnet is a net-based marketer of mutual funds, with a marketing strategy—including no-load funds and low minimum automatic investment programs—aimed at a young market (see Chapter Ten for more on Nomura's strategy and Fundnet).

Discounters

This category was filling up even before discounting became possible in October 1999. Representative is Matsui Securities, based in Tokyo, which,

Table 4.3

Comparison of Pre-and Postliberalization Stock Trading Commissions

Trade value (Yen)	Fixed commission (prior to Oct. 99)	Typical large broker		DLJ direct commission	
		Internet trades	Telephone trades	Internet trades	Telephone trades
500,000	5,750	3,000	4,500	1,900*	2,900*
1,000,000	11,500	3,000	6,000	2,500#	3,500#
5,000,000	47,500	15,000	30,000		
10,000,000	82,500	30,000	60,000	2,900*	3,900*
30,000,000	197,500	90,000	150,000	3,500#	4,500#

Source: DLJ Direct SFG Securities, Inc.
Note: *Indicates trades at market. # indicates trades at designated prices.

in May 1999, was already announcing that it would offer up to 74 percent discount on normal, prederegulation commissions for stock trading. Matsui was among the first to adopt a no-salesmen, no-office, internet-only service. Another scrappy competitor adopting the direct marketing model is Iwai Securities, based in Osaka. In June 1999 Iwai was promising across-the-board discounts of 70 percent for internet trades and 50 percent for call center trades. H.I.S. Company, previously a travel discounter, entered the discount brokerage business in 1999 with H.I.S. Kyoritsu Securities.

DLJ Direct SFG Throws Down the Gauntlet in Internet Discount Services

The shadow over the Japanese brokerage industry darkened—and the light for consumers brightened—in July 1999 when DLJ Direct SFG unveiled its commission discounting strategy. In a move clearly aimed at grabbing a significant market share in advance of the inevitable shareout (see Chapters Seventeen and Eighteen), the company announced a flat commission schedule with a basic rate of $15.83 (¥1,900) per trade (if executed on-line), which was dramatically cheaper than anything offered by the major securities companies (Table 4.3). In addition, it was offering free initial subscription periods for a range of highly valuable information services, offered on an economical "to order" basis.

Further Propelling the Market Toward the Internet

The exceptionally cheap (and, by Japanese industry standards, revolutionary) marketing strategy exemplified by DLJ Direct SFG was certainly something the "established" Japanese securities industry could not ignore. It is not surprising, then, that in July 1999 it was determined that thirty-one Japanese securities had already established internet trading services and twenty more were preparing to do so. The fifty-one companies included the Big Three—Nomura, Daiwa, Nikko—and several of the second tier players— New Japan, Kankaku, Okasan, Tokai Maruman, Yamatane, Universal, and Meiko National—as well as such new entrants as Orix (*Nihon Keizai Shimbun*, August 4, 1999). The one full-service foreign broker, Merrill Lynch Japan Securities, was introducing internet information services in fall 1999 and planned to upgrade services to include trading in 2000.

What all this means, besides more brutal competition, is unclear. What is clear is that the dire straits of Japan's securities industry have created great opportunities for foreign entrants. In this there are similarities to Japan's massive insurance marketplace, to which we now turn.

Chapter Five

Insurance Industry in Crisis

During the 1980s Japan's two dozen life insurance companies came to symbolize the country's raw financial power. By contrast, in early 1999 the life insurance industry was in crisis, with declining revenues and mounting losses, a victim of Japan's postbubble financial decline and the Bank of Japan's (BOJ) desperate need to rescue the banking system by pursuing a superlow interest rate policy. At mid-1999 the BOJ's "zero interest rate policy" was finally buoying the Japanese stock market, and rising values of stock portfolios were beginning to buoy the spirits of the recently demoralized life insurers. But the damage done in this industry, and its many structural and market competitiveness problems, would not easily or quickly be repaired.

Overview of the Insurance Industry

Japan's life insurance industry is still huge, with total assets of US$1.6 trillion (¥193 trillion). Japanese individuals hold some 26 percent of their financial assets in insurance, an amount second only to holdings of bank deposits. Annual premium revenues in the Japanese market in FY97 were US$292 billion. Japanese people on average pay annually some US$4,000 in all types of insurance premiums—three times the world average—in a country with a generous national health insurance system.

But signs of trouble and change are everywhere. In 1997 Nissan Life Insurance failed, the first failure of a life insurance company since World War II. In June 1999 the Financial Supervisory Agency (FSA) ordered Toho Life Insurance to suspend operations due to financial weakness. These closures would have been unthinkable only a few years before, as the life insurance industry, more even than banking, was protected and cosseted by Ministry of Finance (MOF) regulations and the "convoy system." But the severe structural weakness of the industry now portends more such closings, and a drastic sector-wide restructuring seems inevitable.

The restructuring has started, and the weakness of the large Japanese companies has given foreign companies like GE and ManuLife, as well as some innovative local players, the opportunity to make market entries. Given the size of Japan's insurance market and the advent of market-opening big bang reforms, this sector holds high promise of profits for companies that can compete.

Life Insurers—Bedrock of the System (Now Underwater)

The Japanese life insurance industry is generally divided into five groups: the seven biggest companies; the next eleven companies, with a subcategory for the smallest three; the life insurance subsidiaries of nonlife companies; nonforeign katakana companies; and foreign companies.

Japan's largest life insurers are also the oldest, most having been formed between 1880 and 1920, often as elements of the key industrial-commercial-financial combines (*zaibatsu*) of the time. All Japan's large life insurers are mutuals, meaning that they are owned mutually by their policyholders. As mutuals, they seek to meet dividend commitments to policyholders, rather than to achieve high current operating earnings or net income. It is normal for management to calculate the required dividend and then to sell sufficient securities to achieve the requisite capital gains. For this reason, in looking at performance we will focus on policies in force (the difference between new policies booked and cancellations and payouts), new policies written, and premium revenues. Table 5.1 provides the figures for total assets, policies in force, and new policies written for the big seven mutuals.

Dominance of the Big Seven

Table 5.1 provides key data for the eighteen largest Japanese life companies (Toho Life is excluded). It shows that the big seven life insurers dominate the industry, and that Nippon Life towers above them all. Figure 5.1 presents the market share, comparing company figures with BOJ figures for the total industry at year-end 1998. Here we see that the big seven, with $1.2 trillion (¥146 trillion) in assets, accounted for 75.7 percent of total assets of the life insurance industry (Figure 5.1). The assets of the top 18 companies accounted for 93.8 percent of total industry assets.

In terms of policies in force, the top seven, with $9.8 trillion (¥1,178 trillion) in force, accounted for 61.1 percent of the total industry; the combined total of ¥1,402 for the top 18 accounted for 72.7 percent. In terms of new policies, the top seven, with a total of ¥95,812 billion, took 58.9 percent of the market; and the top 18 companies took 74.0 percent of the market.

The largest life insurers have massive sales networks of both direct sales-

Table 5.1

Key Data for Major Japanese Life Insurance Companies for FY98 (March 31, 1999)
(Yen billions, percent)

Company	Total assets	Policies in force	Percentage change	New policies	Percentage change	Premium income	Percentage change
Nippon Life	42,682	337,382	−5	24,049	−28	5,823	−7
Dai-Ichi Life	29,741	238,772	−3	20,685	−11	3,991	−1
Sumitomo Life	24,165	221,166	−4	20,215	−9	3,339	−2
Meiji Life	17,282	136,178	−5	10,399	−23	2,526	−8
Asahi Life	12,148	92,368	−6	6,590	−19	1,583	−8
Mitsui Life	10,115	73,761	−6	6,358	−19	1,575	−11
Yasuda Life	9,745	78,444	−4	7,516	−8	1,524	−11
Total Big Seven	**145,878**	**1,178,071**		**95,812**		**20,361**	
Taiyo Life	6,969	15,129	0	1,857	−7	1,235	−7
Daido Life	5,483	39,284	0	4,773	1	1,193	2
Kyoei Life	5,080	46,376	−5	5,022	−10	727	−3
Fukoku Life	4,469	36,256	1	3,509	−4	728	−9
Chiyoda Life	4,360	37,443	−9	3,593	−11	599	−23
Nihon Dantai	3,657	15,736	−4	1,485	−15	588	−11
Daihyaku Life	2,467	19,611	−9	2,653	4	415	−7
Tokyo Life	1,240	6,947	−7	693	−21	208	−1
Heiwa Life	546	3,495	−5	260	−15	75	−4
Yamato Life	300	2,104	−6	440	n/a	55	−6
Taisho Life	232	1,335	−3	143	−49	51	7
Total next eleven	**34,803**	**223,716**		**24,428**		**5,874**	
Total top eighteen	**180,681**	**1,401,787**		**120,240**		**26,235**	

Sources: Weekly Toyo Keizai, June 26, 1999. Weekly Economist, June 29, 1999.

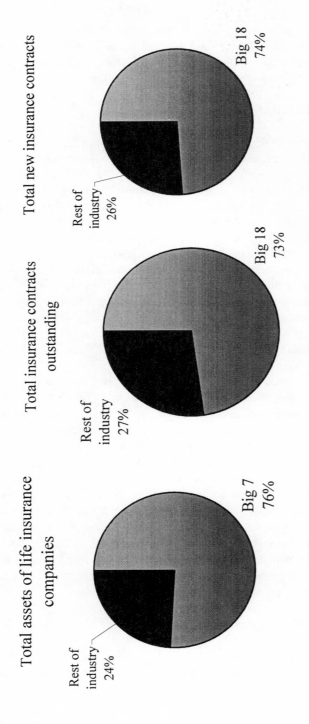

Figure 5.1 **Share of Market of Big Eighteen Japanese Life Insurers**

Total assets of life insurance companies

Rest of industry 24%

Big 7 76%

Total insurance contracts outstanding

Rest of industry 27%

Big 18 73%

Total new insurance contracts

Rest of industry 26%

Big 18 74%

Source: Company reports (balance at 3/31/99) and BOJ statistics (1998 year end).

people, and agents. Nippon Life is renowned for its nationwide legion of some 60,000 "sales ladies" and a total staff of 71,000 employees. Dai-Ichi Life has a sales force of some 50,000 and a total staff of 65,000. Sumitomo Life and Meiji Life employ 67,000 and 40,000, respectively.

Life Subsidiaries of Nonlife Companies

Since October 1996, nonlife insurance companies have been permitted to enter the life business through separately capitalized subsidiaries. In 2001 the barrier between life and nonlife will be fully removed. As of September 1998 there were eleven subsidiaries competing in the market (Table 5.2). Total assets were $3.4 billion (¥409.8 billion), and total policies in force some $39.2 billion (¥4.7 trillion). As a portion of the total life insurance industry, the share of policies was small, only some 0.6 percent, but a year earlier it had been just 0.3 percent, indicating the relatively fast growth (from a small base) of these companies. The life subsidiaries of nonlife companies have the advantage of the extensive sell agency network of the parents. For example, of Tokio Fire & Marine's 80,000 agent offices, some 17,000 have been commissioned to sell life insurance (*Kaneko 1999*, p. 21).

Japanese Katakana *Companies*

Nonforeign-owned *katakana* life companies are generally newer companies formed by nontraditional entrants to the industry, often initially in a joint venture with a foreign life insurer. Sony Life, the largest *katakana* life company, began business as a joint venture with Prudential (see Chapter Seventeen). Orico Life began as a JV between Orient Corporation and Mutual of Omaha, before Orient bought out its partner in 1992. Nikos Life started in 1986 as a joint venture between Occidental Life of the United States and Nihon Shimpan, before it was fully acquired by Nihon Shimpan in 1997. Having been started as joint ventures, usually with the foreign partner transferring product and management knowhow, *katakana* life insurers have acquired a reputation for innovative approaches to the market. Sony Life, in particular, claims to have introduced and to be the paragon of "consultative" selling. In terms of market share, the Japanese *katakana* insurers possess a still small but growing share of about 1.8 percent of the total market for personal policies.

Foreign Firms Now the Third Largest Factor

Foreign life insurers make up the final category. Table 5.2 provides a view of assets and policies in force levels of the leading *katakana* and foreign life

Table 5.2

Comparison of Subsidiaries of Nonlife Companies, *Katakana* Life Insurers and Foreign Life Companies
(data for March 31, 1999. Yen billions)

Life insurance subsidiaries of nonlife companies

	Total assets	Policies in force
Tokio Fire & Marine		
Anshin Life	186	4,396
Nichido Life	39	961
Daitokyo Shiawase Life	24	1,146
Sumitomo Fire & Marine Life		
Yuyu Life	69	1,701
Dowa Life	28	667
Mitsui Mirai Life	67	1,438
Fuji Life	23	834
Chiyoda Fire & Casualty		
Ebisu Life	26	712
Koa Fire & Casualty		
Magokoro Life	22	743
Kyoei Fire & Casualty		
Shinrai Life	20	500
Nihon Fire & Casualty		
Partner Life	21	726
Total	**525**	**13,824**

Katakana Life companies

	Total assets	Policies in force
Sony Life	881	17,113
Saison Life	550	4,131
Orix Life	375	2,704
Nikos Life	106	2,473
Orico Japan	95	780
Total	**2,007**	**27,201**

Foreign Life companies

	Total assets	Policies in force
American Family Life	2,550	40,077
Alico Japan	943	12,120
ING Life	308	3,073
Prudential Life	333	10,750
INA Himawari Life	280	4,957
AXA Life	30	587
Skandia Life	12	55
Zurich Life	3	56
GE Edison	327	9,027
Total	**4,786**	**80,702**

Source: Weekly Economist, June 29, 1999, p. 33.

companies. It shows that, by March 1999, the foreign companies held about 4.5 percent of the market for individual life insurance products. This data shows that foreign life insurers are now the third most important factor in the Japanese life insurance marketplace, significantly larger, in terms of both assets and policies in force, than the *katakana* companies and the subsidiaries of nonlife companies (see below for profiles and products of major foreign companies).

The rising tier position of the foreign life companies is a phenomenon of the last two to three years of the 1990s. In 1997 the U.S. Chamber of Commerce was complaining that foreign insurers occupied only a 1.6 percent share of the life insurance market, much lower than that normally captured by foreign companies in developed markets. Market share in the nonlife market was only 2.9 percent, also very low by international standards (*ACCJ 1999*, p. 139). What was evident by 1999 was that foreign companies were advancing quickly and increasing share, while Japanese firms were stagnating or shrinking.

Why the Life Industry Is in Trouble

To an extent much greater than in the United States, Japan's life insurers have played the role of savings and investment vehicles for Japan's high-saving and risk-averse population. Most policies, whether term or whole life, have offered a fixed dividend payout. In a market with limited savings and investment options—the case in Japan during the 1980s and 1990s—life insurance savings were a popular choice. This was particularly true because life insurance companies—aided by MOF regulations and accounting conveniences—were able to offer higher rates than banks. It was explicitly the policy of government to support the industry and to protect policy holders from loss, so risk was never an issue.

Negative Carrying Cost on Savings Policies

All the major insurers tried to expand rapidly in the early and mid-1990s by selling high-yielding annuities for a single upfront lump sum payment. To pay the high, fixed dividends—which were a contractual obligation—the insurance companies had to invest the funds at a higher rate of yield. As the general interest rate environment declined throughout the 1990s, this became much more difficult to do without taking large risks. By 1997 and 1998, it was impossible, and all the major insurance companies began to register high rates of "negative interest carry" on their policies.

Table 5.3 shows the extent of negative interest spread burden on the major life insurers in FY97 and FY98. For the top seven companies, which dominate the market, the negative carry was a massive $10.6 billion (¥1,276 billion) in FY98. Although the average guaranteed yield of the company's savings products was seen to decline slightly in FY98, the negative spread actually increased. This was an indication of the severity of the investment environment.

Problems with Investment and Loan Asset Quality

But there are problems as well. Many of the securities, real estate, and credit-lending investments of the major insurance companies have soured, meaning that the companies are sitting upon substantial realized losses. On March 31, 1998, total industry-wide assets of life insurers stood at $1.6 trillion (¥190 trillion). Some 50 percent was in securities, while about 40 percent of these assets, $658 billion (¥79 trillion), was in real estate and loans. In June, under new disclosure requirements, the seven largest life insurers, plus Chiyoda, announced that their nonperforming asset levels as of March 31, 1999, had risen to $9.3 billion (¥1,111 billion) (*Nihon Keizai Shimbun*, June 10, 1999). Moody's on June 10 downgraded Chiyoda from BC to Caa1, which indicates very poor financial security. In 1998, before the stricter disclosure and classification standards for nonperforming loans (NPLs) were introduced, Nippon Life reported a relatively manageable ratio of 0.46 percent of total assets. This is almost certainly a gross underestimation. Even applying the lax standards of 1998, some insurers reported heavy NPL burdens. The worst was Heiwa Life at 4.56 percent. Almost as bad was Chiyoda Life, at 4.21 percent. In June 1999 Chiyoda, Daihyaku, and Kyoei were all downgraded by Moody's ratings service to Caa1, meaning "impaired ability to meet payment obligations" (*Nihon Keizai Shimbun*, June 10, 1999).

The weight of negative spread was heavy on Nissan and Toho Life, but what sunk them finally were the unrecognized losses in their investment portfolios, especially from bad loans and real estate. The stock market in Japan is expected to recover in 1999 and 2000, but the postbubble residue of bad loan assets and undisclosed losses (the scale and nature of which are seen clearly in the cases of Long Term Credit Bank and Nippon Credit Bank) will continue to hang over the insurance industry for years. Notwithstanding the prospect of an increase in securities gains, the rating agencies Moody's and Standard & Poor's are negative on Japan's life insurers. They believe that the extent of these companies' bad loan losses is much higher than so far disclosed and therefore see solvency ratios as overstated. They believe that FSA inspections, which have not yet begun in earnest, will uncover vast amounts of bad loans and unrealized losses, requiring massive write-downs in equity values (Moody's Investors Service, June 8, 1999).

Table 5.3

Negative Interest Spread, Average Yield, Bad Loans, and Credit Ratings of Major Life Insurers for FY98 (March 31, 1999)

Company	Negative interest spread (Yen billions)		Average guaranteed yield (percent)		Non-performing loan burden* % of assets	Solvency ratio	S&P rating
	FY98	FY97	FY98	FY97			
Nippon Life	360	330	4.1	4.2	0.46	850	AA
Dai-Ichi Life	240	210	4.1	4.2	0.75	662	A
Sumitomo Life	230	220	4.1	4.2	0.80	590	BBB–
Meiji Life	150	130	3.8	4.0	0.61	706	A+
Asahi Life	130	110	4.1	4.2	0.79	689	BB+
Mitsui Life	87	83	4.0	4.1	1.27	520	BB+
Yasuda Life	79	67	3.8	3.9	0.60	727	A–
Subtotal	**1,276**	**1,150**					
Taiyo Life	90	86	4.4	4.6	1.38	869	A
Daido Life	12	10	3.6	3.7	0.96	998	A+
Kyoei Life	70	70	4.3	4.4	1.37	343	B+
Fukoku Life	35	30	3.8	4.1	0.88	821	A–

Chiyoda Life	44	41	3.9	3.9	4.21	396	Bpi
Nihon Dantai	25	11	4.0	4.0	1.78	378	Bpi
Daihyaku Life	35	25	4.4	4.5	2.71	305	—
Tokyo Life	12	13	4.3	4.4	1.73	479	Bpi
Heiwa Life	n/a	n/a	n/a	n/a	4.56	578	
Yamato Life	n/a	n/a	n/a	n/a	3.62	755	BBB–
Taiso Life	n/a	n/a	n/a	n/a	4.30	385	

Sources: *Weekly Toyo Keizai,* June 26, 1999. *Weekly Economist,* June 29, 1999. *Kaneko Seiho Anzendo Ranking 1999,* p. 10.
Note: *Loans under special risk management as percent of total assets (as of September 30, 1998).

All Eyes on Solvency Ratios

A measure of insurers' ability to cover losses and claims is the solvency ratio. Regulations consider a ratio of 200 percent or less to indicate high risk of default. In March 1999 a number of second tier insurers showed solvency ratios of 300 to 400 percent. This was a clear indication of weakness. At 305 percent, Daihyaku would have been unviable without the support received in a government-encouraged tie-up with a foreign company, ManuLife (see below).

The final issue with Japan's major life insurers is that they are losing business. In 1997 the number of new policies written declined for the first time since World War II. The decline of the leading eight companies reached a shocking 17 percent in 1998 (Table 5.1), and recovery is not in sight. In general, Japanese people are overinsured with the kind of standard life and pension products that have characterized the offerings of the industry. Japanese consumers are increasingly finding alternatives that are more attractive from foreign providers or from products like mutual funds. Add to this the concern of policy holders about the solvency of life insurers, and we can conclude that an epochal change is at hand.

When Disaster Struck: The Cases of Nissan (Aoba) and Toho and Daihyaku

Nissan Life failed in April 1997. Under supervision of MOF, its business was taken over by the Life Insurance Association. The management was dismissed and an investigation conducted. Good assets—policies and loans—were segregated and the business license was transferred to a new company, Aoba Life, on October 1, 1997. Nissan Life was put into liquidation. Net negative assets were some $2.5 billion (¥300 billion). Because Nissan Life had failed, the guaranteed rates on existing policies could be lowered upon transfer to Aoba, so negative spread was not such a problem for the receiving company.

Forty-five members of the Life Insurance Association, the industry association, injected $1.67 billion (¥200 billion) into the new company, Aoba Life, for the value of its earning assets. Another $83 million (¥100 billion) was expended in the bailout, and this was deemed "goodwill" in the new company. Nippon Life contributed the largest share. The purpose of the company was to serve existing policy holders. It is a run-off company, not soliciting new business.

In May 1998 American Insurance Group (AIG) approached the Association with a request to begin a preacquisition due diligence investigation in Aoba. The Association retained Morgan Stanley to represent the sellers and, pursuant to Morgan Stanley's advice, decided to offer Aoba for sale publicly in an auction. The Association had three objectives: in order of priority, to derive benefits for the Association members—that is, recovery of their investment; to protect policy holders; and to maintain employment for employees.

Bids were received during the fall, from AIG and the French company Artemis, among others, but the sellers deemed them unsatisfactory. The process was terminated in February 1999.

Aoba did not sell because the sellers were demanding too high a price. Essentially, they wanted the acquirer to assume costs and liabilities which they, as industry representatives, acting under MOF direction, had been compelled to accept. But assumption of such liabilities could not be justified from a business perspective.

Toho Life was ordered by FSA to cease operations on June 6, 1999, after its auditor had insisted that assets be written down and the company was deemed to have net liabilities of $1.67 billion (¥200 billion). Weakened by bad loans and negative spread, and swamped by policy cancellations, Toho had sold its business license to GE Capital for some $583 million (¥70 billion) in 1998, and formed a JV company, GE Capital Edison Life, for new business development (see Chapter Fourteen). The remaining Toho was operating virtually as administrator of existing contracts and was accepting no new business, except for offering reinsurance for GE Capital Edison.

Toho suffered inordinately from negative spreads, since it was one of the aggressive sellers of single premium savings policies when guaranteed rates were as high as 6 percent. Unlike Aoba, it was unable, since it was not officially bankrupt, to lower these guaranteed rates. But what sunk the company finally was having to recognize the unrealized losses in its balance sheet, as it began to dispose of assets to meet payment obligations. Toho's bankruptcy will release it and its successors from the contractual premium rate obligation, but whether any taker of its remaining assets can be found is questionable. Very likely the policies will be transferred to the Policyholders' Protection Fund, an industry body set up in December 1998.

The Daihyaku Life case looks like a repeat of the Toho saga. By 1998 this company was exceptionally weak, with a solvency ratio approaching 200 percent. With policy cancellations and operating losses increasing, the company was forced to find aid. It found it in ManuLife of Canada, which agreed to buy Daihyaku's business license, thereby providing some $333 million (¥40 billion) in needed capital, and to form a joint venture for new business development. The new venture, ManuLife Century Life, was licensed and began operation in March 1999. What will happen now to Daihyaku? It will probably repeat the pattern of Toho: be declared insolvent by regulators and then be absorbed by its offspring, ManuLife Century.

Conversion of Mutual Companies to Limited Stock Companies

One of the issues with restructuring of the life insurance industry is corporate organization, the fact that of the top eighteen insurers, none of the top seven, and only four of the remaining eleven (Kyoei, Nihon Dantai, Heiwa, and Taisho), are limited stock companies. All the rest are mutual life associations. It is difficult for mutuals to increase capital—to grow, cover losses, and restructure—except by calling upon policy holders. The method of gaining capital and forming strategic alliances through equity tie-ups is blocked (one reason for the formation of JV companies by Toho and Daihyaku). Also, organization as mutuals makes it difficult for insurers to adopt the holding company structure that will be one of the more effective ways to manage growth in the post-big bang financial marketplace. For these same reasons, many U.S. insurance companies converted themselves from mutuals to limited liability stock companies and listed on the stock exchanges.

The severe capital and restructuring issues have compelled some Japanese mutuals to act to change their structures. As at June 1999 the managements of Mitsui, Yasuda, Daido, and Taiyo had decided to seek policy holder approval to convert to limited stock companies. Other companies surely will follow.

Overview of the Nonlife Insurance Industry

The nonlife insurance industry in Japan is much smaller than the life insurance industry, but it is no less undergoing change. One difference is that the industry is generally healthy. But deregulation has released competition, and foreign insurers are making significant inroads. Fourteen listed nonlife insurers dominate the industry.

In July 1998 the law regulating nonlife premium rates was amended, abolishing mandatory industry-wide rates. For the first time in memory, rate competition became a factor in the industry. A consequence of this change, plus the generally weak economy, was a pronounced decline in premium revenues, underwriting profits, and net income for the industry (Table 5.4). In FY98 all of the listed nonlife companies saw net premiums decline, usually between 4 and 5 percent. The largest company and market leader, Tokio Marine & Fire, experienced a 3.8 percent decline.

Automobile insurance is the main contributor of premiums. In the period April to October 1998 automobile premiums accounted for 51.6 percent of premium revenue; compulsory automobile liability premiums 13.7 percent of premium revenue; fire insurance premiums 13.5 percent of premium revenue; "new types" 17 percent; and marine insurance 4.3 percent. The automobile insurance marketplace is thus a major battlefield among the nonlife insurers.

Deregulation legislation provides a transition period, until June 2000, during which insurers can continue to apply fixed premium rates as before. This the fourteen major companies decided to do, except for new product introductions. It is now necessary that companies innovate in both sales approaches and products and attempt to create value, rather than simply to increase sales of undifferentiated products. Insurers are rushing to cut costs in advance of rate declines. More market entrants using innovate approaches are expected.

In 2001, the barriers preventing life/nonlife service providers will be abolished. In order to gain market and product knowledge, in 1996 life insurance companies established nonlife subsidiaries. The performance of these subsidiaries in FY98 is presented in Table 5.4.

Foreign Nonlife Companies: AIG Way Ahead

Table 5.4 lists the top six (out of twenty-six) foreign nonlife companies in Japan in terms of net premiums. As we will examine in detail in Chapter Twelve, AIG, with its long history in Japan, is by far the market leader. Its premium income topped $1.9 billion (¥233 billion). This was down slightly from the previous year, reflecting market conditions. The next company, American Home, is an affiliate of AIG. What this short list indicates is that the pure nonlife sector has been a difficult one in which to build critical mass for most foreign companies. The greatest penetration by foreign insurers has been in the third sector (below), and the vehicle has been a life insurance company.

In addition to cost cutting and new product development, deregulation is pushing Japanese nonlife companies to seek tie-ups with other financial institutions or manufacturing companies. Tokio Marine & Fire, the industry leader, will be launching a joint venture mutual funds company with Charles Schwab (see Chapter Four). The basic strategy of the firm is to have group operations include a life insurance subsidiary and an investment trust subsidiary and generally to leverage its huge distribution network and financial strength. Yasuda Fire & Marine formed a joint venture with Cigna of the U.S. in preparation for entering the 401(k) market. Sumitomo Marine & Fire has taken an equity position in the asset management company of Sumitomo Bank and Daiwa Securities. Chiyoda Fire & Marine effected a capital increase allocation to Toyota Motors in September 1998. Toyota purchased additional shares in Chiyoda to increase its equity ownership share from 34

Table 5.4

Revenue and Profit Performance of Listed Nonlife Companies and Nonlife Subsidiaries of Life Companies. Leading Foreign Nonlife Companies by Net Premiums Received (FY 98)

	Staff, assets, revenue, and profit performance of fourteen listed nonlife companies in FY 98 (Yen billions, figures for YoY change in percent)						Performance of nonlife subsidiaries of life insurance companies (Yen billions, percent)			
Company	Staff	Total assets	Net premiums received	Net profit after tax	Percentage change	Company	Net premiums received	Percentage change YoY	Recurring profit	Net profit after tax
Tokio Marine & Fire	13,751	5,371	1,285	32	−5	Nessei	28	38	−3	−3
Yasuda Fire & Marine	11,319	3,698	902	12	−9	Sumisei	15	38	−2	−2
Mitsui Marine & Fire	7,815	2,873	615	10	−10	Da-Ichi Life	12	65	−2	−2
Sumitomo Marine & Fire	7,514	2,858	540	11	−11	Meiji	10	41	−2	−3
Dai Tokyo Fire & Marine	5,202	1,574	422	6	−6	Yasuda Life	8	48	−2	−2
Nippon Fire & Marine	5,908	1,890	413	7	−6	Mitsui Life	8	60	−2	−2
Nichido Fire & Marine	7,490	1,731	392	9	−10	Total	81	45	−14	−14
Chiyoda Fire & Marine	5,352	1,308	382	5	−3	Leading foreign nonlife companies by net premiums received				
Fuji Fire & Marine	8,696	1,273	341	4	1					
Kao Fire & Marine	4,992	1,329	278	5	3					
Nissan Fire & Marine	4,116	996	269	4	−3	AIU	233.0	−3.3		
Dowa Fire & Marine	3,681	1,039	223	5	−2	American Home	22.0	40		
Nisshin Fire & Marine	2,722	557	151	3	−3	Zurich	11.0	59		
Tasei Fire & Marine	1,913	415	94	1	−9	Generali	7.0	73		
Total	90,471	26,912	6,307	113	−6	Royal Sun Alliance	7.9	32		
						Winterthur	6.1	−59		

Sources: Nihon Keizai Shimbun, May 21, 1999. Company reports. Nonlife Insurers' Association.

percent to 44 percent. Chiyoda has clearly become a house vehicle for Toyota and will develop products and strategies for Toyota vehicles to realize this synergy.

The "Third Sector": U.S.-Japanese Agreement

Prior to 1996, Japan's insurance market regulations had strictly defined and segregated life and nonlife (fire, casualty, and marine) insurance product areas, ensuring through licensing that there was no crossover by companies in one area into the other. However, this separation had left a gap: the so-called "third sector," which included special health (cancer, stroke), disability, hospitalization, long-term care, and unemployment insurance. Well before domestic firms, foreign firms perceived an opportunity in this "third sector" and began to exploit it. Large domestic firms, feeling hemmed in by regulations and having no appropriate products, sat out the competition.

In the late 1980s and early 1990s, some American companies, notably AIG's subsidiary Alico Japan, AFLAC's American Family, and INA's INA Himawari Life, were highly successful in selling "third sector" products, often capturing large market shares. For example, American Family began business selling cancer insurance. By year end 1997 it had written 12.5 million policies and achieved 90 percent market share (see Chapter Seventeen for a profile of American Family's business).

It became apparent to the Japanese industry and its regulator, MOF, that there was a significant market opportunity in the third area. In the late 1980s and early 1990s the MOF began drawing up plans to change regulations to specifically open entry to large Japanese firms. The U.S. firms involved brought this potential competitive threat to the attention of the U.S. government, specially the Office of the U.S. Trade Representative (USTR), which put the issue on the agenda of bilateral market access negotiations.

The results of negotiations were the 1994 U.S.-Japan Insurance Framework Agreement and the 1996 Supplementary Measures (together "Agreements"). The purpose of the Agreements was to protect the so-called third sector pioneered by foreign insurance companies from "radical change" until such time as the first sector life and second sector nonlife insurance markets were liberalized and a sufficient period had elapsed for the foreign companies to establish themselves. Liberalization of the first sector markets was deemed to require full dismantling of the "rating organization" regime in which rates were set by fiat and no competition for differentiation was allowed. The Supplementary Measures recognized the "sufficient period" to be two and one-half years (*ACCJ 1998*).

The Agreements constituted a negotiated bureaucratic standoff, that is, a freezing of the status quo. The MOF was enjoined to reverse its plan to liberalize the third sector before liberalizing the primary life insurance and nonlife insurance sectors. The Agreements essentially provided foreign firms unchallenged access to the market for "third sector" products until the year 2001, until they were permitted to participate equally in deregulated primary life and nonlife product areas.

By 1999, the Agreements were wearing thin. Japanese companies were finding ways to compete with the foreign firms, and foreign firms were finding openings in the primary product areas. Cigna Insurance's plan to sell a majority of INA Himawari Life to Yasuda Fire & Marine, thereby giving the latter entry into the third sector, incited passions and politics worthy of theater. In general it may be said that foreign, particularly U.S., companies did benefit from the preferred access accorded in the Agreements. By late 1999 all serious players were focusing on the future.

Foreign Insurance Companies

For many years some foreign insurance companies complained of being shut out of the primary life and nonlife markets by a combination of MOF guidance or regulations discouraging innovative product development, pricing, and distribution, regulations that favored entrenched Japanese firms; self-serving and anticompetitive industry associations dominated by large domestic firms; and corporate buying practices based on *keiretsu* and cross-shareholdings *(ACCJ 1999*, p. 139). This was not the case in the "third sector" so foreign companies excelled in this area.

Success in the "third sector" has allowed foreign firms not just to make money, but also to distinguish themselves in the marketplace, which is of greater long-term strategic importance. According to one Japanese analyst, foreign insurance companies in Japan have differentiated themselves from local competitors in four ways:

1. *Prevalence of no-dividend insurance.* When virtually all products offered by domestic companies were of the dividend-paying type, thereby requiring higher premiums, foreign companies normally offered no-dividend insurance (the exception now is GE Capital Edison).
2. *Variety of sales channels.* Zurich Life is using telemarketing exclusively. Alico Japan uses a multichannel approach including agents, in-house salesmen, telemarketing, and department store counter sales. In the past, foreign insurers were distinguished by their consultative sales approach, but now most Japanese insurers are emulating this, calling their sales staff "life planners" and providing specialized sales training

and tools. AXA has tried to raise the service level to "counseling." Telemarketing has been particularly successful for sales of cancer insurance and term life insurance. American Home began selling travel insurance over the internet in April 1999.

3. *Focus on key products*. Many foreign insurers have focused on specific products. Skandia Life has offered a guaranteed minimum rate, variable life product, essentially an insurance product that invests in mutual funds, where the policyholder can choose among equity and bond funds. Alico Japan, Prudential Life, and Nicos Life also have products allowing policyholders to choose investments. American Family began business in Japan selling cancer insurance. Zurich Life adopted cancer insurance as its main product when it started business in October 1996. American Family also pioneered nursing home care insurance and by 1998 had achieved over 90 percent market share. Maine-based disability company UNUM Corporation announced in March 1999 that it would form a JV with Chiyoda Life to sell individual long-term disability insurance through Chiyoda's sales outlets.

4. *Introduction of unique products*. In most cases, new products in the Japanese market have been introduced by foreign insurers. For example, INA Himawari Life has offered pregnancy insurance to cover hereditary diseases and defects. Alico Japan has offered term life insurance for persons rejected by other insurers and special insurance for nonsmokers. While GE Capital Edison Life continues to offer the main product inherited from Toho Life, discounted premiums are offered for people who meet certain conditions, and sales are by telemarketing. In December 1998 GE Capital Edison began to offer customers a choice between U.S. dollar and yen denominated personal pension plans. ManuLife's new JV with Daihyaku, ManuLife Century, will focus on life annuity and investment products, rather than death payment products traditional in Japan. (*Gaishikei Kinyu Kikan no Katsuyoho*, pp. 108–116)

Table 5.5 presents details of the major foreign insurance companies operating in Japan. American Family Life, a branch of Georgia-based AFLAC, established in Japan for 25 years, is the strongest (see Chapter Seventeen for details of AFLAC's business). American Family has the best name recognition among foreign insurers.

Alico Japan, a subsidiary of American Life Insurance (part of AIG), has been in Japan since 1973. Alico is renowned for its consultative selling and life planning approach, as well as for new product development. It previously introduced sickness insurance and long-term disability insurance. In

Table 5.5

Foreign Life Insurance Companies

Name	Start business	Country of parent	Group affiliation	Paid in capital	Ownership structure	Staff
INA Himawari Life	1982	USA	Cigna Group	Yen 7.25 billion	Cigna Group 61% Yasuda Fire & Casualty 39%	823
ING Life	1995	Netherlands	ING Group	Yen 8 billion	ING Insurance Int'l B.V. 100%	668
AXA Life	1995	France	AXA Group	Yen 14 billion	AXA S.A. 100%	551
American Family Life	1974	USA	AFLAC	—	AFLAC 100%	1,731
ALICO Japan	1973	USA	AIG Group	—	AIG Group Japan Branch 100%	3,819
GE Capital Edison Life	1998	USA	GE Group	Yen 36 billion	GE Capital 50% Toho Life 50% (voting rights 90% GE)	n/a
Skandia Life	1996	Sweden	Skandia Group	Yen 10 billion	Skandia Group 100%	n/a
Zurich Life	1996	Switzerland	Zurich Insurance Group	Yen 5.5 billion	Zurich Insurance Group	n/a
Prudential Life	1988	USA	Prudential Group	Yen 10 billion	The Prudential Insurance Co. of America 100%	1,780
Manulife Century Life	1999	Canada	Manulife Financial			5,000 (approx.)

Sources: Gaishikei Kinyu Kikan no Katsuyoho, p. 117. Company reports.

August 1998 it introduced a term life insurance product open to anyone aged fifty to eighty and requiring no proof of insurability. (See Chapter Twelve for a discussion of AIG's life and nonlife businesses.)

Prudential Life is a newcomer, but is growing at double digits. It does not employ agents, but invests much training to create a high-quality "life planner" sales force (see Chapter Seventeen).

GE Capital Edison Life plans to target markets and products and sales channels, while fully leveraging the broad direct and agent sales force inherited from Toho (see Chapter Fourteen for details).

ManuLife Century Life (the JV between ManuLife and Daihyaku) was licensed to begin business in March 1999. Having acquired the business license of Daihyaku, it also began with 6,000 former Daihyaku sales people.

ING Life has been growing quickly, focusing on the corporate market. In April 1999 it introduced a variable annuity product aimed primarily at corporations for inclusion in 401(k)-type investment menus for staff. ING has emphasized staff training in order to offer a value-added consulting relationship to customers.

Looking Toward 2001: New Entrants and a More Open Market

When competition in premiums became possible in automobile insurance in July 1998, AIG Group company American Home launched a television and newspaper ad campaign offering to reduce auto insurance premiums as much as 30 percent. In March 1999 Mitsui Marine and AIU came out with policies to provide income, hospitalization and education expense support, insuring against the risk of becoming unemployed through company bankruptcy or downsizing. By July 1999 AIU, GE Edison, Prudential Life, and Alico Japan were offering foreign currency denominated accident, variable annuity, whole life, and pension products. The insurance market in Japan is definitely changing, with new competitors and new products. It will only become more varied in the future.

As Japan's insurance marketplace moves toward full deregulation in 2001, the key factors will be the strategic advances of the major market participants and the entries of some key global players, like Citigroup, that have not yet taken a serious position in the marketplace.

We will review in Chapter Nine the likely alliances and groupings of Japan's largest players. As in the banking and securities industries, the financial meltdown of the 1990s is certain to leave behind fewer companies in the insurance field.

Chapter Six

The Pension Market: The Asset Management Industry

Overview of the Japanese Pension Market

In most developed countries, including Japan, access to pension assets is the El Dorado of the financial services industry. Pension assets are long-term and patient capital, with a need to grow faster than inflation. The amounts are usually so huge that any kind of investment usually can find a place in a portfolio or risk diversification strategy. To be a significant manager or recipient of pension asset investments can be hugely rewarding.

For the period ending December 1997, the total fund assets of the Japanese pension market were approximately US$2,382 billion. In terms of size, Japan is the second largest pension market in the world, behind the United States.

In some countries, pensions are largely private affairs. In most countries, however, including Japan, they are a mix of public and private, with heavy regulation and direction from public agencies. The United States has a mixed system, with mandatory public Social Security existing alongside discretionary private pension programs of individuals and corporations, including 401(k) plans established through corporations.

To understand Japan's pension market and the roles of intermediaries, we should first gain an understanding of the pension system as a whole.

Japan's Pension System

The pension system in Japan has been designed and structured by regulation to be all-inclusive, but with differentiation according to employment. The system contains both public elements and private elements. Government policy is to encourage people to conceive of the pension system as a "three-legged stool," with a basic government pension, work-related pensions, and individuals' own savings and pension plans. In fall 2000, a very important

Figure 6.1 **Schematic of Japan's Pension System**

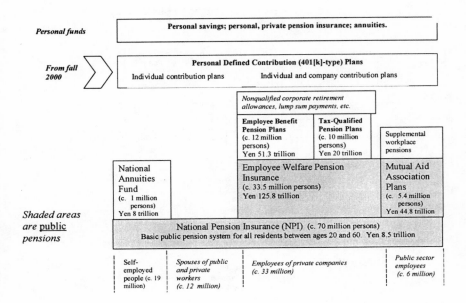

Sources: Ministry of Health and Welfare, *Health and Welfare White Paper (Kosei Hakusho)*, 1997. Mitaka, P. 23. *Nihon Keizai Shimbun*, July 28, 1999.

Note: Values for tax-qualified plans at March 31, 1999; all others at March 31, 1998.

new scheme will be added to strengthen the last two "legs" of the stool: a defined contribution pension scheme, similar to 401(k) programs in the United States. Figure 6.1 provides a schematic presentation of Japan's pension system. Figure 6.2 helps distinguish between public and private pension schemes.

Public Pension Schemes

The base of the system is National Pension Insurance (NPI), which covers all residents ages 20 to 60. This is equivalent to Social Security in the United States, except that the payments are really only subsistence level. Substantial pension payments are provided through work-place plans, supervised or administered by the government, Employee Welfare Pension Insurance (EWPI) for salaried employees of corporations, and the Mutual Aid Association Plans (MAA) for public sector employees.

The Employee Welfare Pension Insurance is the largest public pension

Figure 6.2 **Public and Private Pension Schemes**

Current and Prospective 401(k)-Type Pension Schemes

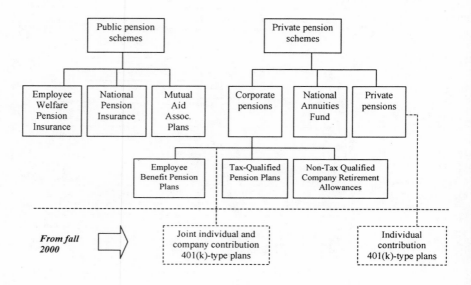

Sources: Ministry of Health and Welfare. *Health and Welfare White Paper.* Mitaka, p. 23. *Nenkin no Shikumi,* p. 21. Figure 6.1

plan in Japan with approximately $1,05 billion (¥125.8 trillion) in March 1999, approximately 70 percent of total public sector pension funds. Funds are accumulated in the EWPI program from withholdings from salary, similar to Social Security. A separate category of public pension is the 98 Mutual Aid Associations established for national and local public employees. In 1998 assets in these associations totalled some $373.3 billion (¥44.8 trillion).

Private Pension Schemes

Private pension schemes include corporate pension plans, the National Annuities Fund for self-employed individuals, and private pension plans purchased from life insurance companies and other sources. The National Annuities Fund (NAF) was established in 1991 because nonsalaried employees did not have a plan to supplement the basic national pension insurance. Joining the plan was voluntary and was opened up to all self-employed workers and others (except public employees) not covered by EWPI. NAF has been popular, with participants in 1999 rising to over one million. Assets in 1998 were some $70 billion (¥8.5 trillion). Assessments are made on a fixed monthly basis to plan participants.

As shown in Figures 6.1 and 6.2, there are three types of corporate pension schemes: Tax-Qualified Pension Plans (TQP); Employee Benefit Pension Plans (EBP), and Non-Tax Qualified Plans (NTQP). There were some 93,000 Tax-Qualified Plans sponsored by corporations in 1998, with total assets of some $166.7 billion (¥20 trillion). Most of the sponsors were typically small- and medium-sized corporations with relatively few employees, but some large corporates also sponsor such plans (see Table 6.1). There were only about 1,900 sponsors of EBP, but these were large companies and groups with thousands of employees. Under the pension system's rules, EBPs pay and manage a portion of the NPI funds. This has led to rapid growth in EBP assets, so that it is the largest of the private sector plans, with some $427.5 billion (¥51.3 trillion) in assets in 1998. NTQP were sponsored by 19,000 companies but, lacking tax advantages, are less popular than the other schemes. In 1997 total assets amounted to some $142 billion (¥17 trillion).

All EBPs are required to be members of the Pension Fund Association (PFA). The PFA serves as an industry association for EBPs and also performs services for members and beneficiaries such as in-house management of pension assets of vested employees who terminate employment before retirement age or who are members of EBPs that have ceased operations due to company bankruptcy.

The Government Superstructure: MOF's Trust Fund Bureau and MHW's *Nenpuku*

By law, funds flowing into the public pension programs—that is, NPI and EWPI—are handed over to the government's Fiscal Investment and Loan Program (FILP) and form—along with postal savings—the bulk resources for this massive program. The FILP is essentially a second, "off the books" budget for funding multifarious government agencies and programs. By the early 1990s the FILP had grown in size to over 50 percent of the General Account Budget. (For a clear explanation of the FILP, see Ishi 1993).

Responsibility for actual management of the funds within the FILP is invested in the Trust Fund Bureau of the Ministry of Finance (MOF). The Trust Fund Bureau is obligated to return a yield on the pension funds based

Table 6.1

Total Pension Market, Public and Private Sponsors

Total Pension Market, Public and Private Sector Sponsors

	Amount Yen tril.	$ bil.	Number of plans
Total Pension Markets	**305.3**	**2,544**	
Public Sector	**179.9**	**1,499**	
EWPI	125.8	1,048	1
MAA	44.8	373	98
NPI	8.5	71	1
Other*	0.8	7	1
Private Corp. Plans	**80.4**	**670**	
EBP	51.3	428	1,883
TQP	20	167	92,500
NTQP*	17	142	19,000
Personal Pension Plans	**45**	**375**	
Private insurers*	15.3	128	14,300,000
Gojo Nenkin*	10	83	98
Other*	19.7	164	9,000,000
Defined Contribution			
Introduced in 2000	?	?	?

Sources: *Nenkin Joho*, October 19, 1998. Mitaka, p. 23.
Note: Data totals for FY98. *Indicates data for FY97.

Top Ten Pension Sponsors in Each Category

Public Sector Sponsors

	Yen tril.	$ bil.
Employee Welfare Pension Ins.	**125**	**104.8**
Mutual Aid Associations	**44.8**	**373.3**
Mutual aid of public servants	10.15	88.3
National government employees	7.58	65.9
Public school personnel	6.72	58.4
Private school teachers & staff	2.56	22.3
NTT	2.0	17.4
Agric., forestry & fishery workers	1.92	16.7
National police personnel	1.8	15.6
Local public service personnel	1.77	15.4
Designated cities personnel	1.48	12.9
National municipal personnel	1.45	12.6

Note: Data for sponsors for FY1996.

Private Sector Sponsors

	Yen bil.	$ bil.
Employee Benefit Plans	**51,300**	**427.5**
Hitachi	786	6.6
Matsushita Electric Ind.	671	5.6
Toshiba	591	4.9
NEC	532	4.4
Mitsubishi Electric	532	4.4
Honda Motor	531	4.4
Toyota Motor	511	4.3
Fujitsu	493	4.1
Zenshinren	319	2.7
Nissan	311	2.6

Tax Qual. Plans

	Yen bil.	$ bil.
Tax Qual. Plans	**20,000**	**166.7**
Mitsubishi Heavy	146	1.217
Nissan	109	0.908
NKK	83	0.692
Fuji Xerox	72	0.600
Shionogi Pharm.	67	0.558
Sumitomo Corp.	60	0.500
Fuji Photo Film	51	0.425
Nikon	42	0.350
Showa Denko	39	0.325
Nihon Sekiyu	39	0.325

Source: Data for FY97 from *Nenkin Joho*, October 19, 1998.

upon the rate for ten-year Japanese government bonds (JGBs). The Trust Fund Bureau channels most of the funds into JGBs and into the operating accounts of some nine public finance corporations, the Japan Development bank and the Export-Import Bank of Japan, and a variety of other uses (Ishi 1993, p. 93).

A certain portion of funds are allocated by the Trust Fund Bureau to an agency, the Pension and Welfare Service Corporation (popularly called *Nenpuku*), which is controlled by the Ministry of Health and Welfare (MHW). To some extent *Nenpuku* is doubtless the MHW's bureaucratic bid to deny MOF sole control over Japan's huge pension assets. More charitably, we may view it as MHW's highly responsible effort to achieve a better return on the assets of a pension system which is MHW's to administer.

Nenpuku technically "borrows" funds from the Trust Fund Bureau, paying the same rate to the Trust Fund Bureau as the latter has guaranteed to the public pension programs. In recent years, *Nenpuku* has taken over some 20 percent of the total assets of the public programs (NPI and EWPI). *Nenpuku* seeks to achieve a return on funds higher than its cost by commissioning trust banks and life insurance companies to manage the funds on a discretionary basis and also by managing a certain part of the funds in-house, with the assistance of investment advisory companies and consultants. Earnings on investment in excess of the cost of borrowing from the Trust Fund Bureau are credited to a Special Pension Account in the national budget. This complicated system is presented in Figures 6.3 and 6.4.

Review of Deregulation

Management of pension fund assets has historically been, and to some extent remains, highly regulated. Prior to 1990 all pension funds, public or private, were required to entrust management of pension assets either to trust banks (eight domestic and nine foreign), to be managed in special pension trusts, or to life insurance companies (twenty-three domestic), which offered only comingled management in general accounts. From 1990, in the interest of increasing efficiency and performance, plan sponsors were allowed for "new money" (up to one third of cumulative assets) to offer discretionary mandates to investment advisory companies (see below); to set up "number two special mandates" with life insurers; and to establish individually managed money trusts with trust banks. By 1998 the limits had been raised and the distinction between new and old money discarded. In 1999 all restrictions were removed.

A second key restriction on the industry, phased out after February 1996

Figure 6.3 **Schematic of Flow of Funds from Pension System to the Fiscal Investment and Loan Program, Trust Fund Bureau, and Pension and Welfare Service Corporation (*Nenpuku*)**

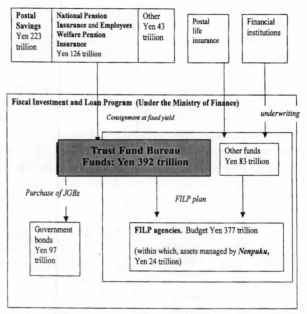

Sources: Ministry of Finance, *FILP Report 1997*. Ministry of Health and Welfare, *Nenkin Hakusho*, p. 98.
Note: Figures for FY96.

and fully removed in January 1998, was the famous 5–3–3–2 rule. This rule required that:

- No less than 50 percent of assets could be invested in "guaranteed principal" investments such as domestic cash equivalents, bonds, loans, and certain types of convertible bonds.
- No more than 30 percent of assets could be invested in domestic equities.
- No more than 30 percent of assets could be invested in foreign currency denominated securities.
- No more than 20 percent of assets could be invested in real estate.

Prior to 1990 the 5–3–3–2 rule was applied at both the sponsors' level (for all pension assets) and at the managers' level (for portfolios).

Deregulation began for investment advisors in 1990 when they were allowed to offer services to EBPs for "new money." In April 1996 in-

Figure 6.4 **Schematic of *Nenpuku* Funds Management**

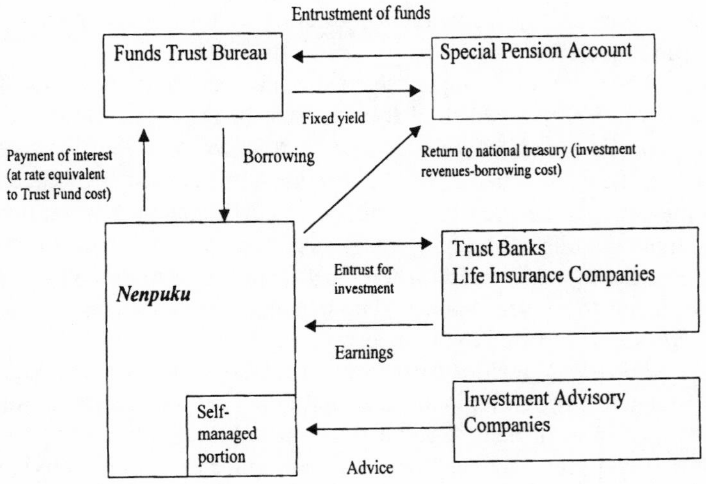

Sources: Ministry of Health and Welfare, *Report of the Study Commission on In-House Pension Fund Management.* Ministry of Health and Welfare. *Nenkin Hakusho,* p. 101.

vestment advisors were allowed to offer services to *Nenpuku* and NPI funds. In October 1997 investment advisors were allowed to offer services to TQPs.

Management of Pension Funds

Asset Managers and Products

In Japan, three types of asset managers are present in the pension market. They are the traditional managers, life insurance companies and trust banks, and the Securities Investment Advisory Companies (Investment Advisors) who have entered the market since 1990.

Life insurance companies. Some twenty-three life insurers are present in the market, but the top eight insurers occupy 90 percent of their market service category. Nippon Life is the largest pension fund manager with over ¥10 trillion under management. Life insurers have traditionally offered "guaranteed" yield and return of capital products through general accounts in which various sponsors' assets are pooled and sponsors cannot direct investments. Insurers also offer special accounts which are separately managed and do not provide a guaranteed yield or return of capital. Until 1997 various asset classes were pooled within a special account, but since 1997 separate accounts (e.g., for domestic equities) have been permitted. An innovation since 1997 has been No. 2 special accounts set up for a specific sponsor to meet specific objectives.

Trust banks. There are eight Japanese trust banks and nine (ten with the addition of BNP in 1999) established foreign trust banks. Trust banks offer pension trusts, special mandates, and pension *tokkin* accounts. Pension trusts are comingled funds, but can be highly differentiated in terms of asset classes. Actual asset allocation is decided in consultation with the client. Special mandates are accounts established for individual customers and designed to meet specific customer needs. Pension *tokkin* accounts are accounts required by regulations to be established between sponsors, trust banks, and investment advisors to actually hold assets entrusted to the investment advisors for management.

Investment advisors. Securities investment advisors were formally legitimized and regulated through legislation adopted in 1986. These companies explicitly do not broker or deal in securities, but only provide advice for a fee pursuant to a contract. Japanese regulations require investment advisors to register with the Financial Reconstruction Commission (FRC) if their business is advice only. If advisors seek to provide discretionary asset management services, that is, to make judgments and adjust portfolio position independently in accordance with general customer guidelines, they must qualify for and receive a discretionary investment management (DIM) license from the FRC. One of the qualifications for investment advisors to handle discretionary investment accounts is that they must be engaged exclusively in the investment advisory business and their directors are barred from holding other offices.

By the end of 1998 some 604 companies had registered as investment advisors in Japan. Some 136 companies, including fifty-one foreign companies, had received licenses from the FRC to engage in discretionary investment management.

Who Is Managing Pension Assets?

Table 6.2 presents the market shares of pension asset managers historically, in 1998, and projected for the future by Goldman Sachs. In 1987 domestic trust banks and life insurance companies provided all the pension fund management service, except for a 0.3 percent share held by foreign trust banks in the corporate sector. Investment advisors were allowed into the EBP market in 1990, but not into the public market until 1996. Until the mid-1990s the ten-year head start by trust banks and insurers helped them to limit the share of investment advisors in the EBP market to under 4 percent.

Table 6.2

Pension Fund Asset Management Shares and Top Ten Investment Advisors

Market share (in %)

Employee benefit plan	1987	1995	1998	2003 projected
Trust banks	68.7	57.9	54.4	50
of which foreign	0.3	1.0	1.9	5
Life insurers	31.3	38.2	31.9	28
Investment advisor	0.0	3.8	13.8	22
of which foreign	0.0	0.6	4.9	12
Public pension assets				
Trust banks	65.0		56.9	54
of which foreign	0.3		9.7	15
Life insurers	35.0		31.4	28
Investment advisor	0.0		11.7	18
of which foreign	0.0		2.5	5

Sources: Nenkin Joho, various issues. Industry sources.

Top ten investment advisors in FY 98 (ended March 31, 1999)
(in US$ billions)

	Public	Private	Total
Nomura Asset Management	20.5	7.8	28.2
IBJ NW Asset Management	1.9	4.7	15.7
Nikko International Capital Management	9.4	4.3	13.7
Daiwa International Capital Management	5.2	4.7	9.9
SB Yamaichi Asset Management	6.5	2.7	9.2
Schroder Investment Advisor	3.8	5.3	9.1
Nissay Asset Management Co.	2.3	6.8	9.1
UBS Brinson Investment Advisory	4.8	3.9	8.7
Merrill Lynch Mercury Inv. Trust Mgmt.	2.4	5.9	8.3
Barclays Nikko Global Investors	3.0	3.6	7.6
Total:	68.8	50.7	119.5

Source: Nenkin Joho, July 5, 1999.

By 1998 major changes were evident in the market. The share of private assets managed by trust banks had declined to some 54.4 percent, of which foreign banks now took about 2 percent. Insurance companies (all domestic) now had some 32 percent, down from about 38 percent in 1995. On the other hand, investment advisors had greatly increased market share to almost 14 percent, of which foreign advisors occupied a significant 4.9 percent. In the public pension fund management field, by 1998 trust banks captured about 60 percent of the business (down from 65 percent in 1987), with foreign banks' share approaching 10 percent. Life insurers provided about 31 percent of services, down from 35 percent in 1987. Similarly to the case with private plans, investment advisors had by 1998 become a major service provider, with almost 12 percent of the service market, of which 2.5 percent was provided by foreign firms.

The Top Ten Investment Advisors

Table 6.2 shows that the four largest domestic investment advisors were Nomura Asset Management, IBJ NW Asset Management, Nikko International Capital Management, and Daiwa International Capital Management. A remarkable finding in this list is that more than half of the top ten advisors are foreign owned or joint ventures. This testifies to the competitiveness of foreign firms in this technically challenging business. The top ten advisors managed some $119 billion in public and private funds in 1998. According to statistics from the Securities Investment Advisors Industry Association, at March 31, 1999 all investment advisors managed $212 billion (¥25.5 trillion) under 5,488 discretionary mandates and provided advice covering another ¥38.6 trillion under 6,259 advisory contracts (*Nenkin Joho*, July 5, 1999).

Growth in Investment Advisors

The steady decline of the traditional asset managers—trust banks and life insurers—and the growth of investment advisors are attributable to a change in the market and in the different responses to this change. A fundamental change has been the lifting of the 5–3–3–2 rule and other restrictions and barriers to entry. Lifting these restrictions allowed advisors to fashion "special mandates" in which the advisor's particular expertise and performance were a selling point. This was particularly true for foreign advisors whose expertise has often been in foreign products and markets.

Pension sponsors have become more sophisticated, demanding, and professional. In awarding mandates, particularly at the margin, they are inclined to respond positively to sales presentations emphasizing performance and skill, rather than "relationship." Sponsors have been educated in the fundamentals of asset-liability management and are responsible for it. They are therefore looking for "solutions" to key ALM issues and in-depth knowledge of investment products as well as the pension system and regulations. Sponsors are increasingly using consultants to screen potential managers and products. Investment advisory companies, including foreign companies, have been quicker to see and respond to this market need than the entrenched and somewhat complacent traditional managers.

Table 6.2 forecasts that by 2003 investment advisors will capture 22 percent of the private market and 18 percent of the public market, with foreign companies' shares at 12 percent and 5 percent respectively. This constitutes dramatic growth in share and, particularly, absolute volume. It suggests that substantial earnings are in prospect for the firms that can compete effectively for this business.

Performance of Foreign Asset Managers

Table 6.3 displays the performance and rankings of all the foreign trust banks and the top ten foreign investment managers in the period March to September 1998. As of September 31, 1998, foreign trust banks, led by Bankers Trust, were managing some US$73 billion public pension assets and US$14 billion in private pension assets. For the top five banks, Bankers Trust, CitiTrust, Morgan Trust, Credit Suisse, and Barclays, this was significant business. The relative preponderance of public to private assets owes to the trust banks' early entry into this market and the tendency of *Nenpuku* to give large mandates. Overall, compared with the previous year's period, the foreign trust banks registered some 24 percent growth in public assets under management and 25 percent growth in private assets under management. These were respectable performance figures, considering that trust banks as a whole were losing business during this period.

In 1998 the top ten foreign investment advisors, with US$38 billion under management, occupied about 70 percent of this sector. The leaders were Schroder, Merrill Lynch Mercury, Goldman Sachs, Deutsche Morgan Grenfell, Jardine Fleming, Morgan Stanley, Fidelity, Capital International, Invesco, and Scudder.

Asset Management Economics

It is interesting to note that foreign investment advisors have almost equivalent assets from the public and private sectors, while foreign trust banks have a much larger scale of business with public pension sponsors. This disparity results from the economics of the asset management business. Traditionally, while offering big mandates, public sponsors would pay only a level of fees "recommended" by the Pension Fund Association. In a mandate of $416 million (¥50 billion), the PFA rate for a special mandate was some seven basis points for a domestic bond mandate, thirteen basis points for a mixed domestic equity and foreign bond mandate, and sixteen basis points for a foreign equity mandate. Trust banks, established to do this business and with substantial fixed costs, sought public pension business, even at low fees, because public sponsors tended to offer very large mandates.

Table 6.3

Performance of Foreign Pension Fund Managers

Foreign trust banks—all banks
for March–September 1998

	AUM $ billion			Asset growth %		
	Public	Private	Total	Public	Private	Total
Bankers Trust	15.9	3.2	19.1	23	10	21
CitiTrust	13.4	0.9	14.3	41	66	42
Morgan Trust	9.2	3.7	12.9	24	19	22
Credit Suisse	10.9	1.5	12.3	17	25	18
Barclays	9.2	2.7	11.9	21	44	26
UBS	6.0	0.6	6.6	31	23	30
State Street	5.1	0.6	5.6	8	83	13
Chase	3.6	0.3	3.9	12	32	13
Deutsche Morgan Grenfell	0.0	0.2	0.3	41	−10	−7
Total	73.2	13.7	86.9	24	25	24

Sources: Nenkin Joho, various issues.

Foreign investment advisors—top ten performance
for March–September 1998

	AUM $ billion			Asset growth %		
	Public	Private	Total	Public	Private	Total
Schroder	3.6	4.6	8.2	31	48	40
Merrill Lynch Mercury	2.1	5.3	7.4	4	7	6
Goldman Sachs	4.6	1.1	5.7	71	78	72
Deutsche Morgan Grenfell	2.6	2.3	4.9	5	25	13
Jardine Fleming	2.6	1.1	3.7	11	33	16
Morgan Stanley	1.9	0.3	2.3	13	62	18
Fidelity	0.0	1.9	1.9	0	61	61
Capital International	0.0	1.7	1.7	0	65	65
Invesco	1.0	0.6	1.6	15	−4	8
Scudder	0.3	0.6	0.9	0	50	28
Total	18.9	19.4	38.3			

Sources: Nenkin Joho, various issues.

In the mid- to late 1990s both public and private pension sponsors sought and received discounted fees from both trust banks and investment advisors. Many large private sponsors demanded and received services—including a guaranteed rate of return—for free and actually got such service from domestic managers. Foreign banks and advisors were less willing than domestic players to discount, but some did. In the late 1990s, as private sponsors began to come under pressure to improve performance, and performance became extremely difficult in the essentially zero interest rate domestic environment, they became—seemingly overnight—prepared to pay reasonable fees to companies with credible track records and capabilities. Public sponsors felt less pressure to perform and remained less willing to pay reasonable fees.

Fidelity and Capital International never discounted, being subject to a global pricing standard imposed by their headquarters. For this reason, neither was willing or able to win mandates from public sponsors, but both were experiencing rapid growth in the private market.

Advent of 401(k) Plans and Reform of the Pension System

Until 1999, all public and private pension sponsors were required by regulation to offer fixed future benefit schedules and rates under defined benefit (DB) scheme. For corporations with large numbers of retired and retiring employees, rewarded under traditional seniority pay systems, and a smaller number of young workers, the burden of DB pension systems began to be felt in the 1990s. Further, with investment returns on their assets falling chronically below committed levels of benefit payments, Japanese corporations have been required to "top up" funds to make current payments. At the same time, companies are accumulating huge unfunded liabilities for future pension payment obligations.

The seriousness of this situation can hardly be exaggerated. Using U.S. GAAP accounting standards, it was calculated that in March 1998 the unfunded accumulated benefits obligation of the companies listed on the first section of the Tokyo Stock Exchange was a staggering $450 billion (¥54 trillion) (Mitaka 1999, p. 21). Finding solutions to deal with this shortfall became more pressing when, in 1999, new corporate disclosure and accounting regulations required Japanese companies to declare publicly their future benefit obligations in financial statements for the year ending March 31, 2000.

Defined Contribution Solution to Corporate and Government Shortfalls

This critical situation, as well as analogous problems with Japan's public plans, caused the government in 1999 to decide to legalize (and then to promote heavily) the introduction of "defined contribution" (DC) pension schemes in Japan, to begin in fall 2000. Under these schemes, participants—employees and employers—will make regular contributions to plans, but the pension benefits available for payment to retirees will depend upon investment performance. There will be no fixed, committed level of annuity or lump sum payments at or after retirement.

The system, like that in the United States, will involve the establishment of 401(k)-type plans in the names of individuals. Companies and employees will contribute to the plan. The plan accounts will be opened with a financial institution—bank, trust bank, life insurance company, or securities company. Some specialized companies will provide the record-keeping services for the plans.

Investments in funds in Japanese 401(k)-type plans will be decided by the individual plan holder, from options provided by the financial institutions, subject to regulatory limitations and restrictions. As in the United States, Japanese 401(k) plans are expected to prove a fillip and a boon to development of the asset management industry and particularly to the mutual fund industry (as was the case in the United States). One foreign Japanese JV asset manager estimates that assets in Japanese DC plans will increase to the equivalent of US$500 billion equivalent in 2010 from zero in 1998. The entire pool of pension assets is expected to increase to over US$3.6 trillion, offering vast potential for the asset management industry.

Creating a Huge New Asset Management Market

The need to prepare for introduction of 401(k)-type plans has created a flurry of activity among Japanese and foreign financial institutions. Many new mutual funds have been launched or are under development with a view to serving the DC market. Foreign companies that have sought or are seeking alliances with major Japanese institutions or groups with a view to entering the DC market include Charles Schwab, DLJ Direct, Bank of New York, Credit Suisse, State Street, Goldman Sachs, and Societe Generale. Surely others will follow.

At the same time, Japanese banks and securities companies, sensing the great earnings potential of the DC business, are increasing equity positions in affiliated asset management companies, trying to ensure both control and a reliable group capability in this business. During FY98, DKB increased its equity in DKB Asahi Investment Trust Investment Advisory Company from 5.6 percent to 63.4 percent; Sanwa Bank increased equity in Partners Investment Trust Management from 49.3 percent to 50.2 percent; Sumitomo Life increased ownership of Sumisei Global Investment Trust Management from zero to 50 percent; Nikko Securities increased equity in Nikko Asset Management from 4.9 percent to 39.7 percent (total Nikko group holdings are 66.2 percent); and Fuji Bank increased ownership in Fuji Investment Trust Investment Advisory Company from 7.8 percent to 38.6 percent (*The Nikkei Financial Daily*, June 30, 1999).

Table 6.4

Groupings for Development of Pension Fund Management Systems

Mitsubishi-Sumitomo Grouping	**IBJ Nomura Grouping**
Bank of Tokyo-Mitsubishi	IBJ
Mitsubishi Trust and Banking	Nomura Securities
Meiji Life	Da-Ichi Life
Tokio Marine and Fire	Sanwa Bank
Sumitomo Bank	Toyo Trust and Banking
Sumitomo Trust and Banking	Daiwa Bank
Sumitomo Life	Sakura Bank
Daiwa Securities	Tokai Bank
Nikko Securities	Asahi Bank
IBM Japan	Mitsui Trust and Banking
Others	DKB
	Fuji Bank
	NTT
	Fujitsu
	Goldman Sachs
Nippon Life Grouping	Societe Generale
Nippon Life	State Street
IBM Japan	Others
Hitachi	
NTT Data	
Others	

Source: Nihon Keizai Shimbun, April 10, 1999.

Forming Groups for Record Keeping

The enormous job of record keeping for DC plans will require development of an extensive computer software systems. Therefore, given the huge cost of this development, Japanese financial institutions have agreed to share burdens and earnings in three large groups (Table 6.4). Leadership of the groupings is, in one case, with Mitsubishi and Sumitomo financial companies; in the second with IBJ and Nomura Securities; and in the third, Nippon Life. Such record-keeping abilities will give financial institutions a chance to offer comprehensive DC services to corporate sponsors. Relationship, particularly group affiliation, will be an important consideration of sponsors when deciding upon a supplier of services. All *keiretsu* financial institutions feel compelled to have a full-service capability so as to defend their relationship markets.

In an interesting contrary move, Fidelity of the United States announced in mid-1999 that it would not join one of the three groups developing record-keeping systems. Rather, it would adapt the system it is using in the United States (by building a Japan market-compatible "front end") and would market directly to selected customer segments (see Chapter Seventeen). Fidelity, with a wealth of experience in the business in the United States was reluctant to "write a blank check" to systems developers in Japan when the size and the shape of the market opportunity was still unclear.

Reform of the Pension Fund Management System

The advent of DC plans is only one part of a drastic overhaul of Japan's strained pension system planned in the near future. In 2000 or 2001 it is expected that the current system—inextricably linked to the FILP program and the discretion of the Trust Fund Bureau of MOF—will be replaced by a new system. The new system will transfer administration of National Pension Insurance and EWPI funds to an Investment Council subordinate to the Minister of Health and Welfare. Determination of investment policy will be made by the Minister of Health and Welfare through consultation with a newly constituted advisory body, the Asset Management Council.

The Investment Council will manage funds in accordance with policy guidelines, either by entrusting funds to money managers (trust banks, life insurers, or investment advisors) or by conducting its own in-house investment.

The new system is likely to increase the professionalism and activity of pension fund management. It can only be good news for providers of asset management services.

Chapter Seven

The Mutual Fund Industry

From Bust to Boom?

A Dismal Market in 1998, Following a Dismal Decade, But . . .

In late 1998 and early 1999, nothing in Japan's financial marketplace appeared to foreign financial companies to be more incongruous, and more exciting, than the minuscule level of Japanese investment in mutual funds. (In Japan mutual funds are usually called *investment trusts*. We will use the two terms interchangeably below.) As we saw in Chapter One, in 1998 Japanese individual financial assets were overwhelmingly held in bank deposits and savings-type guaranteed-rate insurance products. Stocks and bonds made up a paltry 6 percent of individual financial asset portfolios, and mutual funds accounted for only 2 percent (Figure 1.5). Not only was this a very small relative and absolute number, it was substantially lower than it had been a few years earlier. In other words, for a decade, Japanese individuals had been steadily disinvesting in mutual funds. Mutual funds were unpopular and poorly understood.

Figures 7.1 and 7.2 illustrate the sad state of the mutual funds industry in late 1998. The total value of assets in Japanese mutual funds—having stagnated during the prior five years—stood at $370 billion (¥44,400 billion). This was in stark contrast to the United States, where steady growth since 1993 had powered the value of U.S. mutual funds to some $4 trillion, more than ten times the level in Japan. From Figure 7.2 we can also observe that Japanese mutual funds (or investment trusts) were fairly insignificant in terms of Japan's financial marketplace. Mutual funds held less than 2 percent of shares on the stock exchanges, only about 4 percent of bonds, and less than 2 percent of convertible bonds. The only market in which investment trusts made a difference was in the money market, suggesting that the funds' managers could not think of anything better to do with the money.

Figure 7.1 **Comparative Growth in Value of Mutual Funds in Japan vs. the United States**

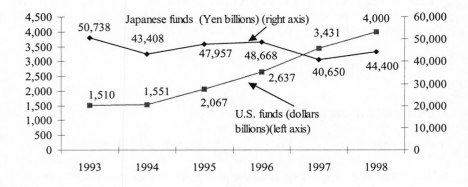

Source: Report on Investment Trusts, July 1999.

Figure 7.2 **Position of Investment Trusts in Japan's Financial Marketplace at End 1998**

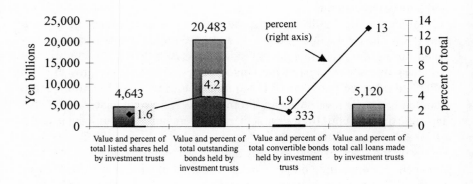

Source: Report on Investment Trusts, July 1999.

December 1998 Big Bang Reform Expands Distribution Channels . . .

For the participants in the industry, particularly foreign companies, this was all good news. Notwithstanding the bleak present, many signs pointed to a promising future. The big bang reforms introduced on December 1, 1998, greatly expanded channels for marketing investment trusts and relaxed restrictions on types of funds that could be offered. Prior to December 1, only Japanese securities companies could sell mutual funds. From December 1, the market was opened to banks, trust banks, and life insurance companies. At one stroke this change increased the number of mutual funds sales representatives from 64,000 to 210,000. It also had the effect of producing a "little bang" in mutual fund promotion. New market participants touted their arrival and their array of products and, importantly, made substantial efforts through media advertising, seminars, direct mail solicitations, and consultation by counter staff to educate the public about the merits of long-term, diversified investing through mutual funds.

Energizing Both "Manufacturers" and "Distributors" of Mutual Funds

The half year before and after December 1, 1998, witnessed a flurry of activity by participants in the mutual funds industry. Generally speaking, the imperatives and actions of the players depended upon where they fit in the marketing chain. Were they "manufacturers" of mutual funds who "owned products" and earned money for managing assets? Or were they "distributors" who "owned customers" and whose strengths were a sales force or other distribution network—branches or agents—or, in some cases, a niche in direct marketing, and who earned money by distributing products for manufacturers for a fee.

The situation was complicated, because the roles were often not exclusive, particularly in Japan's *keiretsu* context. In a pure sense, Japan's securities companies were and are the quintessential mutual funds distributors. They own hundreds of thousands of customers by virtue of their retail strategies and extensive branch networks and sales forces. At the same time, however, all the major securities houses (as required by Japanese law) have set up investment trust management (ITM) companies. These ITM companies are quintessential manufacturers. Banks and insurance companies—natural distributors because of their client bases—have their affiliated ITM companies to provide products.

As in any other market, client relationship and distribution is a key business driver, so distributors have held the stronger position. Foreign companies entering the mutual funds market, with a few exceptions (like Citibank,

Figure 7.3 **Portfolio Composition of Investment Trust Assets in 1998**

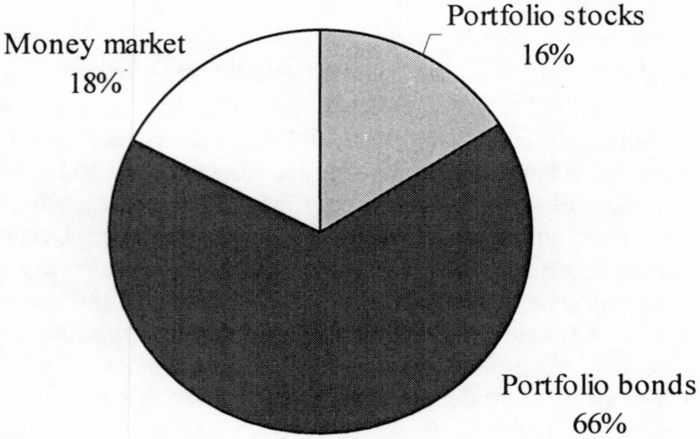

Source: *Report on Investment Trusts*, July 1999.

American Express, and Merrill Lynch), have been pure manufacturers of products. They have had no choice but to tie up with and rely upon Japanese distributors, and the price paid for this access has been high, as we shall see.

Expansion of Distribution Channels Gives New Prominence to Products, Favoring Growth of Foreign Manufacturers

But the balance of negotiating power has been changing in favor of the manufacturers. Particularly after December 1 and the entry of many new distributors, particularly banks, distributors have needed to differentiate themselves in a crowded and competitive market. For this they have needed attractive and well-performing products. Part of the reason for the depressed Japanese mutual funds market before 1998 was that securities companies—the only distributors—tended to offer customers little choice. Brokers pushed almost exclusively the mutual funds manufactured by the securities company's affiliated ITM company. In most cases, the funds selection was limited to a few generic classes, and clients had no ability to switch investments. The funds tended to perform miserably, and fees were high. The allocation of assets in Japanese mutual funds has been and continues to be in bonds, rather than stocks (Figure 7.3).

By 1999 no one, including the companies themselves, was denying that Japanese ITM companies had been pathetic performers who, like asset managers in the pension asset management field, were lacking in skills and knowhow compared with foreign players. Such companies as Goldman Sachs, Fidelity, Morgan Stanley, Alliance, and Merrill Lynch Mercury had shown that they were better and more innovative in managing money in mutual funds—not only for foreign stock and bond portfolios, but also for Japanese stock and bond portfolios! This appreciation, in the new, competitive post-big bang environment, caused many domestic ITM companies to seek alliances with foreign companies and caused distributors, securities companies, banks, and insurance companies to seek distribution relationships with the foreign companies.

On December 1, 1998, Japanese banks filled the financial press with advertisements touting their new mutual fund products. Of course, they were only distributors, and the products were provided under distribution agreements with manufacturers. Nomura Securities' ITM company, Nomura Asset Management, had tied up with 65 banks; Daiwa's ITM had tied up with 41 banks; Nikko's ITM, Nikko Asset Management, with 39 banks; Fidelity with 27; Partners with 20; Credit Suisse with 18; Bankers Trust with 17; Merrill Lynch Mercury with 16; Goldman Sachs with 15; Morgan Stanley with 13; and others with 50.

Major Market Players in March 1999

Table 7.1 presents the ranking of ITM companies by assets as of March 31, 1999, as well as a comparison with the previous year. ITM companies associated with Japan's Big Three securities companies, Daiwa Securities ITM, Nomura Asset Management, and Nikko Asset Management, continue to dominate the market, accounting together for some 66 percent of total investment trust assets. However, we should note that a large portion of the funds sold by these companies were domestic yen money market funds, on which neither customers nor the companies make much money. Daiwa reportedly offered a particularly high (and, for itself, money-losing) 0.635 percent yield for its MMF product during the year, which helped attract $8.3 billion (¥1 trillion) (*The Nikkei Financial Daily*, April 15, 1999). This would account for most of its assets increase during the year.

The big news in the ranking was the increase in assets of foreign companies, which cumulatively acquired 10.3 percent of the market. The leader was Goldman Sachs with $12.7 billion (¥1,519 billion). This figure was up 96 percent from the previous year and constituted some 3.6 percent of the market, which can only be described as spectacular performance. Other leading foreign companies like Credit Suisse, Merrill Lynch Mercury, Invesco, Fidelity, Rothschild, and Morgan Stanley experienced double or triple digit growth.

Another interesting finding in this ranking was the lackluster performance of the newcomers in the market—banks and life insurers. Cumulatively, in the four months following deregulation on December 1, 1999, their ITM companies had sold only $4.9 billion (¥589.6 billion) in funds, a mere 1.4 percent

Table 7.1

Ranking of Investment Trust Companies by Net Assets Outstanding on March 31, 1999

Rank 3/99	Rank 3/98	Company	Net assets outstanding at 3/31/98 (Yen billions)	Increase (decrease) over 3/3/98 (%)	Percent of total market
1	2	Daiwa	11,110	17	26.0
2	1	Nomura	9,825	1	23.0
3	3	Nikko	7,942	9	18.6
4	4	Kokusai	1,584	11	3.7
5	9	Goldman Sachs	1,519	96	3.6
6	6	Taiyo	1,182	16	2.8
7	8	Partners	1,098	27	2.6
8	7	Dai-Ichi Kangyo Asahi	935	4	2.2
9	5	Shin Waco	747	−47	1.7
10	11	Nochu	552	26	1.3
11	10	Alliance Capital	514	−2	1.2
12	13	Japan	442	14	1.0
13	12	Cosmo	389	−10	0.9
14	17	Credit Suisse	347	54	0.8
15	23	Merrill Lynch Mercury	342	132	0.8
16	18	Universal	339	58	0.8
17	30	Invesco	329	293	0.8
18	29	Fidelity	249	188	0.6
19	14	IBJ	239	−13	0.6
20	26	Taiheiyo	236	77	0.6
21	15	Nissay	234	−13	0.5
22	22	Tokai	222	42	0.5
23	37	Rothschild	215	371	0.5
24	20	Morgan Stanley	214	27	0.5
25	19	Asahi Tokyo	213	16	0.5
26	28	Sanyo	209	88	0.5
27	16	Daido Life	171	−27	0.4
28	21	Fuji	152	−6	0.4

Source: The Nikkei Financial Daily, April 15, 1999.

of the market. However, this does not reflect all of their sales activity. When the banks sold the funds of another ITM company, the assets flowed to the manufacturer, and therefore the manufacturer was able to record the asset. For bankers, selling only for commission and not to gather or lend funds for the bank is an alien concept. As such, it helps to explain the banks' poor performance and to cast doubt on their importance as a distribution channel in the future.

The assets outstanding for all the ITM companies at the end of FY98 were $356 billion (¥42,753 billion), up 11 percent from the previous year. The total number of ITM companies increased by 13 to 55.

Table 7.1 (continued)

Rank 3/99	Rank 3/98	Company	Net assets outstanding at 3/31/98 (Yen billions)	Increase (decrease) over 3/3/98 (%)
29	24	Tokyo Mitsubishi	139	−4
30	27	Jardine Fleming	136	6
31	32	Deutsche Morgen Grenfell	136	95
32		Dai-Ichi Life	124	
33	25	Sakura	94	−34
34		Salomon Smith Barney	80	
35	33	AIMIC	71	13
36	31	Schroders	63	−21
37	39	Bankers Trust	55	232
38		Pictet	50	1,468
39	35	NCG	41	−25
40	36	Maple	39	−28
41	38	Barings	38	−8
42	34	SBIM	26	−54
43		Yasuda Fire & Marine	24	
44		Shinkin	20	
45		Prudential Mitsui	15	
46		Credit Lyonnais	14	
47		Tokai Marine	12	
48		UBS	11	
49		Commerz	10	
50		Toyo Trust	6	
51		State Street	2	
52		Scudder	2	
53		HSBC	2	
54		Pincus	1	
55		Barclays	0	
		Total market		42,754

Goldman Sachs Leads the Pack

The relatively fast growth of foreign ITM companies owes primarily to their ability to manufacture and offer attractive products for distributors. Having a famous name has helped, too. Goldman Sachs was the most successful in the field in 1999 for the second year running. Table 7.2 presents the lineup of products offered by Goldman as of June 1999 as well as the distributors it is serving.

At the end of May 1999 Goldman Sachs ITM had some $11.7 billion (¥1,402 billion) under management, sold through alliances with twenty

Table 7.2

Products, Volumes, and Distribution Relationships of Goldman Sachs Investment Trust Management Company (June 1999)

Type	Fund name	Main investments	Standard FX hedge	Net assets at May 31, 1999 (Yen billions)	Designated distributors
Balanced	Da Vinci	Global equity + global bonds + short-term yen instruments	100%	126.0	Nikko Securities, Shizuoka Bank
Balanced	GS Pascal	Global equity + global bonds	100%	13.6	Fuji Bank
Balanced	Europia	European bonds + European equity	50%	3.1	Advisortech Securities, Kankaku Securities, New Japan Securities, Tokai Maruman Securities, Marusan Securities, Waco Securities
		Subtotal balanced		**142.7**	
Bonds	Variety Open	Foreign bonds + currencies	50%	460.0	Kokusai Securities
Bonds	Galileo	Instruments	100%	338.0	Nikko Securities, Skzuoka Bank
Bonds	GS Global Bond Open (Hedged)	Global bonds	100%	66.5	Nomura Securities, Nomura Fund Net Securities
Bonds	GS Global Bond Open (Unhedged)	Global bonds	0%	107.0	Nomura Securities, Nomura Fund Net Securities

Bonds	Asahi/GS Global Bond Fund *Takarajima* Global Bond	Global bonds	100%	7.2	Asahi Bank
Bonds	Mona Lisa	Global bonds	100%	5.2	Advisortech Securities, American Express Securities, Shizuoka Bank
	Subtotal bonds			**983.9**	
Equity	GS Japan Equity Fund *Ushiwakamaru*	Japanese stocks	n/a	21.0	Imakawa Misawaya Securities, Okusan Securities, Orix Securities, Kankaku Securities, New Japan Securities, Dai-Ichi Securities, Daiwa Securities, Daiwa SBCM, Tokai Maruman Securities, Tokyo Securities, Meiko National Securities, Japan Investors Securities, Maruko Daika Securities, Marusan Securities, Yamatane Securities, Yasuda Trust Bank
Equity	GS Japan Equity Fund *Ushiwakamaru* (continuous)	Japanese stocks	n/a	1.7	Advisortech Securities, Shizuoka Bank, Sakura Bank, Toyo Trust Bank, Japan Investors Securities
Equity	GS Global Stock Fund Marco Polo	Global stocks	50%	8	Advisortech Securities, Daiwa Securities, Daiwa SBCM, Okusan Securities, Maruko Daika Securities, Japan Investors Securities, Shizuoka Bank, Sony Life Insurance, 23 Shinyo Kinko nationwide

(continued)

Table 7.2 (continued)

Type	Fund name	Main investments	Standard FX hedge	Net assets at May 31, 1999 (Yen billions)	Designated distributors
Equity	GS Global Equity Fund Caesar	Global stocks + short-term yen instruments	100%	2.6	Kokusai Securities
Equity	GS American Open (limited FX hedge)	U.S. stocks	100%	3.3	Nomura Securities, Nomura Fund Net Securities
Equity	GS American Open (FX unhedged)	U.S. stocks	n/a	0.7	Nomura Securities, Nomura Fund Net Securities
		Subtotal equity **Total open type**		**37.3** **1,164.0**	
Bonds	Galileo-Aria	Global bonds	100%	54.3	Nikko Securities
Bonds	New Variety	Global bonds + currencies	variable	7.4	Kokusai Securities
Bonds	Variety	Global bonds + currencies	75%	151.3	Not presently soliciting funds
Bonds	GS Floater Fund Excel	U.S. high yield bonds, emerging market bonds, mortgage backed bonds	100%	25.4	Not presently soliciting funds
		Total unit type		**238.4**	

Source: Goldman Sachs Investment Trust Management Company, Ltd.

securities companies, six banks and trust banks, and one life insurance company. Over \$9.7 billion (¥1,164 billion) was in open type funds. Over \$10.2 billion (¥1,222 billion), or 87 percent of Goldman's assets, were in bond funds. Most of these funds offered foreign exchange risk hedges to protect value in yen. What these figures suggest is that, in 1999, the way to satisfy the needs of Japanese investors was largely to offer nonequity products that were also hedged against FX risk. The combinations of investments and hedging options evidences Goldman's capabilities and its strategy of giving the market what it asked for, which, for foreign companies, has required development of new products or approaches.

Another important factor in Goldman's success has been its ability and willingness to produce and package products for a particular distributor or class of distributors. Giving a distributor a "unique" product and exclusive marketing rights can often help motivate the distributor to produce greater sales. We see this strategy in the Da Vinci balanced fund, distributed exclusively through Nikko Securities and Shizuoka Bank, and in the GS Pascal balanced fund, distributed only by Fuji Bank. We also see the strategy in the case of Variety Open, distributed highly successfully and exclusively by Kokusai Securities, and with the Galileo fund, distributed again by Nikko Securities and Shizuoka Bank.

Goldman naturally has had to gauge the appetite of the market for its products before deciding whether to take a risk that one or a few distributors could sell enough of a product to justify the investment in product development and, particularly, ongoing maintenance and customer service. It has also had to consider whether a more attractive market opportunity would present itself through marketing through multiple distributors. Goldman has been flexible and opportunistic enough to develop products for general as well as exclusive distribution. We see this in particular with its equity funds, *Ushiwakamaru* and Marco Polo.

It is interesting to note that in most cases Goldman Sachs has eschewed establishing distribution relationships with banks. This is probably because Goldman believes that banks are relatively weak in selling risk products, and it wants to concentrate its efforts on supporting sales organizations that can sell. From the initial results of counter sales by banks, we are inclined to concur in Goldman's negative judgment.

Industry Economics: Who Makes Money

The mutual fund industry anywhere makes money from managing clients' assets over time. Persistency (the length of time clients' funds stay with the manager) is strongly correlated with profitability. Not surprisingly, persistency—buying and holding the fund—has also been the way that investors made money in funds.

Traditionally, the mutual fund industry in Japan has been fundamentally unhealthy—both for asset managers and for investors—because of short persistency. Average redemptions in a year have been 45 to 60 percent vs. 15 percent in the United States. The average holding period has been measured in weeks rather than months or years. And, bizarrely, the better the performance of a particular fund, the shorter has been its average holding period.

The reason for this apparent incongruity is simple: mutual funds were distributed by stock brokers in securities houses whose earnings came from sales commissions or "loads" on the funds. During the 1990s it was typical for a Japanese broker to sell a mutual fund to a client one week, collecting the sales load, and, in the next week, if the fund had appreciated in value, to call and advise the client to sell it to raise cash to buy the broker's next product (on which he hoped to earn another commission). Brokers were not compensated or rewarded for persistency or assets under management, but only for selling. This resulted in a rapid turnover of the better performing funds and the inevitable buildup of client assets in underperforming funds. When a fund went down, the broker was embarrassed to call the client.

Distributors are still paid by manufacturers to sell their products, and in Japan the "give up" is larger than in the United States. Typically a manufacturer of equity funds like Goldman Sachs, Fidelity or Merrill Lynch (or any of the Japanese ITMs) will allow distributors to charge a 3 percent sales load on the value of a fund sale. This load will be fully paid to the distributors. For balances and bond funds, sales loads are typically 1.5 to 3 percent. This is all kept by the distributors.

In addition, manufacturers will pay the distributor a cut of the ongoing management fee. This is also the case in the United States, but in Japan the cut can be 50 to 60 percent of gross fees, vs. 10 to 20 basis points in the United States. Mailing and advertising costs, which are borne by manufacturers, are 2 to 4 times United States rates (Sotorp 1998).

All this means that the mutual funds market in Japan is, at this stage, fairly rich for distributors and difficult for manufacturers.

Other Foreign Companies Target the Market: Merrill Lynch, Citibank, Fidelity, American Express, Charles Schwab, J.P. Morgan

The way to benefit most from the system is to be both a manufacturer and distributor. This is accomplished by the Japanese financial institutions that have ITMs providing products for and through affiliated brokers. It is also accomplished by—and is a major strategy of—such companies as Merrill Lynch, Citibank, Fidelity, and American Express, which possess both distribution and manufacturing capability. As noted above, the key is client relationships. Merrill Lynch has acquired such relationships by virtue of running a thousand-man sales operation out of thirty offices throughout Japan. Citibank has acquired relationships through its retail banking strategy. Fidelity has painstakingly built a direct marketing customer base of some 4,000 clients through years of telemarketing and print advertising. American Express has a loyal group of some 800,000 card members who are effectively reached by mail.

As we will examine more closely in later chapters, Merrill Lynch reaches its customers with a variety of proprietary mutual funds distributed exclusively through its sales force, which is trained and compensated to achieve high levels of persistency. Citibank distributes its proprietary Citifunds through twenty branches and via a telemarketing center. American Express distributes proprietary funds established in an offshore "umbrella fund" vehicle.

Fidelity sells funds predominantly through Japanese distributors. As of March 1999 it had signed up to distribute through three life and nonlife insurance companies, nine securities companies, and twenty-five banks. This reliance on distributors has made it difficult for Fidelity to differentiate its direct service to customers. It has been unable, for example, to discount sales commissions below those charged by its distributors, even though there is little justification for such loads (except that the market will bear them) when there is no salesman to compensate.

Selling Funds as a Commodity: Nomura Fundnet, E-Trade, and Charles Schwab

It is inevitable that the high sales loads collected on mutual funds sales will be driven down by competition. This, in combination with the deregulation and reduction of brokerage commissions, will force securities companies and other distributors to adopt lower cost distribution and sales structures.

The mutual funds market is seeing the advent of companies using new distribution channels. This includes, of course, the internet. All major and many minor brokers will soon offer internet trading. Banks like Sakura, Sumitomo, and Fuji are taking to the web to sell mutual funds (*Nihon Keizai Shimbun*, August 2, 1999). Many others will surely follow. A number of internet boutiques, like DLJ Direct SFG (Chapter Seventeen), have entered the market and will be formidable competition.

Nomura Fundnet, 100 percent-owned by Nomura Securities, is likely to set the pace for success. This company is using direct marketing (a relatively low-cost infrastructure) and such innovative strategies as subscription through monthly bank account debiting to build a customer base with low cost. It offers dozens of proprietary and nonproprietary funds at attractively discounted rates and targets young people and beginning investors, hoping to build volume over the long term (see Chapter Ten).

Another interesting 1999 entrant is E-Trade Japan Securities, an online broker. This JV between E-Trade in the United States and Softbank in Japan (Chapter Eleven) burst into the market in mid-1999, offering 177 equity funds, the most of any domestic company, including those managed by large domestic ITMs (*The Nikkei Financial Daily*, July 15, 1999). The interest of so many manufactures in distribution through E-Trade evidences the manufacturers' confidence that E-Trade will be reaching a large and fairly exclusive market segment.

Another example of a new approach is the joint venture securities company established by Charles Schwab and Tokio Marine and Fire. The company will be an online discount broker with a twenty-four-hour call center, offering mutual funds as well as other securities. J.P. Morgan Investment Management formed a fifty-fifty joint venture with Dai-Ichi Kang yo Bank (DKB) in March 1999. This venture will exploit the retail customer relationships of DKB and manufacture tailored products for this market.

The discount broker *cum* mutual funds distributor market will certainly get increasingly crowded in 1999 and 2000. We expect a major shakeout (Chapter Eighteen), which will also present many opportunities.

Offshore Funds

In July 1998 the total value of domestic mutual funds produced by ITMs was $373.2 billion (¥44,784 billion). At the same time, securities companies were distributing $24.3 billion (¥2,917 billion) in foreign currency-denominated funds manufactured and domiciled offshore, mainly in Luxembourg. Offshore funds as a category have been growing in popularity, and the big bang reforms have further widened the scope for such funds in the Japanese market.

It was possible in 1999 for a securities company to get into the mutual funds business in Japan without incurring the substantial costs of setting up an ITM company. The securities company could simply establish an investment trust company in a place like Luxembourg and bring the product into Japan, following highly simplified post-big bang registration procedures with the Financial Supervisory Agency (FSA). This was in fact the method by which American Express Financial Advisors Japan launched its business (with a Luxembourg-domiciled U.S. dollar money market fund) in March 1999. It was reported in March 1999 that Daiwa Securities, Sumitomo Bank, T. Rowe

Price, and U.K. Fleming Group would similarly be setting up a new offshore company to manage investment trusts and to produce products for the Japanese market.

In what is probably a harbinger of things to come, Nomura Securities launched in May 1999 a Luxembourg-domiciled yen-denominated "fund of funds"—a structure newly allowed by big bang deregulation. The mother fund would allow investment in subfunds managed by nine foreign asset management companies.

On the Cusp of a 401(k) Boom?

As mentioned earlier, it was the advent of individual retirement accounts (IRAs) and 401(k) plans that fueled the boom in the U.S. mutual fund industry. Will something similar occur in Japan? The smart money says that it will. AIMIC, AIG's asset management joint venture with Mitsubishi Trust, estimated in late 1998 that within ten years the asset management opportunity from 401(k)-type plans would be equivalent to $200 to 400 billion, and in mutual funds the opportunity would be equivalent to some $200 to 300 billion (Sotorp 1998).

We believe that this is conservative. In mid-1999 the signs are that the optimism of foreign financial firms about prospects for the industry are justified. Japanese investors appear to be awakening from a long and troubled sleep. What they are waking up to is a more professional, client-oriented market where even firms like Nomura and Daiwa are preaching long-term investing and diversification. They have become serious about selling mutual funds.

The post-big bang proliferation of mutual fund manufacturers and distributors means that Japanese investors are being offered a dramatically new and improved set of mutual fund investment options. With a new dedication in the industry to raising investor knowledge and understanding, it is only a matter of time before the market takes off. The advent of 401(k)-type plans will, as in the United States, prove an important fillip. But the more substantial and fundamental driver of the coming boom in mutual funds will be Japanese investors moving money out of postal savings and bank deposit accounts.

The outlook for mutual funds is indeed bright. It could provide a future version of what has been Japan's sole financial services moneymaker in the recent past. That has been consumer credit, to which we now turn.

Chapter Eight

The Outsiders: The Consumer Finance Industry

> In a country where financial firms are either recording anemic profits (mainly in insurance and regional banking) or stunning losses (in money-center banking and securities), consumer finance ROEs seem almost . . . Western.

So wrote a securities analyst in Tokyo (Altherr 1998). And, indeed, when we look at the consumer finance industry in Japan, we do see something more familiar to Western eyes than, say, the banking system. Why is this so?

The key reason Japanese consumer finance looks like that of other countries is that it grew up largely outside of the strict regulation—and industrial nation-building vision—of Japan's Ministry of Finance (MOF). The MOF's banking bureau tightly regulated products, services, branching, and (together with the Bank of Japan) interest rates for Japan's commercial banks. Consumer finance companies, which did not take deposits from the public and therefore had no direct influence on the general availability of credit, were categorized as nonbanks and supervised largely by the Ministry of International Trade and Industry (MITI) under the company law. This meant that the consumer finance companies were much less restricted in establishing offices and outlets (like cashing machines) and, critically, that they could set interest rates at levels high enough to justify taking risk on consumers. (Another category of nonbanks is commercial finance companies, including leasing companies. We shall not be covering this sector except to note in Chapter Fourteen that it is also seeing important investment by foreign players—particularly GE Capital's acquisition of Japan Lease in 1999.)

Japan's commercial banks—because of MOF controls, a conceit that their mission was to finance Japanese industry, and a certain disdain for the consumer finance business—for decades virtually surrendered this market to the consumer finance companies (see Chapter Three). The opportunity cost of such surrender has been huge for the banks. To a significant degree, their future survival and prosperity depend upon their success at building a significant presence in this market.

Sizing the Consumer Credit Market

New consumer credit extended in Japan in the year ended March 1998 totaled some $640 billion (¥77 trillion). Consumer credit outstanding was some $620 billion (¥74.3 trillion) at the fiscal year end. Figure 8.1 presents the major components of new credit extensions during the year by type of product. From this we see that consumer credit comprises credit extended to finance purchase of specific goods (shopping credit) and nonspecific consumer lending. Shopping credit is further divided into credit card shopping credit (for customers buying an item in a store with a credit card) and credit contract shopping credit (extending a credit line to customers who have filled out an application and been approved to make an installment payment purchase). In FY97 new credit shopping credit extensions totaled $151 billion, were credit contract extensions totaled $124 billion. New consumer lending totaled $362 billion. As for loans, some $192 billion were largely unsecured loans from consumer finance companies. Another $171 billion were loans secured by deposits, usually extended by banks.

Largest Outside the United States

The point to be made about the consumer credit market is that it is large—the largest in the world outside the United States—and that it has been expanding steadily, although at a slow pace in FY97 and FY98 because of the depressing effect on consumer spending of Japan's recession. When the economy recovers, we can expect a pickup in growth. The market is shared, as in the United States, by a number of players who as a whole constitute the industry.

An interesting particularity in Japan's credit market is the place of cash. Japanese consumers carry and use cash to a much greater extent than in the United States, where payment by check or credit card is the norm. Customers of consumer credit companies seem particularly prone to want cash. This market preference has led the providers of consumer loans to create an extensive infrastructure of "cashing" machines (like automatic teller machines—ATMs) where persons who have established a relationship with the companies can draw down on credit lines, make repayments, and inquire as to the status of their accounts. Some companies even allow customers to apply for loans through ATMs and, if they qualify, to immediately draw cash advances.

The credit card market, with over 230 million credit cards issued—on average three cards per consumer—is second in size only to that of the United States (see below). Credit card shopping turnover expanded by an average of 6.8 percent per annum between 1993 and 1998, making credit cards one of the fastest growing segments of financial services. In the year ended March 31, 1998, spending by credit card exceeded $151 billion (¥18.1 trillion).

Figure 8.1 Japan's Consumer Credit Market
(US$ billions)

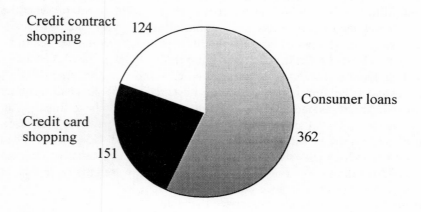

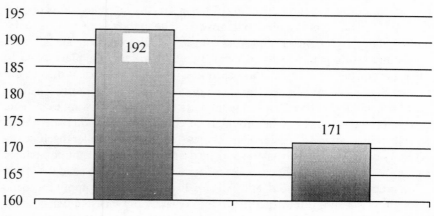

Overview of the Consumer Finance Industry Players

Japan's consumer finance industry can be understood as having three major player segments. These are sales finance companies (*shinpan*) and retailers—providing the bulk of credit shopping, consumer lenders, and credit card companies. This segmentation reflects the original business niches of the key players. In recent years, however, the players have all tended to expand their franchises across the three segments. In particular, *shinpan* companies, retailers, and consumer lenders have all become card issuers. Still, the segmentation remains a way of viewing product and market strategies.

Another way of looking at consumer finance is how players approach the key driver of credit risk management. From this perspective, we find two major industry segments: secured lenders, including companies offering consumer product sales finance and charge cards (debit cards without lines of credit); and unsecured lenders, including companies offering credit cards (cards with revolving credit lines).

Let us examine each player segment in turn.

Shinpan *and Retailers*

The largest and most famous of the *shinpan* companies is Nippon Shinpan. Nippon Shinpan dominates its traditional sector of providing sales finance services to vendors. It is now also the largest credit card issuer, with some twenty-four million cards in force. Other important *shinpan* companies are Orico, JACCS, Aplus, Central Finance, and Life. The most prominent retailer is Credit Saison, the shopping credit lender and card issuer for the large Saison Group, whose retail flagship is Seibu Department Store. Credit Saison has become the leading retailer-affiliated card company, with 17 million cards issued, including international branded and nonbranded cards. Credit Saison has also become the market's leading credit card service company, selling this service to such companies as Associates First Capital Corporation, which operates in Japan as AIC and the card business of GE Capital. Other prominent retailers—all of which provide credit shopping service and issue cards—are Marui department store, whose card name is Marui One; Daiei, which issues the Daiei OMC card; Jusco, which issues the Aeon Credit Service card; and Mycal.

Consumer Lenders

These are the purest of Japan's consumer finance companies. The largest and most prominent got their start after World War II in Osaka, where a number of entrepreneurial, but common-class businessmen saw a clear market opportunity (completely dismissed by banks) to lend small sums to people like themselves. The purpose of the loans—and one reason banks disdained them—was generally for consumption: buying a television or giving a banquet. Through at least the 1960s, this kind of consumption was still considered profligate and somewhat shameful. Japan was beginning to develop a consumer culture but did not have a consumer finance industry. The Osaka entrepreneurs stepped in to fill the gap.

For years the consumer finance companies were pejoratively referred to as *sarakin* (short for "salary man finance") and had a disreputable reputation of encouraging uncontrolled borrowing by low-paid Japanese workers and housewives so as to earn usurious rates of interest. The interest rates are still high—in the neighborhood of 30 percent—but the press seems less interested in publicizing horror stories of overborrowing and more interested in following the strong stock performances and exemplary service standards maintained by these companies. Consumer lending is where U.S. companies like Associates First Capital and GE Capital have seen and, in the former case, already successfully exploited opportunities.

Table 8.1 profiles the leading consumer lenders. The leader is Takefuji, whose total loans outstanding approach $11 billion. The top seven companies include five companies listed on the Tokyo Stock Exchange and two private companies—Lake, purchased by GE Capital in November 1998, and AIC, a subsidiary of Associates First Capital of the United States. These companies serve nearly 12 million customers in Japan, primarily through a vast network of owned and jointly-accessed ATMs and cash dispensers. Total loans outstanding for the seven leaders as of March 31, 1998, were some $45.6 billion.

This was about 15 percent of total consumer loans outstanding, which is evidence of a highly fragmented market. The market is consolidating, however, as every month brings news of mergers and acquisitions among the dozens of small, local lenders around Japan. Opportunities continue to arrive, therefore, for foreign firms, like GE Capital and Associates First Capital, to expand through acquisition. The strategies of these two firms are examined in Chapters Fourteen and Sixteen below.

Credit Card Companies

As mentioned, most of the shinpan and retailer-related credit companies, and some of the consumer lenders, have issued credit cards. There are also a host of pure credit card companies, as well as bank issuers. Roughly half of cards issued are still connected to one location. Others are private "house"

Table 8.1

Top Twenty Consumer Lenders

Top consumer lenders	Loans			Total accounts	Sales offices	Owned ATMs	Joint CDs/ATMs	Average account loan balance ($)	Maximum interest rate p.a.
	Total ($millions)	Unsecured (%)	Secured (%)						
Takefuji	10,806	100	0	2,634,106	1,266	1,457	20,525	3,925	27.375
ACOM	9,763	94	6	2,550,077	1,483	1,782	12,563	3,666	27.375
Promise	7,938	99	1	2,226,081	1,135	1,455	19,059	3,375	25.550
Aiful	6,688	84	16	1,809,371	961	1,083	11,072	3,675	29.200
Lake (GE)	4,410	92	8	1,409,675	564	917	10,060	3,125	29.200
AIC (Associates)	4,170	54	46	500,000	635	500	6,000	6,467	29.000
Sanyo Shinpan	1,862	99	1	596,737	328	363	7,883	3,025	39.800
Total	45,637			11,726,047	6,372	7,557	87,162		

Sources: The Consumer Credit Monthly, March, September, and December 1998 issues and industry sources.

Table 8.2

Cards Issued, Turnover, and Revenues of Credit Card Issuers
(turnover and revenue values in yen billions)

Issuing company segment	Cards issued (millions)	Credit card shopping turnover	Total operating revenues		Revenue from sales financing (installment and revolving credit)
Total	244.4	18,124	1,200.0 ⇧	⇐	149
Banks	98.2	9,040	493.0	⇐	49
Shinpan companies	65.4	3,090	41.1% 359.3	⇐	45
Department stores, retailers	63.7	4,435	29.9% 256.2	⇐	26
Others	17.6	1,559	21.4% 91.4	⇐	30
Percent of total			7.6% 100.0%		

Sources: The Consumer Credit Card Monthly, March 1999; Perry, "Credit Cards."
Note: Data for FY1997.

cards issued under five international brands, MasterCard, Visa, JCB, American Express, and Diners Club. Table 8.2 provides a breakdown of cards issued and turnover by segment. What we observe is that bank-affiliated companies have issued the most cards, some 98 million. *Shinpan* companies and department stores and retailers have issued roughly an equivalent number, 65.4 million and 63.7 million cards, respectively.

Table 8.3 presents the leading issuers of cards. The leading two companies, and four of the top ten, are owned by a grouping of banks. JCB is owned by Sanwa Bank, Asahi Bank, and Daiwa Bank. Visa Japan is controlled by Sumitomo Credit, under Sumitomo Bank. (There are formally seven members of the Visa Japan association. They are Credit Saison, Nikos, Daiei OMC, Sumitomo Credit, UC, DC, and MC.) UC Group is owned by Dai-Ichi Kangyo Bank (DKB), Fuji Bank, Asahi Bank, and Sakura Bank. DC Group is owned by Bank of Tokyo-Mitsubishi. As we noted above, the leading *shinpan* company is Nippon Shinpan. Orico and Aplus are previous spinoffs of Nippon Shinpan. Retailer-related issuers include Credit Saison, Daiei MC, Aeon Credit Service, and Marui.

Table 8.2 *(continued)*

% of total	Revenues from consumer lending (cashing commission)	% of total	Revenues from vendor commissions	% of total	Revenues from card members' fees	% of total
12.4	559	46.6	324	27.0	168	14.0
9.9	146	29.6	169	34.2	130	26.3
12.5	234	65.2	62	17.2	19	5.1
10.0	159	61.9	58	22.5	14	5.5
32.5	20	21.9	36	39.5	6	6.2

American Express, with some 1.1 million cards in force in Japan, did not make the list. AMEX has a special niche in the market that we will examine more closely—along with the business of Associates First Capital—in Chapter Sixteen.

Business Drivers and Competitive Strategies

The relatively unregulated marketplace for consumer finance has fostered a highly competitive industry in which participants have been quick to adapt to competitive challenges. A key challenge has been the Japanese consumer's increasing desire for convenience, as well as credit. This has driven all participants toward providing credit card services and access to cash dispensers.

Retailers and Shinpans Expand Through Cards

Retailers began by offering credit for customers to purchase items in their stores. They have seen the opportunity to increase customer loyalty and ex-

Table 8.3

Top Twenty Credit Card Issuers

Issuer	Card holders (millions)	Shopping loans (Yen (billion)	Cash advances (Yen billion)	Total sales (Yen (billion)	Merchant acceptors (thousands)
JCB Group	38.1	3,510	770	4,280	5,300
Visa Japan	29.3	2,780	680	3,460	2,777
Nippon Shinpan	27.8	1,380	690	2,070	1,002
Credit Saison*	17.5	1,020	680	1,700	450
UC Group	13.8	1,610	650	2,260	1,848
Orico	7.5	220	230	450	293
DC Group	7.4	1,220	380	1,600	1,188
Aeon Credit*	7.0	340	300	640	200
Life	6.8	150	120	270	634
JACCS	6.2	260	180	440	268
MC Group	6.0	660	300	960	1,161
Daiei OMC*	5.5	570	460	1,030	262
Michael Card*	5.1	90	80	170	71
JAL Card*	4.7	275	0	280	18
Aplus	4.4	80	60	130	268
Central Finance	4.3	240	80	320	428
Marui*	3.7	140	320	460	n/a
Takashimaya*	3.2	360	10	370	11
Nissenren*	3.1	300	160	460	108
Isetan Finance*	3.1	200	10	210	0
Total	204.5	15,405	6,160	21,560	16,287

Source: The Consumer Credit Monthly, September 1998.
Notes: *Indicates retailer-related issuers. Data as of March 31, 1998.

pand volumes by issuing cards. The cards can be used at both their own and affiliated-vendors' stores (often entitling the user to substantial discounts). Recently, retail-affiliated issuers have joined larger card service networks (e.g., with MasterCard, Visa, DC, JCB, UC) so that cards can be used widely, including in nationwide ATM systems. *Shinpan* companies developed the market for credit contracts, and have issued cards as a customer-friendly extension of this business and also to defend their customer bases from competition. Naturally, a customer who desires credit to buy products is likely also to be short of cash, so companies have sought to offer cash advance services.

Bank-affiliated issuers, the largest group, have tended to offer cards as part of a banking service relationship to account holders, rather than as a profit center business. Fees charged were generally uniform and low. Bank issuers have been able to offer shopping utility and convenience by virtue of their having extensive relationships with vendors.

Consumer Lenders Target ATMs and Cash Advances

While credit cards have been natural extensions of business strategies for *shinpans*, retailers, and even banks, this has not been so clearly the case with consumer lenders. Their traditional business has not been directly related to purchasing goods, but rather to providing cash. Their profitability was all about net spread on lending borrowed funds, after credit loss reserves, and had nothing to do with additional earnings from product sales. As of late 1999, Takefuji, the market leader, did not offer a credit card. Nor did Lake, but market speculation was that GE Capital management would soon add a card to Lake's strategy.

For consumer lenders, what the market's desire for convenience has meant is increasing the availability, accessibility, and functionality of ATMs and cash dispensing (CD) machines. Table 8.1 provides figures for the ATM and CD networks of the largest consumer lenders. The leader was Takefuji with 20,525 machines. Lake, the new acquisition of GE Capital, provides service from over 10,000 machines. In the case of AIC, a customer can apply for a credit line, be approved, and draw down cash in a matter of minutes at any of its ATM machines. Repayment is also made at ATMs in cash.

One of the reasons that consumer lenders have been slow in providing credit cards is that the convention in Japan has been for card balances to be settled the following month. Today the convention is that the "default" is full repayment every month, and customers must specifically request "revolving" facilities if they so desire. Without the ability to offer revolving credit, cards did not clearly fit into the consumer lenders' business lines. Today revolving credit is possible, and some companies—including AIC—make revolving the "default" in new applications. Other issuers are likely to follow.

ACOM's New Card-Based Strategy

A significant innovation among consumer lenders was introduced by ACOM, number two in the industry, in April 1999. This is a revolving ACOM MasterCard. The card provides no statements. It is entirely ATM-based. (This is considered in the industry a highly desirable marketing advantage, because it provides confidentiality. Many borrowers do not want statements sent to their homes to be possibly inspected by spouses. This is another reason that banks would have difficulty serving this market.) Customers can check their account status, draw down cash, and make repayments, in cash, through ATMs. ACOM's card has no default except a minimum payment, like revolving cards in the United States, and lines can revolve indefinitely. The ACOM card is expected to revolutionize the credit card and consumer finance business. Each interaction with customers at ATM "shops" will allow cross-selling of other products. The upfront investment will be large, but the payoff could be substantial.

Industry Economics: "Cashing" Is King

For credit card issuers in Japan, operating revenues come from four sources: sales financing (installment sales credit interest), consumer lending (interest on cash advances), vendor commissions, and card members' fees. In mid-1999 the rate of interest on revolving or installment sales credit balances was some 12 to 15 percent per annum. Interest "commission" on cash advances—accrued from the day of the drawdown and paid the month following use of the credit card or on outstanding balances that revolve—was some 16 to 30 percent per annum. Revenue from vendors (generally withheld by the issuers) was 0.5 to 5.0 percent. Membership fees for the typical card were $10.42 (¥1,250). Gold or premium cards would charge a higher fee. Some companies were waiving fees. (For complete discussion, see Suefuji 1999, pp. 70–71.)

Table 8.2 provides a breakdown of these revenues for Japanese issuers, by category of issuers, in FY97. The results are interesting. We observe that, for the industry as a whole, interest spread on cashing accounted for a massive 46.6 percent of total operating revenues! The next largest revenue contributor was from vendor commissions at 27 percent, followed by card members' fees of 14 percent. Revenues from interest on revolving credit were only 12.4 percent of the total, the smallest contributor.

There are differences among the issuers in these revenue categories. Banks received an exceptionally small share of revenues from cashing commissions and a relatively large share from vendor commissions, compared with *shinpan* and retailers. Banks also collected a larger percentage of membership fees than either the *shinpan* or department store issuers.

These figures reinforce our sense of how business has been driven among issuer and customer segments. Banks have leveraged large customer bases and vendor relationships to offer convenient shopping service, but not necessarily credit. *Shinpan* companies have pursued credit cards as an extension of their credit contract business for people with cash borrowing needs. Retailers have used the service to push product sales and to offer credit shopping.

Managing Risk: Making Money by Banking the Unbanked

The key business driver for the consumer lenders like Takefuji, ACOM, Lake and AIC is risk management, because, to a greater or lesser extent, they are unsecured lenders. The success of these companies over time is a testament to how effectively they have learned to control credit risks in good times and bad. How they do this is evidenced in Table 8.1, showing total accounts, average loan balance, and maximum interest rate. The consumer lenders have proven adept at risk profiling and other actuarial and database marketing techniques to manage exposures. Their very high interest rates also provide a big cushion for borrower defaults. Average loan loss provisions among the industry leaders was about 3.6 percent of loans in the first half of FY98. Net write-offs for the period were about 3.0 percent, meaning that the companies were conservative.

The key is the companies' lending margins, which, particularly given low money market funding costs, often exceed 25 percent. Such wide margins and credit controls, have driven an industry return on assets of some 3.5 to 4 percent. These economics have driven strong profitability for the major players in the industry, including U.S. players like AIC. For the year ended March 31, 1998, AIC reported pretax earnings of $201 million on equity of $479 million. This was before the merger with DIC.

Open, Compelling Market for New Entrants

The consumer finance industry is crowded, like many others, but it is also open. Providing consumer credit using sophisticated risk modeling and control systems is an area of specialty for many U.S. companies. We should expect new foreign entrants into the market as well as continued expansion by the two foreign leaders, AIC and GE Capital.

It could be years before the shakeout in Japan's corporate banking sector is complete and industry economics become attractive, but in consumer finance, they are attractive today and expected to remain so. The market should be compelling for companies seeking to break out of limited franchises, like AIG or Chase, or to further exploit and develop existing franchises, the case of Citibank. The most important requirement will be the ability to manage across significant cultural and social divides, as has been done with great success already by Associates First Capital (Chapter Sixteen).

Part Three

Choosing Sides and Closing Ranks

Chapter Nine

Japan Marketplace Financial Groups and Affiliations

The Tradition of Grouping—*Zaibatsu* and *Keiretsu*

Being independent in Japan has traditionally been a prescription for early demise, at least in business. For whatever reason—a cultural group orientation, regional or family ties, a defensive approach to market development, the need for mutual financial support and risk sharing, or the desire for horizontal and vertical process integration—Japanese companies have banded into groups. Before World War II, the largest corporate groups were the famous *zaibatsu* trusts with names like Yasuda, Mitsubishi, Mitsui, and Sumitomo. The *zaibatsu* were broken up by the Allied occupation administration, and the trust and holding company structure that supported them was prohibited. In the 1950s the groups came together again, however, in the form of *keiretsu*—group affiliations based upon cross-holdings of shares and close coordination of group development policies through the mechanism of "informal" "Presidents' Clubs"—regularly scheduled and highly formalized meetings of the senior managements of the group's companies.

Old and New Groupings

The largest of Japanese groups have fallen into one of two categories. In one category are groups that fall into the prewar pattern of industrial and trading companies surrounding and linked to and by several core financial institutions, particularly a main bank, trust bank, and life insurance company. Examples of these groups today are the Mitsui Group, the Bank of Tokyo-Mitsubishi (read: Mitsubishi Group), the Fuyo (formerly Yasuda) Group, and the Sumitomo Group. In the second category are groups—usually grown up after World War II—of which the leading company is a manufacturer. The best examples are Toyota Motor and Honda Motor.

Japanese corporate groups have been inseparable from Japan's economic development for all the reasons suggested above and more. But the most critical reason that groups have been indispensable in Japanese business is that they have ensured the availability and persistence of the most important resource—capital. Being a member of a group has meant access to capital in good times and bad from the core financial institutions—and particularly from the group's main bank.

For at least the last twenty-five years, commentators—and particularly those from the United States—have been opining that Japan's groups and main bank relationships are anachronisms with little relevance to businesses in Japan's modern marketplace. They have predicted, on the one hand, a Darwinian decline in such obeisance these relationships receive (e.g., in the form of stable cross-holdings of shares) and, on the other, an increase in Western-style "arm's length" behavior. In the view of the author, nothing could be farther from the truth in Japan. *Keiretsu* relationships and behaviors are as strong as ever. And, for new as well as old reasons, so is the importance of the financial institutions at the center of most of the groups.

Financial Groupings and the Big Bang

This is not to say that the financial institution cores of many groups are not strained and challenged by today's environment in Japan. On the contrary, as seen in earlier chapters, Japan's financial institutions have been, without exception, severely weakened by the post-bubble recession and collapse in collateral asset values. Some institutions have been compelled by their weakness, and the behest of regulators, to seek merger partners. Inevitably, where this has happened, group ties have been complicated and in some cases diluted, even as groupings have expanded in size. As new consolidations occur this problem of dilution is likely to increase. A good example is the Mizuho Financial Group megabank, to be fully operational in spring 2002. The megabank will embrace the relationships of the former *zaibatsu*-origin Fuyu Group (Fuji Bank), which includes Nissan Motors, Fuji Heavy Industries, and Marubeni Corporation, plus the extensive cross-group relationships of IBJ, which originated as a government-sponsored, long-term credit bank. DKB's relationships, including such companies as Isuzu Motors and C. Itoh, will also be brought in. Even for a bank as massive as the new megabank, some weakening of relationships will be inevitable when, for example, it becomes necessary to allocate credit exposure in the general trading company sector, and both Marubeni and C. Itoh are desiring greater financial support.

But the larger challenge for the financial institutions of Japan's groups is the big bang and financial deregulation. Since World War II, the groups' key financial institutions—commercial banks, trust banks, life and nonlife insurance companies—have been able to serve the needs of their "captive" group companies with little fear of competition from financial service suppliers outside the group. Moreover, due to strict segmentation of financial services by the Ministry of Finance (MOF), the financial service suppliers—be they banks, trust banks, life or nonlife insurers—did not have to contend with competition across service segments from other financial institutions within the group.

As a legacy of the piecemeal deregulation since 1993, which allowed limited cross-sector entry through subsidiaries, the financial landscape is littered with special-purpose subsidiaries and affiliates of financial institutions. As big bang deregulation removes restrictions on direct entry, it is necessary to decide which of these subsidiaries or affiliates to keep and which to discard or merge. Within a group, there are often four or five competitive subsidiaries or affiliates in the same area. What to do?

Within the three-year period 1998 to 2001, the world as it was known to Japan's group financial institutions will change entirely, requiring a fundamental adjustment and adaptation from the financial institutions themselves. We are witnessing the change begin.

The Challenge of Rationalizing Cross-Sectoral Services

The key issues for financial groups in 1999 and 2000 are and will be the following: (1) How to best organize and deliver services competitively when—with cross-sector entry deregulation—many more choices of corporate vehicle can be used. Ultimately, it may be possible to deliver most or all services from one corporate vehicle or, at minimum, to achieve the same effect through a holding company structure. (2) How to acquire and maintain the expertise and product innovation capability—i.e., specialization—needed to compete as deregulation allows new products and the marketplace demands them. (3) How to set and manage overall corporate or group strategy and manage risk. And, ideally, all these issues have to be addressed and resolved with a view toward maintaining the cohesion and efficacy of group relationships and for the greater advancement of group interests. Let us review the situations of each of the groups. The specific strategies of key industry players will be examined in Chapter Ten.

Mizuho Financial Group: A Model for Others?

The reorganization and restructuring issues for Japanese financial groups are vividly presented in the case of the new Mizuho Financial Group holding company. As seen in Table 9.1, a new holding company structure

Table 9.1

Cross-Sector Reorganization and Restructuring Issues for the Mizuho Financial Group Holding Company

Separate Group Affiliations in 1999

	Wholesale securities	Wholesale retail banking	Retail securities	Mutual funds (investment trusts)	Institutional asset management	Trust banking	Life Insurance	Nonlife insurance
IBJ Group	IBJ Securities (100%)	Industrial Bank of Japan	New Japan Securities Waco Securities	**DL-IBJ Asset Management** Co. (50/50) Dai-Ichi Life and IBJ		**IBJ Trust & Banking** (100%)	**Dai-Ichi Life**	
Fuyo (Fuji Bank) Group	Fuji Securities (100%)	Fuji Bank	Daito Securities	**Fuji Investment Managemement** (38.6% Fuji Bank; 42.7% Fuyo Group)		**DKB-Fuji Trust & Banking** (50/50)	Yasuda Mutual Life	Yasuda Fire & Marine (YFM)
				DKB-Fuji Trust & Banking	Yasuda Kasai Global Asset Management Co.	Yasuda Trust & Banking (56.3% by Fuji Bank)		
DKB Group	DKB Securities (100%)	Dai-Ichi Kangyo Bank	Kankaku Securities (54% group ownership)	**Dai-Ichi Kangyo Asset Management** (63.4% DKB; 73.4% group).		**DKB-Fuji Trust & Banking** (50/50)	Asahi Mutual Life	Taisei Fire & Marine
				Asahi Life Management			Fukoku Life	Nissan Fire & Marine
Joint Holding Company	Three wholesale securities subsidiaries to merge during 2000. **Combined capital $2.7 billion.**	Business operations of three banks to be combined into separate entities under holding co.: 1. **Customer and Consumer Bank;** 3. **Corporate Bank; 3. Investment Bank.** By fall 2000.	New Japan and Waco to merge 4/2000. **All companies to merge** by fall 2002 **in New Securities** Co. under holding co.	*Changes in connection with Mizuho Financial Group Holding Company Structure 2000-2003* Asset management and mutual funds (investment trust) vehicles must be rationalized. One issue will be how to handle joint ventures and tie-ups with foreign companies. **IBJ Group (including Dai-Ichi Life)** was already the fourth largest broker and mutual funds company. After combination it is among the **largest asset managers.**		All trust banking operations to be combined into **New Trust Bank** under the holding company. By fall 2002.	Holding company likely to take equity positions in demutualized life companies. Companies likely to merge and to integrate life and nonlife businesses. Insurance tie-ups will create powerful entity.	

Background, Issues, and Relationships in 1999

IBJ Securities in alliance with **Nomura** in derivatives. Alliance with Macquarie Bank (Aust.) in derivatives	IBJ in JV with 3i of the U.K. to do MBOs. IBJ 40% In private banking focus, **IBJ** agreed to give **Dai-Ichi Life's** life planners corner in IBJ branches	**New Japan Securities** (NJS) (from 4/2000). IBJ Securities agreed to take 25% equity. Will sell products of **Dai-Ichi Life's nonlife subsidiary**	**IBJ Trust & Banking** (100%)	**Dai-Ichi Life Comprehensive** tie-up with IBJ announced October 1998. Emphasis in cross-selling of products and asset management
		DL-IBJ Asset Management Co. (50/50%) Dai-Ichi Life and IBJ. Created by merger of IBJ NW Asset Management Co., IBJ Investment Trust Management Co., and Dai-Ichi Life Asset Management Co. Plan to absorb ITM and asset management companies of merged **New Japan Securities and Waco** in FY 2001. Joint product development with **Nomura Securities.** Tie-up with Nomura Securities in 401(k) system development ITM JV **Yasuda Paine Webber Mutual Fund Co.** New company, **Yasuda Fire Cigna Securities** 50/50 JV YFM and Cigna to develop DC pension products and sell mutual funds		
Fuji Securities absorbed securities subsidiary of Yasuda Trust	**Fuji Bank** and **Yasuda Trust** will merge branch operations over 2-3 years		**DKB-Fuji Trust** will absorb pension fund business from **Yasuda Trust.** Targeting wholesale pension and securities agency business nationwide	
Yasuda Trust and **Fuji Bank** agreed to eliminate overlapping operations				**Yasuda Fire & Marine** increased investment in INA Himawari Life (Cigna) to 39 percent
Kankaku Securities (54% DKB group ownership)	**DKB-J.P. Morgan Investment Management Co.** (50/50). Capital $24.4 million. **Asahi Envest Investments** established June 1999 (AML/MetLife)			**Asahi Mutual Life** tie-up with **U.S. MetLife** in asset management

Within 1999 IBJ's securities affiliates will begin selling products of **Dai-Ichi Life's** nonlife subsidiary

Source: Author.

will provide a framework and driving force for a series of rationalizations and reorganizations of the many historical entities and relationships brought to the new structure (also see Chapter Three for an explanation of the plans for the merger of business operations in 2002).

The challenge for the new megabank will be to achieve synergies and to grow stronger, as well as bigger, in the new holding company structure. One critical requirement will be to ensure that rationalization and specialization— for example, the merger of three wholesale securities companies by 2000— is not pursued to the detriment of relationships and arrangements like those with Dai-Ichi Life. The model for the post-big bang financial group ultimately is a "supermarket" of financial products, tailored to marketplace niches and delivered efficiently through the broadest possible channels. As part of a comprehensive tie-up agreement, which includes asset management, IBJ and Dai-Ichi Life began in 1999 to jointly sell each other's products, as permitted, and IBJ opened its branches to Dai-Ichi Life's financial planners. Dai-Ichi began to place IBJ's debentures with insurance clients. In 1999 IBJ began combining resources with Dai-Ichi Life in asset management, combining IBJ's own investment trust management and investment advisory companies with those of Dai-Ichi Life. IBJ will go further in FY2001 and integrate the asset management operations of its affiliated securities companies, New Japan and Waco, into the new combined Dai-Ichi Life-IBJ asset management JV.

The challenge will be to ensure that this integration strategy is given full play within the broader megabank holding company framework. Very likely this will happen and will include also the life insurance companies in the former Fuji Bank and DKB groups, Yasuda Life, and Asahi Life and Fukoku Life, respectively.

The joint holding company structure could also facilitate an enhanced level of integration with group insurance arms, through equity holding. Until the mutual life companies are converted to shareholder corporations, equity participation will be one-way, with the insurers taking equity in the megabank holding company. Subsequently, the holding company would take equity in the corporatized insurer. Conceivably, a holding company could acquire all the shares of an insurer, bringing the insurer completely under the group.

Integration and rationalization issues for Mizuho Financial Group include rationalization of duplicated or overlapping business entities. As mentioned earlier, an immediate step, by fall 2000, will be the merger of the three banks' 100 percent-owned wholesale securities companies. In the longer term, by spring 2002, it is planned to merge the retail securities affiliates (see Chapter Four). Asset management, investment trusts, and trust banking also present vast opportunities for continuing a process of rationalization started by the banks in 1999 (Table 9.1, lower panel).

By 1999 the financial weakness of Fuyo Group financial firms Fuji Bank and Yasuda Trust had already forced substantial group restructuring. Under the supervision of the Financial Reconstruction Commission, Fuji Bank in 1999 invested funds in Yasuda Trust sufficient to turn Yasuda Trust into a subsidiary. Following this, Fuji Bank orchestrated a restructuring of Yasuda's operations, transferring its pension fund business to DKB-Fuji Trust & Banking, a new joint venture with DKB.

Yasuda Trust's securities subsidiary was absorbed into Fuji Securities.

Under the new megabank holding company structure, Yasuda Trust's remaining branches and operations—corporate and retail banking—are likely to be absorbed first into Fuji Bank and then into the combined new corporate and retail banking entities from spring 2002. Yasuda Trust will cease to exist. Fuyo Group's trust and pension management activities will be conducted through the combined trust bank and asset management entities of the new megabank.

One interesting, though minor issue will be how to handle the relationships existing with foreign firms. In asset management and investment trusts, the megabank will have legacy relationships with J.P. Morgan, Paine Webber, and Cigna, among others. Very likely, the new situation will hasten the dissolution or buyout by one party of most of these joint ventures.

The Bank of Tokyo-Mitsubishi Group

Due in part to its financial strength (Chapter Ten) and in part to its conservatism, in 1999 the Bank of Tokyo-Mitsubishi (BOTM) Group remained the least changed and most representative of the old-line *zaibatsu* groups (Table 9.2). Its financial pillars—the bank, Meiji Life, Tokio Fire & Marine, and Mitsubishi Trust—were at the top of their traditional segments. BOTM was the only city bank strong enough to be able to turn down a public funds bailout. This strength is both an advantage and a disadvantage in the context of the big bang. BOTM management is known to see clearly the need for change, but it is less compelled than others to act quickly. Inevitably, the lack of a sense of urgency breeds complacency, inertia, and perfunctory rather than purposeful action.

Perhaps this is why we sense that the BOTM Group has only just started to rationalize itself and that it is proceeding cautiously in small steps. In fall 1998 the BOTM, Mitsubishi Trust, Meiji Life, and Tokio Fire & Marine publicly announced that they would coordinate their strategies and undertake joint activities. By 1999 some initiatives were begun, but the impression was that coordination was weak.

In the trust banking area, three entities still existed. It was expected that in

Table 9.2

Affiliations of Bank of Tokyo-Mitsubishi Group

Wholesale securities	Wholesale banking	Retail banking	Retail securities	Mutual funds (investment trusts)	Institutional asset management	Trust banking	Life insurance	Nonlife insurance
Tokyo-Mitsubishi Securities (TMS) Yen 150 billion capital	**Bank of Tokyo-Mitsubishi**	**Bank of Tokyo-Mitsubishi**	**Tokyo Mitsubishi Personal Securities**	**Tokyo-Mitsubishi Asset Management** **Tokio Marine Asset Management**		**Mitsubishi Trust & Banking** (MTB) **Nippon Credit Bank** (78%) **Toyo Trust Bank** (100%)	**Meiji Life** (ML) **Tokio Marine Anshin Life** **Tokio Marine Anshin Life** is a 100% subsidiary of TFM	**Tokio Fire & Marine** (TFM)
TFM and ML each to take 5% equity in TMS. TMS absorbed Mitsubishi Shin Securities, subsidiary of MTB. MTB acquired 9.3% equity in TMS.	Transfer M&A operations to TMS?		Merged entity of Ryoki and Dai Nana Securities					
			BOTM, TFM, MTB, and ML jointly take 50% of on-line brokerage with Charles Schwab	AIMIC Investment Management (MTB JV with AIG). BOTM tie-up with Dreyfus in mutual funds. BOTM cooperation in pension funds with Frank Russell Associates		TFM to invest 30% in online broker with Charles Schwab. BOTM, ML, and MTB to take equity participation.		

Source: Author.

a few years Nippon Credit Bank and Toyo Trust Bank would be merged into Mitsubishi Trust. In the asset management and mutual funds area, BOTM Group was still without a clear strategy or coordinated institutional approach. AIMIC, the JV with AIG, seemed to be adding little economic or strategic value. BOTM had formed an alliance with Frank Russell of the United States in an apparent effort to gain mutual funds and asset management technology.

BOTM was more proactive in the area of wholesale securities, perhaps spurred to action by the forceful competition of IBJ, Sumitomo/Daiwa, and Nikko/Citigroup. In 1999 BOTM moved to strengthen Tokyo-Mitsubishi Securities (TMS) by raising its capital and rationalizing some operations (see Chapter Ten). TMS absorbed the securities subsidiary of Mitsubishi Trust Bank. In retail securities, we saw less activity and less clarity of direction. Tokyo-Mitsubishi Personal Securities was created from the merger of two smaller firms. The market strategy and position of this company remained unclear, as did BOTM's overall corporate strategy.

In early 1999 BOTM hired A.T. Kearney to help it forge a long-term, comprehensive strategy for its group operations. The market was told to expect the results of the strategy review in later 1999.

Sumitomo Bank Group

Whereas observers of the BOTM Group sensed indecision in 1999, in the Sumitomo Group they saw boldness (Table 9.3). Sumitomo Bank has traditionally been a trendsetter with a proactive, results-oriented management style. By 1999 Sumitomo Bank had drastically restructured its retail business to achieve profitability. It sought to achieve the same kind of focus on corporate business through its JV with Daiwa Securities to form Daiwa SB Capital Markets (DSBCM). DSBCM was positioned to be competitive with IBJ, Nomura, Nikko/Citigroup, and others in providing debt and equity underwriting for corporate customers and in offering sophisticated financial products like derivatives (see Chapter Ten).

Sumitomo Group was actively pursuing consolidation and cooperation across the group in asset management. We can expect more of the same in this area and in trust banking. In terms of cooperation with foreign firms, Sumitomo Bank for years leveraged its equity relationship with Goldman Sachs to train staff. The entire group participated in the joint venture with DLJ Direct to offer online, discount trading and information. We can expect to see more initiatives from this dynamic group.

Sanwa Bank Group

Sanwa Bank Group appeared in 1999 to have relatively clear strategy for facing the post-big bang marketplace. In July 1999 six group companies,

Table 9.3

Affiliations of Sumitomo Bank Group
(alliance with Daiwa Securities) (six percent equity in Goldman Sachs)

Wholesale Securities	Wholesale banking	Retail banking	Retail securities	Mutual funds (investment trusts)	Institutional asset management	Trust banking	Life insurance	Nonlife insurance
Daiwa SB Capital Markets (40% Sumitomo Bank)	**Sumitomo Bank** (SB)	**Sumitomo Bank**	**Meiko National Securities**	**Daiwa SB Investments** (DSBI)		**Sumitomo Trust & Banking** (STB)	**Sumitomo Mutual Life** (SML)	**Sumitomo Fire & Marine** (SFM)
			Daiwa Securities	**Sumisei Global Investment Trust Management** (SGITM) (50% by SML)		**Sumigin Trust & Banking** (100% SB)	**Sumitomo Marine YuYu Life**	
Joint venture with Daiwa International Group. Part of comprehensive tie-up. Capital Yen 408 billion. 1,400 staff.			Link with Daiwa Securities through group shareholding, synergy with wholesale securities JV	Daiwa Asset Management and two asset management affiliates of Sumitomo Bank merged in April 1999 to form DSAM. Will accept investment from T. Rowe Price.		Sumigin Trust & Banking expected to be merged into STB	Sumitomo Marine YuYu Life is the 100% subsidiary of SFM	
			JV with DLJ Direct	T. Rowe Price and U.K. Fleming Group to join DSAM. U.K. Friends, Ivory & Sime partners in SGITM		STB to invest in DLJ Direct JV		

Source: Author.

Table 9.4

Affiliations of Sanwa Bank Group

	Wholesale securities	Wholesale banking	Retail banking	Retail securities	Mutual funds (investment trusts)	Institutional asset management	Trust banking	Life insurance	Nonlife insurance
Sanwa	**Sanwa Securities** (100%) subsidiary. Capital Yen 50 billion	**Sanwa Bank**	**Sanwa Bank**	Four company merger: **Universal Securities**	**Partners Asset Management** (50.2% Sanwa Bank)	**Sanwa Asset Management** **Toyo Trust Asset Management Co.** **Daido Life ITM Co.**	**Toyo Trust & Banking** (TTB) (12% owned by Sanwa Bank)	**Daido Mutual Life** (DML) **Taiyo Life**	**Koa Fire & Marine**
		Sanwa will adopt joint branch strategy with Toyo Trust from October 1999		Dai-Ichi, Universal, Taiheiyo, and Towa Securities to merge April 2000. Combined customer assets Yen 3 trillion. Investment trust license and operations transferred to Partners.	Partners will absorb Universal ITM in fall 1999. All mutual fund development will be done by Partners.	Sanwa Bank, TTB, DML to form new company to develop 401(k) pension business. Comprehensive tie-up between Sanwa and TTB in pension funds.	Former Sanwa Trust & Banking merged into TTB in October 1999. Sanwa will adopt joint branch strategy with Toyo Trust from October 1999.	Daido Life and Taiyo Life announced in January 1999 a comprehensive tie-up to lead to a joint holding company	

Sanwa Group to cooperate with Morgan Stanley Dean Witter in sales and development of mutual funds

Source: Author.

Sanwa Bank, Toyo Trust, Daido Life, Taiyo Life, Koa Fire and Marine, and Universal Securities held a joint press conference to announce a comprehensive tie-up of business strategies, in advance of the establishment of a holding company. Sanwa Bank (Table 9.4) is distinguished for lacking *zaibatsu* roots, and this distinction necessarily influences its strategy. Sanwa Bank is aggressively pursuing a retail, mutual funds and securities distribution-oriented strategy, partly by acquisition (Chapter Ten). In early 1999 it forged a joint business development with Toyo Trust, a likely prelude to an acquisition of Toyo by Sanwa. Sanwa surprised the market with its bold acquisition of Dai-Ichi Securities from Long Term Credit Bank (LTCB) in 1999. This company will be merged with two other securities companies into Universal Securities in April 2000, giving Sanwa a major position in the retail securities marketplace. Mutual fund development is being consolidated in Partners Asset Management and further rationalization of vehicles in this area is likely.

Under a Sanwa Bank Group holding company, the six allied companies will coordinate strategies and cross-sell products with a focus on the retail market. They will also coordinate an approach to the 401(k) asset management business. The Group's management, under the leadership of Sanwa Bank, has demonstrated tactical and strategic skills which bode well for the future of this group. It is possible that Sanwa will decide to absorb Daiwa Bank.

Sakura Bank Group

Sakura Bank is the nucleus of the Mitsui (Table 9.5). This group, with deep *zaibatsu* roots and the backing of major industrial companies like Toyota Motor Corporation, will survive, but its strategy is far from clear. The group is weak in securities, both wholesale and retail. Its trust banking components, Chuo Trust and Mitsui Trust, were forced to merge by regulators following receipt of public funds.

The Group needs to gain competence and delivery capability in the asset management and mutual fund areas. The JV with Prudential is successful on a small scale, but the Group's needs are greater.

Asahi/Tokai Bank Group

The Asahi Bank/Tokai Bank tie-up illustrates some of the possibilities for rationalization and joint efforts when the will exists (Table 9.6). The two will form a joint holding company, probably antecedent to a merger in 2002–2003. The holding company will direct activities of group companies with a view to creating a "supraregional" bank. Some or all of Bank of Yokohama's operations could be integrated into the supraregional operations structure. The structure could also accommodate integration of Daiwa Bank, whose base of operations is in the Osaka region.

Table 9.5

Affiliations of Sakura Bank Group

	Wholesale securities	Wholesale banking	Retail banking	Retail securities	Mutual funds (investment trusts)	Institutional asset management	Trust banking	Life insurance	Nonlife insurance
Sakura Securities	**Sakura Securities**	**Sakura Bank** Toyota Motor Corp. is major shareholder	**Sakura Bank**	**Yamatane** **Shinko Ishino** **Kyokuto Securities** Three companies expected to merge	**Sakura Investment Trust Management** Prudential-Mitsui Trust Investments Co.	**Chuo Mitsui Asset Management** **Mitsui Marine Asset Management Co.** Sakura Bank, Mitsui Trust, MFM to jointly enter DC pension business, to establish JV subsidiary Chuo Trust tie-up with HSBC in asset management	**Chuo Trust & Banking** **Sakura Trust & Banking** (100%) **Chuo Trust & Banking** formed April 2000 by merger of Chuo and Mitsui Trust	**Mitsui Mutual Life** **Mitsui Mirai Life** Mitsui Mirai Life is 100% subsidiary of MFM	**Mitsui Fire & Marine (MFM)**

Source: Author.

Table 9.6

Affiliations of Asahi/Tokai Bank Group
(holding company or merger in 2000–2003) Tie-up with Bank of Yokahama

Wholesale securities	Wholesale banking	Retail banking	Retail securities	Mutual funds (investment trusts)	Institutional asset management	Trust banking	Life insurance	Nonlife insurance
Tokai International Securities	**Tokai Bank**	**Tokai Bank**	**Tokai Maruman Securities**	**Asahi Tokyo Investment Trust Management Co.**		**Tokai Trust & Banking** (100% Tokai)		
	Asahi Bank	**Asahi Bank**	**Okasan Securities**	**Tokai Asset Management Co.**		**Asahi Trust & Banking** (100% Asahi)		
Derivative, special products focus. Bank of Yokohama invested 10% equity. Asahi closed 100% securities subsidiary	Focus on small and medium-sized companies	Tie-up in retail operations, ATM systems, back office, other	**Chiyoda Securities** Tokai Maruman and Okasan are affilliates of Tokai. Chiyoda is affiliated with Asahi	Asahi Tokyo ITM and Asahi Investment Advisory Co. merged March 1999. Tokai and Asahi jointly selling products developed by affilliated ITM companies. Bank of Yokohama transferred asset lmanagement operations to Tokai Group				

Source: Author.

The group's strategy is to be a specialized retail and small enterprise-oriented service provider. A differentiated level of service, including financial consultation and planning services, will be provided to individuals, depending upon needs. Front and back office operations of branches will be rationalized to increase efficiency and avoid overlapping and duplicated functions.

Consolidation of group entities has started in mutual funds and asset management. More will need to be done to rationalize services here and in trust services. In retail securities, merger of group entities can be expected.

Asahi Bank's advertising slogan in mid-1999, aimed at retail customers with assets to manage, was "I Support Your Dream." Having almost failed due to bad corporate debts, Asahi and Tokai are focusing hard on the consumer. Their relatively clear strategy has a good chance of achieving their own dreams as well.

Against a backdrop of deregulation, heightened competition, and technological advance, the watchword for all Japan's major financial groups was in 1999, and will remain for years, revolutionary change. This change will profoundly influence the entire Japanese economic structure, and will have global effects. But to us the greatest interest is to be found in the individual strategies of the major players, to which we now turn.

Chapter Ten

Survival Strategies Among the Japanese Majors

In the last chapter we examined Japan's major financial groups with a view to ascertain how they were adapting to the challenge of a changing marketplace and, especially, to the imperatives of big bang deregulation. Below we take a closer look at several of the leading companies. We look at the strategies of the new megabank members—Industrial Bank of Japan (IBJ), Fuji Bank, and Dai-Ichi Kangyo Bank (DKB)—Bank of Tokyo Mitsubishi, Sumitomo Bank, Sanwa Bank, Nomura Securities, and Nippon Life. We are particularly interested in the extent to which these companies have planned differentiated strategies to leverage their strengths and to defend against threats. We are looking for indications of where these key players—and Japan's financial services marketplace—will be in five to ten years' time.

Mizuho Financial Group—Forming the World's Largest Bank

IBJ—From Wholesale to Universal Bank Model

In summer 1999 IBJ was the only one left of the three Japanese long-term credit banks. The other two had been declared insolvent and nationalized in late 1998 and early 1999. Regulations in Japan's segmented financial system before the big bang gave to long-term credit banks and denied to commercial banks the right to issue debentures, thereby creating a source of medium- to long-term funding. This ability to fund, and then to extend, medium- to long-term loans allowed IBJ to establish itself as a supplier of investment funds for most of Japan's largest corporations. Since Japanese banks could also hold equity shares, and lenders are in a position to ask for and get equity, IBJ was and remains one of the major shareholders of most of Japan's big industrial companies.

The system put Japan's commercial banks and brokers in the position of underwriting the debentures of the long-term credit banks, essentially upstreaming consumer deposits and savings. The system permitted IBJ to meet its funding needs without an extensive branch network, and, indeed, its branching was restricted. Therefore, it never developed either a branch network or a consumer banking services capability. But it did develop superb relationships with Japanese corporations, and a certain expertise in understanding and serving the financing needs of large corporations.

In 1999, after the urgent problem of solvency was dealt with by the infusion of public money, IBJ's management considered two different options for future development: Would the bank continue in the mode, something like J.P. Morgan in the United States, of Japan's purest "wholesale" bank, concentrating on providing top-quality services to big corporations and institutions? Or, alternatively, would it seek or accept the opportunity to join— through merger, acquisition, or in a joint holding company structure—with one or more retail-oriented banks, to become part of a universal bank?

Prior to the Megabank Decision—Hoping to Make Wholesale Banking Pay

Prior to the summer of 1999, IBJ's management had been pursuing a strategy of trying to make wholesale banking pay, even in Japan's structurally flawed market.

Its strategy had three components: strengthening the wholesale securities capability of IBJ Securities, creating a significant retail distribution arm through New Japan Securities, and becoming a major player in asset management in alliance with Dai-Ichi Life.

Building Wholesales Securities and Investment Banking Prowess

In 1999 IBJ increased the capital of its 100 percent securities subsidiary, IBJ Securities (IBJS), to $1.4 billion, making it a highly credible investment banking and capital markets player. IBJ's strong corporate relationships gave IBJS a strong competitive edge in winning mandates to originate debt and equity issues. Alliances with Nomura Securities and Macquarie Bank in development and marketing of derivatives products were formed to keep the company competitive in technology. IBJS proved its strength in underwriting corporate bonds in FY97 and first half FY98 when it underwrote some 10 percent of new straight bond issues. This was the fourth position behind the Big Three securities houses and double the share of the next contender, Tokyo-Mitsubishi Securities. (For a thorough discussion of IBJ's positioning, see Garone et al. 1999.) The president of IBJ, Nishimura Masao, was quoted as forecasting that by March 2003 securities-related business would contribute some 70 percent of revenues (*Nihon Keizai Shimbun*, April 23, 1999).

And Retail Securities Distribution

The key vehicle for IBJ in retail securities distribution was New Japan Securities, which would be the surviving company after the merger of New Japan and Waco Securities, both IBJ affiliates, in April 2000. It was expected that IBJ would increase its equity in the merged New Japan Securities (NJS) from 25 percent to over 50 percent and operate NJS as the group's retail brokerage arm (Garone et al. 1999, p. 4). It was also expected that Dai-Ichi Life would invest in NJS. The combined NJS planned to operate between 90 to 100 branches. This would have been a powerful distribution channel for securities originated by IBJS and for products of other group companies, especially for mutual funds and asset management products.

Alliance with Dai-Ichi Life in Asset Management

The third key strategic initiative of IBJ was the alliance with Dai-Ichi Life in asset management. As of March 1998, Dai-Ichi Life Asset Management managed a total of $6.4 billion in public and private pensions. IBJ managed $17.5 billion. At $23.9 billion combined, IBJ-DL was at the top of the league in terms of discretionary asset management. Looking at mutual funds, as of January 1999, the assets of the investment trust companies affiliates with NJS, Waco, and IBJ totaled $20 billion.

As of March 1998 Dai-Ichi Life had 54,700 insurance agents and 10.5 million policyholders. This constitutes a powerful franchise on which IBJ can capitalize in its securities and asset management strategies. Analysts (Garone et al. 1999) believed that IBJ was well placed to capture a major part of the defined contribution 401(k)-type pension market after its introduction in 2000, since the key to success will be a credible investment product and strong corporate relationships.

Fuji Bank and DKB—Seeking Strength Through Unity

The Fuyo Group, of which Fuji Bank is the nucleus, is relatively weak financially, containing Nissan Motor Corporation among other perennially limping companies. By the late 1990s its main trust bank, Yasuda Trust & Banking, was terminally damaged by credit losses. Fuji Bank's origins, its pride, and its passive, vision-less management made the bank one of the best examples of what has been wrong in the industry. In 1998 it was "all-things-to-all-people," with 340 branches providing the full range of services (unprofitably) to corporate and individual clients. It had an abysmal record of self-assessment in the quality of its credit exposures (Ohara 1999).

By early 1999, when it stood in line for public money, Fuji Bank was beginning some drastic restructuring, but its ability to deliver results and become truly competitive alone was in doubt. The restructuring included forming a group structure under which would operate three major business divisions: customer banking (retail and small- and medium-sized companies), global banking (large corporates), and asset management. In this new structure, Fuji Bank was picking apart and reallocating parts of Yasuda Trust & Banking, its 56.3 percent subsidiary. Beginning in 1999 the branch network of Yasuda Trust was gradually rationalized and combined with that of Fuji Bank. Yasuda Trust's personal and private banking staff and products— deemed more competitive than those of Fuji—were folded into Fuji Bank's customer banking structure, both for individuals and corporations.

While possessing weaker *keiretsu* ties than Fuji Bank, DKB was similar in other respects. It manifested all the shortcomings, particularly low profitability and poor risk control, of the industry. Burdened by bad debts and weak management control, the bank had done little beyond rescuing its affiliate Kankaku Securities, strengthening its securities subsidiary, DKB Securities, and forming the trust banking JV with Fuji Bank, DKB-Fuji Trust, to restructure or reorient itself before being forced to make a plan in exchange for public funds in 1999. The plan, when revealed, looked similar to others. DKB was to concentrate on retail and small- and medium-sized corporate segments, which hopefully could provide a higher ROE. Organizationally, the bank would reorganize into four internal "companies": CCBC—small and medium corporate and individual; CBC—large corporate; IBC—overseas business with non-Japanese companies; and MTC— capital markets and trading business. Each "company" would be given an asset budget and require ROE targets over the next three years. In general, lending to large corporates and, especially, overseas business would be reduced. Domestic lending to individuals and small corporates would be increased. Overall DKB planned to reduce risk assets by $10 billion (¥1.25 trillion), or 3 percent, from FY98 to FY01 and to raise ROA from 0.40 percent to 0.72 percent.

For both DKB and Fuji, the new 50/50 JV, DKB Fuji Trust & Banking, was a key initiative. Fuji Bank would transfer the asset management operations and business license from Yasuda Trust to this new JV. DKB Fuji Trust would operate nationwide through some twenty branches, focusing on corporate pension and securities agency business.

Key Objectives and Benefits of the Megabank Strategy

On August 20, 1999, IBJ, Fuji Bank, and DKB announced that their former plans would be subsumed into a grand new megabank holding company structure (for details, see Figure 3.1). The post-2002 structure of the combined operations of IBJ, Fuji Bank, and DKB under a joint holding company, operating distinct retail, corporate, investment banking, trust and securities businesses, clearly has much to offer all three participants. What can we conclude are the key strategic objectives and benefits of this structure, judged against the preceding strategies of the three banks?

Specialization. The structure of a holding company directing specialized businesses appears to increase opportunities for market- and customer segment-oriented product and services strategies, which will increase competitiveness and profitability.

Economies of scale. The economics of modern banking, with its massive systems requirements, favor large organizations that can broadly apply and defray the costs of technology development. Often articulated as a benefit of the combination was the potential to spend annually $1.3 billion on technology. This was a level of expenditure that was standard among large global banks like Citigroup and Chase, but that the Japanese banks individually had been unable to match. Such economies will be critical in achieving the goal of making retail banking profitable.

Universal product delivery capability. The holding company structure facilitates the offering of the entire range of financial service products. This is the financial supermarket model, which is still favored (and looks something like the "all-things-to-all people") in the Japanese marketplace.

Defensive market positioning. Each bank had deficiencies. IBJ had a limited branch and deposit gathering capability; Fuji was weak in wholesale and securities; DKB was lacking broad corporate relationships. Each area of weakness provided competitors with an opportunity and created a threat to the bank's client bases. The combination of the three banks allows each bank to draw on the others' strengths, in order to defend and, ultimately, expand market position. This is clearest in the cases of Fuji and DKB, who will answer competitive threats to their corporate relations by offering highly competitive wholesale banking and securities services from IBJ.

Broad coverage for asset management. With the importance of asset management and the future of defined benefit 401(k)-type pension schemes, the ability to offer services and to spread systems costs over a broad client base is important. The combination of the client bases of the three banks clearly offers benefits in this respect. For IBJ and its alliance partner, Dai-Ichi Life, the additional access to the large, medium, and small corporate clients of DKB and Fuji was attractive. For the retail market, the opportunity to manufacture and sell mutual funds nationally through the combined channels of the three banks was attractive, as was the opportunity to rationalize asset management operations to increase market share and profitability.

Bank of Tokyo-Mitsubishi

Bank of Tokyo-Mitsubishi (BOTM) was born on April 1, 1996, the result of the merger of Japan's premier global bank, Bank of Tokyo, and the strongest primarily domestic bank, and the core of the venerable Mitsubishi Group, Mitsubishi Bank. In 1999, with assets of $581 billion, 393 branches, including sixty-two overseas branches, and some 17,800 staff members, BOTM towered over its domestic competition in terms of overall reach. (Of course, the advent of the new IBJ, Fuji Bank, and DKB megabank holding company in fall 2002 will relegate BOTM to a position of second in all these categories.) In 1999, BOTM had the most customers, both individual and corporate, the most branches, the biggest staff. It was also the strongest money earner with net operating profit in FY98 of $5.8 billion, more than double the level of any of the other city banks.

With the big bang, the competitive issue going forward will be less of reach, or size, and more of depth and speed—depth of expertise, products, and execution and delivery capability, speed in adapting to changes and seizing new business opportunities. How does BOTM measure up and what is its strategy for the future? Sadly, this seems to be a question more asked than answered within BOTM today. Such is the absence of confidence that senior management in early 1999 engaged consultants A.T. Kearney to conduct a major strategic review.

BOTM, as the biggest player, suffered its share of credit losses from Japan's post-bubble recession. In 1998, in order to cover loan losses, the bank made new equity placement with Mitsubishi Group companies and sold its headquarters building, raising $3.3 billion. It joined the other banks in making further huge provisions in March 1999 and needed additional capital to maintain capital at 10 percent. One source of the new capital was the U.S. market, where BOTM made a public offering of $3 billion in preferred shares in 1999. This was a first for a major Japanese financial institution.

Japan's One Global Bank

BOTM was the one city bank able to resist taking public bailout money from the Financial Reconstruction Commission (FRC) in March 1999. As a result, it did not have to submit a restructuring plan or take many actions—like closing of foreign branches—required of the other city banks. Retaining its premier position in international banking services and its overseas operations was a high priority for BOTM, particularly as the forced reduction of overseas presence by its Japanese rivals created a once-in-a-lifetime opportunity to break into business relationships with Japanese companies through financing their overseas subsidiaries.

At March 31, 1999, some $400 billion, or 65.5 percent, of BOTM's interest-bearing assets were domestic, and $210 billion, or 34.5 percent, foreign. In the year ended March 31, 1999, fully 60 percent of BOTM's revenues came from outside Japan (27 percent from the United States), evidencing both the bank's global reach and the relatively low spreads and commissions it is able to earn in Japan's distorted marketplace. Even in the domestic market, BOTM does better than other banks in earning noninterest income because of its international trade-related services and foreign exchange.

Expansion of the global reach and capabilities of BOTM will be a key strategy for the future. This will include realizing the potential in international business of BOTM's wholesale securities company, Tokyo-Mitsubishi Securities (below).

A major improvement in BOTM's performance is likely to require and relate to a substantial improvement in the economics of banking in Japan, brought about by industry restructuring in the context of deregulation and the big bang.

Domestic Universal Bank

As suggested in the preceding chapter, the relative absence of a crisis and pressure from regulators—owing to BOTM's strength and resources—has allowed the bank's management to approach the issue of future competitive strategy at a leisurely, if not glacial, pace. Observers looking for announcements of decisive, dramatic departures have been disappointed. Indeed, it sometimes seemed that BOTM simply was too big and too bureaucratic to make any decisions about its future.

The reason seems to be that BOTM has a vision of the future, and it is taking a lot of time—and the assistance of outsiders—to translate the vision into a plan. The plan is promised in fall 1999. Already some outlines are clear. In a few words, to BOTM's management the future looks a lot like the past.

By virtue of its financial strength, BOTM is alone in its ability to continue to pursue a universal banking model—that is, a balanced combination of retail banking, wholesale banking, and investment banking and securities.

The Key Problems—Retail and Domestic Business

But having the option and the desire to pursue a universal banking strategy is not the same as successfully doing so. BOTM will need to use its strong revenue streams from corporate lending and foreign exchange trading to fund a buildup of businesses generating fee and commission revenues and securities trading profits. These latter activities contributed respectively only 8 and 9 percent of revenues in 1998. And, like other Japanese banks, it must begin to turn its retail banking franchise into profits.

In FY98 lending to individuals for housing and other purposes accounted for only 9 percent of BOTM's entire lending portfolio. In March 1999 BOTM's residential housing loans totaled $48.6 billion, less than Sakura Bank and not much more than Sumitomo.

In wholesale banking and securities, BOTM is clearly determined to turn its subsidiary, Tokyo Mitsubishi Securities (TMS), into a major domestic and international market force. TMS was allowed to absorb the securities subsidiary of Mitsubishi Trust, in exchange for which Mitsubishi Trust received 9.3 percent of TMS equity and established stronger *keiretsu* ties. The capital of TMS is $1.3 billion, on a par with Japan's second tier brokers. TMS is increasing staff to about 400 to prepare to enter full equity brokerage and underwriting business in October 1999. TMS will increasingly orchestrate and deliver international securities and investment banking activities, like Eurobond underwriting, through Tokyo Mitsubishi International in London, which will be restructured as a TMS subsidiary. Domestically transferring mergers and acquisitions (M&A) operations of BOTM to TMS is under study. In all these moves, BOTM seems to have one eye on the competitive challenge of the tie-up between Nikko and Salomon Smith Barney, and the other eye on its closest rival, Sumitomo Bank, and its tie-up with Daiwa Securities.

BOTM must take steps to strengthen its retail business. In April 1999 affiliates Ryoko Securities and Dainana Securities were merged into Tokyo Mitsubishi Personal Securities, but in terms of outlets and staff, this company is inferior to even the second tier securities firms. Another tie-up, perhaps, with Tokyo Securities—which has strong ties to BOTM—is needed. A particularly high-potential idea would be to revive the traditional relationship with Nikko Securities in the retail area (*Weekly Toyo Keizai*, April 17, 1999).

Sumitomo Bank

The solemn stone edifice on the southern bank of the Yodogawa River in Osaka that is the headquarters of Sumitomo Bank resembles a fortress. The image is appropriate for Sumitomo, which for a century has, in financial and business matters, lorded over the Kansai region as the nucleus of the Sumitomo Group. To be a member of the Sumitomo Group, which meant to have Sumitomo Bank as a main bank and to have one's own company's shares held on a permanent basis by other members of the Sumitomo Group, and to hold other members' shares—in other words, to be part of the Sumitomo *keiretsu*—has been the aim of all major companies and the best insurance possible of survival in good times and bad. And the arbiter of *keiretsu* membership and good standing has always been Sumitomo Bank.

As we approach the twenty-first century, this is still largely the reality.

The power and influence of Sumitomo Bank has been and remains immense. Immense too, was the humiliation of the bank when it was obliged—due to massive bad corporate loan accounts—to accept public bailout funds and to solicit government approval of a restructuring plan in March 1999. What is the course being plotted by the management of Sumitomo Bank?

Sumitomo's Restructuring Plan

In the plan approved by the Financial Reconstruction Commission in March 1999, the bank announced its intention to achieve differentiation by adopting clear strategies and taking quick action. It would in April form a strategic partnership with Daiwa Securities. It would sell California Sumitomo Bank and withdraw from middle market lending in the United States. It would also sell Gottardo Bank in Switzerland. The bank outlined a business strategy emphasizing three business segments: retail banking, banking services for domestic small- and medium-sized corporations, and capital markets operations (*The Nikkei Financial Daily*, March 9, 1999).

Retail Banking

Sumitomo Bank has been relatively aggressive in restructuring its retail banking operation. This is an ongoing process and a key to the bank's success. One key policy is to separate wholesale-corporate and retail operations within and among its branches. This is the first step to implementing clearly targeted product and service programs based on market segmentation. Sumitomo will be offering customized or specialized products targeted to different retail customer segments and needs. It will also reduce costs through rationalizing and standardizing service delivery systems. Electronic banking, ATMs, and other technology applications will be important in this respect.

The challenge the bank is facing to make retail business contribute to profits was revealed by the figures on gross revenues and operating profits released by the bank in July 1999 (*The Nikkei Financial Daily*, July 27, 1999). For the year ended March 31, 1999, the individual client business group, while earning some $1.4 billion (¥170 billion) in gross revenues, contributed only $125 million (¥15 billion) in gross operating profits—less than 10 percent of the total gross operating profits of the bank—after deducting its $1.3 billion (¥155 billion) in direct costs.

The importance of these numbers was not just the bad news. In publishing the internal management accounting figures for six business groups, Sumitomo showed that management is focusing on business segments and clearly seeking to balance costs and revenues. With respect to fixing its consumer business, while it has a long way to go, Sumitomo is well ahead of most of its competitors. One problem being addressed is the large number of inactive retail accounts, which create expenses but provide no revenues. The bank is seeking to close these accounts or to move customers to less expensive delivery platforms like telephone banking, ATMs, and cash dispensers.

Sumitomo was in April 1999 the first city bank to raise handling commissions for funds transfers and to differentiate between transfers initiated through counter service, on which fees were raised, and transfers through telephone banking, the internet, or ATMs, on which fees were lowered (Chapter Three).

On the positive side, the bank began in July 1999 to offer slightly higher rates for large deposits initiated by customers using telephone banking services. For wealthy customers, Sumitomo has begun to offer highly differentiated private banking-type services.

Middle Market Corporate Banking

In order to improve quality of service and management of credit, Sumitomo will consolidate service delivery for small- and medium sized corporations in 110 locations (compared with 248 branches previously). A new department will be established to deal with young business ventures or those in new technology areas.

Capital Markets

The bank announced (and implemented in April) a full strategic partnership with Daiwa Securities in wholesale securities and capital markets business. This entailed new business ventures in capital markets, derivatives, and asset management. Sumitomo Bank invested 40 percent of the $3.4 billion capital in Daiwa SB Capital Markets and transferred its entire wholesale securities and capital markets staff to the JV. This evidenced a real commitment to delivering Sumitomo's customer base to the JV. And given both Daiwa's and Sumitomo's relative strengths in capital markets (Sumitomo's expertise owing in part to staff training by Goldman Sachs, in which Sumitomo Bank is a large shareholder), the new venture is likely to be highly competitive and successful.

In asset management, Sumitomo merged its two asset management affiliates together with Daiwa's investment advisory company into a new company, Daiwa SB Invesments Ltd. This company is expected to accept equity investments from T. Rowe Price and Robert Fleming. In preparation for the advent of 401(k)-type defined contribution pension plans in Japan, Sumitomo Bank is leading the four financial companies of the Sumitomo

Group and Daiwa Securities in an alliance with Mitsubishi Group to develop related systems. When DC plans arrive, Sumitomo Bank will be in an unbeatable position to get business from its corporate customers.

Delivering Above-Average Profitability

Sumitomo Bank's plans would be meaningless unless they promised to deliver a significant return on investment for shareholders. The company forecast that in the year ending March 2003, consolidated results would be gross operating profit of $5.8 billion, consolidated net profit of $1.3 billion, and a consolidated ROE of 7.9 percent. This sounds anemic by U.S. standards, but it is fairly rich by standards in Japan. It is also overly conservative. Sumitomo Bank has many situational and cultural advantages over its competition, and its strategy makes sense. We expect the bank to surprise itself on the upside.

Sanwa Bank

A Dedicated Retail Bank

Lacking *zaibatsu* roots, Sanwa Bank has plotted a largely retail and small- and medium-sized corporate strategy. It has also sought to coordinate its activities with affiliated companies, most importantly Toyo Trust and Banking Corporation, in which Sanwa Bank held 12 percent equity share in 1999. Toyo Trust and Banking is one of the most important trust banks in Japan. Its experience (and corporate relationships) in offering corporate customers pension and securities agency services makes it an attractive partner. In Sanwa Bank's strategy, Toyo Trust will introduced to Sanwa Bank corporate finance clients. Toyo will pursue pension-related business, securities agency, and real estate-related products. In securities agency-related business, Toyo Trust was already boasting market share of over 20 percent (*Yomiuri Shimbun*, August 12, 1999).

There remains the question of how Sanwa, as well as other banks, will deal with the eventual (probably FY 2001) full liberalization of trust banking business by commercial banks (*Nihon Keizai Shimbun*, August 10, 1999). In this case the market opportunities were already being exploited by Toyo Trust alone or in cooperation with Sanwa. Sanwa had the option, when the time came, to continue to pursue trust banking business itself or to leverage (or acquire?) the substantial operations of its affiliate, Toyo Trust.

In an interview with *Nihon Keizai Shimbun* published on July 29, 1999, the president of Sanwa Bank emphasized the bank's focus on retail and small- and medium-sized customers. He also suggested that Sanwa would strive to exploit perceived retail market opportunities in consumer finance. He admitted that the bank was only doing secured mortgage lending. What was needed was an advance into unsecured consumer lending, which might require a separate business vehicle.

Importance of Retail Securities and Insurance Distribution

Retail securities distribution is an inseparable part of Sanwa Bank's strategy. This was the impetus for the purchase in 1999 from bankrupt LTCB of Dai-Ichi Securities. This company will be merged with two other securities companies into Universal Securities in April 2000, giving Sanwa a major position in the retail securities marketplace (see Chapter Four). Mutual fund development will be consolidated in Partners Asset Management.

In August 1999 Sanwa and Morgan Stanley Dean Witter announced that they would cooperate in mutual funds sales and other activities involving mutual funds. This alliance seems to offer significant potential benefits to both parties. Morgan Stanley has made a wise choice in picking a partner that is committed to distributing mutual funds. Sanwa Group can certainly benefit from the expertise of Morgan Stanley in mutual fund development. Part of the agreement was that trainees from Partners would be sent to work in Morgan Stanley's offices in the United States (*Nihon Keizai Shimbun*, August 24, 1999).

The president of Sanwa has indicated the group's interest in distributing insurance products, particularly as insurance product sales over bank counters is fully liberalized in 2001. For a bank like Sanwa, risk-management insurance products might be easily incorporated in a banker's product portfolio. Sanwa's concept was to sell over its counters the insurance products produced by affiliated companies (*The Nikkei Financial Daily*, July 29, 1999).

Ultimately a Holding Company

Ultimately Sanwa Bank sees itself as the head of a holding company. The objective of the company will be to coordinate the activities and strategies of the group. We are favorably impressed by the strategies and actions of Sanwa Bank and, through it, the Sanwa Group. We are prepared for them to continue to do well in the future.

Nomura Securities

Among the Big Three securities firms, Nomura is by far the first among equals. With some 9,800 staff, 125 offices, assets of $101 billion, and capital of $10.4 billion, it is clearly one of the world's leading financial institutions. It has always been, and remains, Japan's premier "universal broker"—equally strong in origination and underwriting of debt and equity securities, in trading, and in retail distribution and brokerage. It has been the closest international competitor in form to America's universal broker, Merrill Lynch. Like Merrill Lynch, it has generally sought to remain independent and in control. It has built up a host of subsidiaries and affiliates into a sizable group.

But looking sideways and forward, Nomura has cause to be nervous. On one side, it sees its closest rival, Daiwa Securities, forming a strategic alliance with the powerful Sumitomo Group in wholesale securities, investment banking, and asset management—the three fastest growing and most profitable industry sectors. On the other side, it sees number three Nikko Securities essentially become an affiliate of Citigroup and then form a joint venture with the awesome Salomon Smith Barney in investment banking and wholesale securities.

Nomura's "go it alone" strategy seems highly risky now that its rivals have formed such powerful alliances. The one alliance formed by Nomura—in derivatives development and marketing, and in 401(k) system development with IBJ—seems tentative and inconsequential in comparison.

Looking forward, deregulation will free commissions and invite a host of discounters into the retail brokerage arena. In FY98 Nomura earned some 57 percent of its revenues from brokerage commissions and 19 percent from financial income. It lost huge money in trading activities, particularly in positions in emerging market debt held in portfolios in overseas offices.

Defending Its Domestic Position

In FY98 Nomura lost $3.2 billion, the most of any brokerage in the world. In mid-1999 Moody's assigned Nomura a credit rating of Baa2, two ranks above junk bond status. Such a low rating hampers Nomura in using its balance sheet to take large trading positions. In July 1999 Nomura president Junichi Ujiie was quoted as saying that the company's low credit rating would force it to refrain "for the next year or so" from active trading activities in foreign markets (*Financial Times*, July 1, 1999). But the issue is more than Nomura's temporary financial weakness. It is the critical need for Nomura to defend and strengthen its domestic business franchises.

Japan's equity market staged a recovery in the first half of 1999 that allowed Nomura, as well as other securities firms, to make substantial brokerage commission earnings. Nomura, with roughly 12 percent of trading volume, is positioned to take advantage of a cyclical recovery. But deregulation of retail brokerage commissions still looms as a major threat to profitability.

Nomura has been losing mandates for debt underwriting and M&A advisory services in its domestic market to U.S. investment banks. Nomura was jolted by losing to Goldman Sachs and Nikko the lead underwriting position in the huge IPO for DoCoMo, the mobile telephone subsidiary of NTT, Japan's telephone company. It sees foreign investment advisors and trust banks making significant inroads in the asset management market.

Strengthening Mutual Funds and Asset Management

Nomura is planning to meet competition—especially from U.S. investment banks—by introducing new products, improving risk control, consolidating and focusing activities, and building assets under management. It is essentially the same strategy adopted by U.S. securities companies when the commissions were deregulated in the 1970s. The company claims not to be interested in entering into the insurance sales business or many other of the new product areas opened by the big bang. It plans to focus resources in broker/dealer, investment banking, and asset management areas. Proprietary trading will be de-emphasized or exited, particularly in international markets.

The key vehicles for Nomura in the future will be Nomura Securities itself, which will remain a wholesale and retail broker/dealer, and Nomura Asset Management. At the end of May 1999 Nomura Asset Management had $9.99 trillion under management in stock and bond investment trusts, $1 trillion in medium term bond funds, and $4.4 trillion in money management funds.

Fundnet: Meeting the Internet Challenge

To meet competition in what could be a long-term growth market in discounted or no-load mutual funds, Nomura has established a 100 percent subsidiary, Nomura Fundnet Securities, which is a direct marketer of mutual funds. Nomura Fundnet offers thirty-two funds managed by Nomura Asset Management and some twenty-six funds managed by other companies, including Merrill Lynch Mercury, Goldman Sachs, Morgan Stanley, Fidelity, Jardine Fleming, Bankers Trust, Credit Suisse, and Schroders. The range of funds includes yen money market funds, domestic and international bond funds, international equity, and emerging markets debt and equity funds. Funds are offered with no loads or reduced loads, and customers can earn "points" on invested balances that can be applied toward further discounting sales loads.

Nomura Fundnet seems to be Nomura's answer to the approach to the market of Fidelity, Vanguard, or T. Rowe Price in the United States. It has no storefronts, offering services only over the phone, by mail, or by internet. It offers a direct debit automatic subscription service with a low ¥10,000 a month minimum. Through Fundnet, Nomura is targeting a new market segment: young, first-time, or small-time investors who might not already have a brokerage account. It hopes that this segment will grow and that it can be served profitably through this new direct sales model.

Nomura will also provide internet trading services to regular customers, at a slight discount, beginning in late 1999.

Nippon Life

With policies outstanding at $2.8 trillion, total assets of $356 billion, and 18 million customers, Nippon Life has long been the undisputed industry leader, dominating the field. Indeed, it is the largest mutual life insurance company in the world. "Nissay's" approach has traditionally been to command legions of nonthreatening and not very expert "Nissay ladies" recruited in every Japanese neighborhood to sell standardized, largely savings-type guaranteed-rate products. The products were designed to compete with bank deposits. Nissay's challenge is a changing competitive marketplace, with new entrants gaining business from increasingly demanding customers.

"The big bang is ultimately a contest for the retail market." Such is the perspective of the head of corporate planning at Nippon Life, quoted in *Shukan Toyo Keizai* (April 17, 1999). In 1999 the evidence was inescapable that Nissay and other insurers were losing the contest, as new policies booked in FY98 declined a dramatic 27.9 percent to $200 billion and cancellations increased 2.1 percent to $259 billion. This decline was in contrast to the relatively robust performance of the newer, particularly foreign, life insurance companies coming to market with new, attractive products and a sophisticated sales approach.

Of course, Nissay is burdened along with the rest of the industry with negative spread on savings-type policies bearing guaranteed dividend payout rates higher than the yields Nissay can earn on investing the capital. Serious as this problem is, it is not Nissay's greatest strategic challenge. That challenge is—as the corporate planning head said—the market.

New Product Development: the Nissay Insurance Account

Like Nomura, Nissay is in a position of needing to defend and strengthen its huge but threatened market position. It needs to meet head-on the challenge presented by competitors offering more tailored products.

An initial response in 1999 has been the launch of the Nissay Insurance

Account. This account reflects a change from product- to customer-focused sales and service. Previously, customers were sold multiple Nissay products, but there was no link between them and no advantage to customers for repeat buying and loyalty.

The Nissay Insurance Account will provide clients with a portfolio approach to products purchased from Nissay. Products of group companies, such as Nissay's nonlife and investment trust subsidiaries, as well as 401(k)-type plan accounts will be offered through the Nissay Insurance Account, and discounted "package" pricing will be offered for multiple product purchases. In the future, the relationship with Nissay will be client-driven, not product-driven, or so says the company.

The Critical Pension and 401(k) Sector

Strategically, Nissay must aggressively defend its pension management franchise, where it has $9.2 billion under discretionary contract. This it is doing through more professional management in its traditional accounts (see Chapter Six). It is also moving quickly and independently to develop systems to accommodate new pension plans. Unlike the Sumitomo-Mitsubishi- and IBJ-Nomura-led groups, which are developing systems specifically to accommodate 401(k)-type defined contribution (DC) plans, Nissay's strategy is to develop a system that will accommodate both defined contribution and the current defined benefit (DB) pension plan types. This will allow Nissay to maintain and enhance service to client corporate pension sponsors that will continue to offer DB plans, or a combination or DB and DC plans, while also anticipating DC plans. Nissay has tied up with IBM Japan, Fujitsu, and NTT Data to develop the system, which it hopes to commercialize in sales to regional banks.

Beyond technology, Nissay will be striving to offer attractive investment products, such as mutual funds to pension sponsors and individuals. To this end it tied up with Putnam in July 1998 to development investment trusts, and with Deutsche Bank in December 1998 in the asset management area. As the largest market player, Nissay is approached regularly by foreign companies offering products and ideas for cooperation. The issue for the company is how to incorporate innovation and change into such a mammoth corporate entity with a legacy of regulatory protection.

Nissay's commitment to the mutual funds business was evidenced in the first half of 1999 when it achieved a level of mutual funds assets under management of $440 million (¥53.3 billion), compared with just $40 million (¥5.1 billion) for its closest rival, Dai-Ichi Life. Yasuda Life had accumulated $70 million (¥7.9 billion) in the same period (*Nihon Keizai Shimbun*,

August 5, 1999). After the prohibition on offering of mutual funds by insurance companies was lifted in December 1998, Nissay began to pursue this business aggressively, targeting its corporate customers and using telephone marketing.

Strengthening Cross-Sector Ties

The big bang reforms will likely dramatically reshape the insurance industry by 2005 (see Chapter Eighteen). Notwithstanding its strong market position, Nissay cannot ignore the challenges and opportunities in the opening of new products and distribution channels. Anticipating the opening of insurance sales over the counters of banks, Nissay and other major insurers are strengthening ties with selected banks. In June 1999 the company increased its shareholding in Sakura Bank by 32 million shares and in Tokai Bank by 16 million shares, while reducing shareholdings in other city banks.

In the struggle for survival and growth in Japan's revolutionary post-big bank marketplace, the biggest players—like those above—have the considerable advantages of size, capital, and tradition. But another feature of today's marketplace is opportunity for new, often smaller players whose lack of size and tradition makes easier one key to future success—innovation. It is to examples of such new players that we now turn.

Chapter Eleven

Mavericks and Upstarts

Over the past thirty years, Japan has been a particularly difficult place for entrepreneurship. Big market players, a bias toward group affiliation, limited access to capital, and pervasive, restrictive regulations have been formidable obstacles to individuals with ideas, energy, and an independent, entrepreneurial spirit. Not surprisingly, the number of such individuals has been small, and the few success stories are tales of mavericks and outsiders who bucked the system, often after spending time outside Japan.

One typical story is that of Hideo Sawada. As a young man, Sawada studied in the United States, where he noticed that a thriving business was done by no-frills travel agencies selling discount tickets. No such business existed in Japan, where custom, attitude, and cartel-like arrangements in the trade, countenanced by regulators, had sustained and protected an inefficient and expensive full-fare, full-service industry. Sawada confronted this system— suffering untold indignities and threats—to found H.I.S., the first big discount travel agency. In the mid-1990s he went further and, against the opposition of Japan's Ministry of Transportation, established a no-frills discount airline named Skymark. Given how Japan's system had ossified, it had been thirty years since the last airline had been founded in Japan.

Sawada, a man who anticipates market trends, values the consumer, and is not afraid of a fight, took advantage of big bang reform to establish H.I.S. Kyoritsu Securities in 1998. This company will also be a discounter and offer services primarily through the internet and telephone.

But Sawada is still small-time. Two companies that have reached massive scale, Orix and Softbank, exemplify how new or unconventional entrants, following different strategies, have been able to enter and increasingly to transform Japan's financial marketplace. Let us look at each of these companies.

Orix Corporation

The Orix Corporation was formed in the 1960s when some of Japan's more international companies, particularly its trading companies, noticed how leasing was becoming a big and profitable business in the United States. Three trading companies and five banks invested jointly in the new company, which was named Orient Lease. The company grew quickly and in 1970 listed on the Tokyo Stock Exchange.

In the relatively unregulated nonbank sector, with sponsorship from several *keiretsu* groups, the company soon achieved and has since held a leadership position in the leasing sector. As of March 31, 1999, the company held $16.5 billion in financial lease assets, some 41 percent of total assets. Operating leases made up 9 percent of assets, and installment loans, totaling $14.9 billion, made up 37 percent of assets. Investment in securities and other operations constituted the remaining 13 percent of assets. From the 1970s the company consistently sought business opportunities abroad. In the year ended March 31, 1999, over 55 percent of the company's net profit came from overseas operations. The main contributor was the United States, where mainly leasing operations earned some $174 million.

Orix has been one of the most transparent and professionally managed financial firms in Japan. This had helped to attract foreign investors, who in 1999 owned about 30 percent of Orix parent stock. Partly in order to accommodate the needs of foreign investors, Orix listed on the New York Stock Exchange in September 1998.

Early on, its particularly entrepreneurial management saw opportunities in serving individual as well as corporate customer segments and in offering a variety of financial products, from consumer loans to securities to life insurance. Orix Credit Corporation, 100 percent-owned, was established in 1979 to provide shopping credit and consumer finance. This was followed by the establishment of a specialized consumer lender, Orix Club Corporation, in 1990. Orix entered the securities business in 1986 with the establishment of Orix Securities as a 100 percent subsidiary. It entered into life insurance by establishing a joint venture with Mutual of Omaha in 1991. In 1992 Orix took over 100 percent of the company named Orix Life Insurance Corporation. Orix had previously established Orix Insurance Services Corporation as an agent for casualty and life insurance. Following the collapse of Yamaichi Securities in 1997, Orix seized the opportunity to purchase Yamaichi's trust banking subsidiary, now renamed Orix Trust & Banking.

Figure 11.1 describes the scope of Orix Group's businesses and the segmentation of its products and markets. More important than its market or product coverage, however, has been the company's leading-edge, innovative, and aggressive approach to business. In Japan's still clubby and largely lock-step marketplace, Orix is shaking up the market.

Figure 11.1 **Schematic of Orix Group**

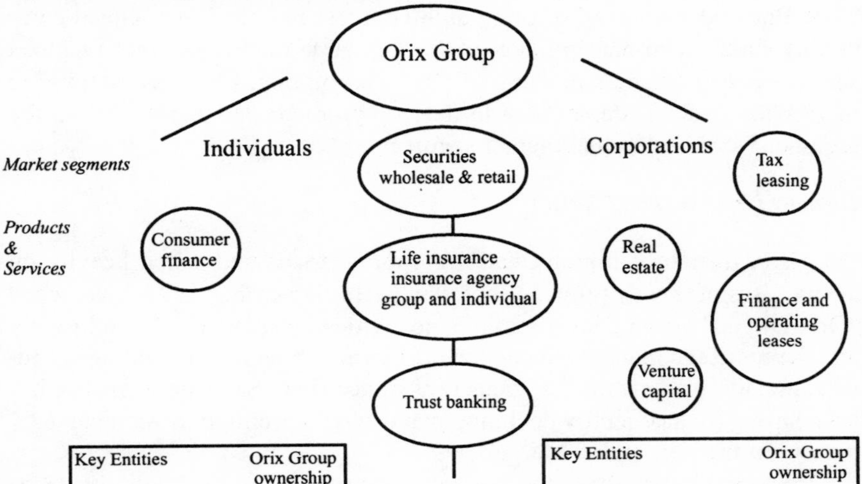

Key Entities	Orix Group ownership
Orix Securities	100%
Orix Life Insurance	100%
Orix Credit Corp.	100%
Orix Trust & Banking	100%
Orix Rent-A-Car	85%
Orix Club Corp.	100%

Key Entities	Orix Group ownership
Orix Auto Leasing	100%
Orix Aircraft Corp.	100%
Orix Capital Corp.	95%
Orix Marine Corp.	100%
Orix Insurance Services Corp.	100%

Others	Orix Group ownership
Skymark Airlines	23%
Orix Baseball Club	100%
Orix Commodities	100%
Orix USA Corp.	100%
Japan Sports Channel Inc.	28%
Banc One Mortgage Capital Markets LLC	45%

Total Orix Group Performance by Segment in FY 1998

Segment	Revenue ($ millions)
Finance leasing	1,209
Installment loans	848
Operating leases	780
Securities brokerage	62
Life Insurance	1,657
Other	458

Source: Orix Corporation Annual Report, 1998.

Orix Trust Bank's Direct Deposits

This was most clearly evidenced in 1999 when Orix began placing ads in Japanese newspapers offering deposits in Orix Trust Bank at rates 10 to 50 basis points higher than the rates offered by other banks. To a skeptical public, the bank explained that it was operating as a new type of depository institution with no branches and no counter operations. Rather it was a "virtual bank," serving depositors only over the telephone and by mail (*Nihon Keizai Shimbun*, June 28, 1999). In a market lacking rate competition, this was a gutsy challenge, which by reports seems to have been quite successful.

As an example of segmented marketing, on the same page as the Orix Trust Bank ad was an ad offering an 80 percent principal guaranteed commodity fund investment product under the name of the personal financial services (PFS) business division of Orix Corporation. PFS was established in 1997 as an R&D department to develop products and approaches to the high-net-worth-individual market segment.

Direct Life Insurance Sales

Orix Life Insurance initially had a corporate focus and relied heavily on agents. Business was growing, but slowly. In September 1997 it launched "Orix Direct," offering low premium, no dividend insurance sold exclusively by telephone and mail. Products included term, whole life and old-age products, including a new kind of cancer insurance rider. Sales performance has been strong (in a generally declining market) with premium revenue up 62.7 percent in the year ended March 1999.

Orix is exploiting fully the big bang's expansion of channels for insurance sales. In 1998 four Orix Group companies were agents for Orix Life Insurance products. Orix Securities became an agent and began to distribute Orix Life's products in April 1999.

New Consumer Credit Initiatives

Equally impressive have been Orix's initiatives in the consumer credit area. In mid-1999 the company launched through its consumer credit subsidiary, Orix Credit, a "VIP Loan Card." The card makes it convenient for customers to borrow money by providing access to some 70,000 cash dispensers and ATM machines nationwide, including those of most major banks and the postal savings system. Borrowing rates are graduated, from 8.7 percent per annum on borrowings equivalent to $20,000 to $25,000, to 12.6 percent for advances of $4,000. Repayment schedules are flexible and can incorporate large repayments two times a year when most Japanese employees receive bonuses. Repayments can be deducted automatically from bank accounts or paid directly by the borrower in cash into ATMs.

The most attractive aspect of these loans, from the borrowers' perspective, is the rate, which is substantially below the industry average (see Chapter Eight). Again Orix is aggressively breaking conventions in order to build customers and to grow its business.

Online Brokerage from Orix Securities

Orix Securities was among the first securities companies to offer services, including trading, over the internet. The service was introduced on May 6,

1999, and Orix Securities was publicly announcing in July its intention to become the number one online broker in Japan, promising to offer big discounts in commissions from October.

Orix is positioned to become an even bigger player in the post-big bang marketplace. It has established companies in the fastest growing segments of the market and appears to have the management skill required to win in competition. What we like most about the company is its somewhat irreverent and impatient style and its clear orientation toward customer needs. These attitudes tend to make Orix a maverick, like Sawada of Skymark Airlines. Maybe this explains why Orix decided to invest in 20 percent of the shares of that upstart company.

Softbank

But for audacity, impatience, and—so far at least—success, there are few businessmen in the world who can match Masayoshi Son, the president of Softbank. People who speak with Son come away with a clear sense of his vision of the future: global interconnectivity over the internet. With this vision firmly in mind, Son has been prepared, when more seasoned businessmen have hesitated, to bet on start-ups and small ventures in and around the internet. As recorded in a profile in *Forbes* Magazine in July 1999, Son has been right, fabulously so, most of the time (Weinberg). Son told *Forbes* that Softbank holds 7 to 8 percent of the publicly listed value of all internet properties. Softbank, founded by Son in 1981 and listed in Japan, is still owned 39.7 percent by him. As of mid-1999, Softbank had a 27 percent ownership share of E-Trade, 28 percent of Yahoo, and 85 percent of ZDNet in the United States. In Japan, Softbank owned 51 percent of Yahoo Japan, which dominates the local internet, and 100 percent of E-Trade Japan.

Son's vision of an interconnected future is combined with a sense that the internet is the perfect medium through which to deliver financial services. He has therefore conceived a strategy for Softbank Group in Japan that includes financial services delivered electronically as a key component.

Nasdaq-Japan

The most dramatic expression of Son's vision is the plan to establish, in a joint venture with the U.S. National Association of Securities Dealers, an electronic exchange using internet technology to trade stocks. The exchange, Nasdaq-Japan, will probably look and operate much like the Nasdaq exchange in the United States. Of course, this competitive challenge is strongly resented by the Tokyo Stock Exchange, already suffering from competition from off-exchange services newly permitted by big bang reforms.

E-Trade Japan Securities

Softbank's internet financial services strategy against the retail market is exemplified by E-Trade Japan Securities, in which Softbank owns a controlling 58 percent interest (the remaining 42 percent is owned by E-Trade U.S.A.). Softbank had been preparing for almost a year to launch E-Trade, buying a failed broker, Osawa Securities, in order to get a full brokerage license and a seat on the stock exchange. E-Trade Japan is offering services and taking a market approach similar to those of E-Trade in the United States. It is offering the largest number of equity mutual funds, some 180 on- and offshore funds as of June 1999, of any Japanese brokerage, two money management funds, and a money reserve fund (which in Japan has transactional characteristics).

E-Trade Japan and other securities-related companies in the Softbank Group, including Morningstar Japan, are under the day-to-day management of Yoshitaka Kitao, Softbank's executive vice president, who came from Nomura Securities. This unified management and Softbank's opportunistic culture explain how the company chose to launch E-Trade Japan Securities services in June 1999 with an "exclusive" offering of new issue bonds from Softbank, IPO shares from Softbank Technologies, and new issue shares from another Softbank group company, Trade Micro K.K.

As of this writing, E-Trade appears inclined to stay with the pack of middle-range discounters, rather than join DLJ Direct SFG at the high discount, low commission end. E-Trade Japan Securities is capitalized at $12.5 million, which suggests some staying power in the coming mutual funds and discount broker shakeout.

Part Four

The Major Foreign Players

Chapter Twelve

The Perennial Players: Citibank and AIG

The One and Only Citi

Japan's market, regulatory structure, culture, and cost base have combined to prevent many if not most putative global financial firms from fully integrating Japan into their global operations. Whereas markets as diverse as Hong Kong, Singapore, the United Kingdom and continental Europe have been viewed and managed more or less uniformly, Japan has often been set apart, seemingly incompatible and impossible to include in global product and market strategies.

It is against this background that industry participants, Japanese as well as foreign, stand in awe of Citibank in Japan. For longer than all others, with greater persistence and willingness to invest, with greater confidence and boldness, Citibank has consistently striven to build in Japan the same businesses on the same models as in other key markets. In this unique approach, the bank has made many missteps, but no one now disputes the wisdom of its vision. Few, it might be said, ever disputed the view that Japan's huge and rich marketplace presents opportunities that any truly global player should try to seize. But other companies have lacked deep-pocketed patience and confidence in their ability to execute a strategy. In both these respects, Citibank has shown itself without peer in the entire global financial sector, its closest rivals nonbanks AIG, Associates First Capital, and, recently, GE Capital, wholesale trading houses like Goldman Sachs, and, sporadically, Merrill Lynch.

As we know, Citicorp merged with Travelers Group to form Citigroup in 1998. We will consider the activities of the group as a whole in Chapter Thirteen. Here we will focus on the business of Citibank and other parts of the former Citigroup in Japan.

Building Franchises Through the 1970s

Citibank traces its origins in Japan to 1902, when its progenitor, the International Banking Corporation, opened a branch in Yokohama (and, at the same time, in Asia's financial center, Shanghai). The International Banking Corporation became First National City Bank of New York and later Citibank, a subsidiary of the bank holding company, Citicorp. Citibank's operations in Japan, mainly related to trade finance, were interrupted during World War II. After the war, Citi returned with the occupation forces, established a branch in Tokyo, and set up two kinds of business—wholesale banking and services to U.S. forces.

In the 1950s Citibank opened branches in Yokohama, Osaka, and Nagoya. The business of these branches was primarily with Japanese banks. The local banks had no international networks through which to conduct trade finance business: they were unknown internationally and had no direct access to international money markets. Citibank's business primarily entailed responding to requests of Japanese banks to borrow foreign currency (which these banks on-lent to local corporations) and opening and settling import letters of credit on behalf of Japanese banks. There were few if any relationships with local corporations, most of which would not have been deemed credit-worthy in any event.

In the 1960s a few Japanese corporations got large enough to become interesting as customers. Citibank began lending foreign currency directly to these companies, usually under the guarantee of Japanese banks. At this time, loans from Citibank and the few other foreign banks in Japan were exclusively in foreign currency. Because they impacted Japan's balance of payments, they were called "impact loans." There were barriers to funding in yen, and the Ministry of Finance (MOF) enforced rules that kept Japanese banks from directly raising foreign capital. Foreign and domestic banks each had their "turf" and everyone made money.

By the 1970s Japanese corporations had become large indeed, and many exported enough to have strong foreign currency cash flows, as well as foreign currency financing requirements. Citibank became a leader in providing loans and trade finance directly to the large Japanese corporations, as well as continuing to offer funding and transactional services to Japanese banks. By the end of the 1970s, competition with Japanese banks began to intensify, first in markets, then in products. MOF was approving overseas branching by Japanese banks, especially Bank of Tokyo, which allowed these banks to cut out Citi in trade finance transactions. Japanese banks were gaining access for U.S. dollar funding, and foreign banks, led by Citibank, were clamoring for more access to yen funding through expansion of swap limits (used to convert foreign currency funding into yen) and approval to issue negotiable CDs (as a way to raise yen funds domestically in the absence of a consumer deposit base).

Exploiting Niches in the 1980s

A mini-big bang of deregulation occurred in the early 1980s in which a level playing field was created for foreign and domestic banks. On the one hand, restrictions on Japanese banks' extension of impact loans were lifted; on the other, foreign banks were able to participate in a new negotiable CD and government bond repurchase markets. (For a full schedule of money market deregulation, see Hall 1998, pp. 89–100.) Always Citi was the biggest foreign player and strongest advocate of reform.

In the 1980s, with a level playing field allowing full competition with Japanese banks in traditional products and markets, Citibank was confronted with two realities: (1) Japanese corporations naturally favored their main local banks for "plain vanilla" services; and (2) margins began to drop, especially for credit products. In other words, the pathologies of the Japanese banking marketplace began to appear. Citi's response was to pursue a high value-added niche strategy of helping clients to solve particular problems in areas where Citi had or could develop some competitive advantage. In this strategy, relationship was helpful, but knowhow and innovation—and sometimes a willingness to challenge regulatory restrictions—were key.

The 1980s were a decade of substantial financial product and market deregulation and innovation, in areas like foreign exchange, options, overseas bond issuance, and swaps. Citibank was first and usually best to market whenever a new product or service was offered. For example, in 1984 rules preventing nonbank corporations from dealing in foreign exchange (buying and selling without an underlying transaction) were scrapped. Citibank became a leading trader of foreign exchange with the major trading companies, one of the few banks to be able to trade lots of $100 million or more. Citi's treasury department also became one of the most successful options and swaps houses. But competition closed in quickly, both from Japanese banks and brokers, and from many of the big trading companies that set up their own finance companies to compete with banks.

From its leading position, Citibank saw more clearly than many both the problems and potential in Japan's marketplace. The problems were clear: an overbanked corporate marketplace where risk was chronically underpriced and unlikely to improve. Unable to move the market, Citibank reduced loans to corporations. Also, Citibank sensed that the credit-driven bubble economy would collapse, so it substantially narrowed the list of Japanese corporations with which it would take any credit exposure. These sophisticated and cost-conscious corporate clients tended to seek disintermediate banks, however, causing Citibank to treat them increasingly as trading counterparties, rather than borrowers or investors. Citibank's corporate banking operation gradually restructured itself into a "boutique" corporate finance and structured finance house, taking a highly disciplined and selective approach to both customer relationships and transactions.

Key Market Initiatives in the 1980s

Along the way, Citibank took quick advantage of such new venture opportunities as were presented, in most cases using the approach of wholly owned subsidiaries of Citicorp offered under Japanese and U.S. banking regulations. In 1978 Citicorp established Citicorp Credit K.K. (CCKK) as a wholly owned consumer credit subsidiary. In 1981 it established a 100 percent leasing subsidiary, Citilease K.K. In 1984, as part of its global expansion into brokerage, Citicorp acquired Vickers da Costa Securities operations in Tokyo, later renaming it Citicorp International Securities. In 1986 it took advantage of a chance to establish a trust bank, Cititrust Trust and Banking. In the same year it set up a Tokyo branch of its global card operations, Citicorp Card Service, which commenced issuing cards in the same year. In the late 1980s, as foreign trading in Japanese equities grew, Citibank established stand-alone custody business within its financial institutions group.

Through these many initiatives and ventures, Citibank executives, including many Japanese, developed a sophisticated understanding of the Japanese marketplace. And they learned many lessons. CCKK expanded quickly, then exploded with huge credit write-offs. Its operations were scaled back. Vickers da Costa was upsized and downsized along with Citi's global equities business. A securities custody business developed quickly and profitably. Leasing proved a stable but slow-moving niche business.

John Reed's Consumer Banking Vision

By the late 1980s, John Reed knew Japan well. He had been coming to Japan about twice a year since ascending to the chairmanship of Citicorp following Walter Wriston's retirement in the early 1980s. John Reed had secured his position at the helm of Citicorp by having successfully built a consumer banking franchise in the United States. That business was now reaching critical mass in revenues and profits and was growing strongly, just as Citibank's traditional corporate business, globally, but especially in the U.S. market, appeared to be stagnating. Another place corporate business was stagnating, for many of the same reasons, was in Japan.

In the 1980s, Reed and Citicorp's board had determined that Citibank could be the one bank in the world to create a global consumer banking business, with a known brand and franchise. The consumer banking business was attractive, compared with corporate business, because of its high margins on risk assets. Also, equally important, in Citibank's global strategic perspective, consumer banking meant funding from consumer deposits and making loans in local currency. This was the solution to the problem of cross-border exposure in foreign currency that had almost bankrupted Citibank in the Latin American debt crisis of the early 1980s.

In certain markets, particularly in Asia (Hong Kong, the Philippines, Taiwan) and South America (Brazil), Citibank had already achieved a significant position in the domestic consumer business. From Citi's global perspective, notwithstanding all the market entry and cost issues, Japan needed to be included in its global consumer strategy. The decision to go ahead with a long-term investment and development strategy was made by John Reed in 1987 and 1988.

Citibank's vision was to serve a segment of the Japanese population—which research showed to be large—that was relatively affluent, sophisticated, globally minded and globally active. This targeted approach called for a limited branch network, use of technology to deliver products both domestically and internationally, premium service and pricing, product packaging and new product development. For senior Citibank executives, the general issues of "how to get there from here" were not unfamiliar. They had been dealt with over the years in markets as diverse as Brazil and Hong Kong. Since Citibank was rolling out a "branded" global consumer banking strategy, the decision was really one of not excluding Japan.

To execute its retail strategy, Citibank in the late 1980s established a separate consumer banking organization and management structuring, reporting to global consumer banking management levels in New York. Executives, including many who had risen through the retail banking management ranks in Citibank operations in other Asian countries, were brought in to head the start-up operations and to transfer knowhow. The first dedicated consumer branches were established in 1988 and 1989. Branching was combined with aggressive expansion of ATM services and innovations (for Japan) like twenty-four-hour service.

Citibank in Japan in 1999

The operations of Citibank in Japan in 1999 are presented in Figure 12.1 (we shall take a broader view of the role of Salomon Smith Barney and former Travelers Group entities in Chapter Thirteen). The structure and content of these operations are the result of management judgments taken over at least the last twenty years. What we see is the current phase of the evolution of Citibank's market positioning and capital allocation strategy.

Figure 12.1 **Citibank (formerly Citicorp) Operations as of June 1999**

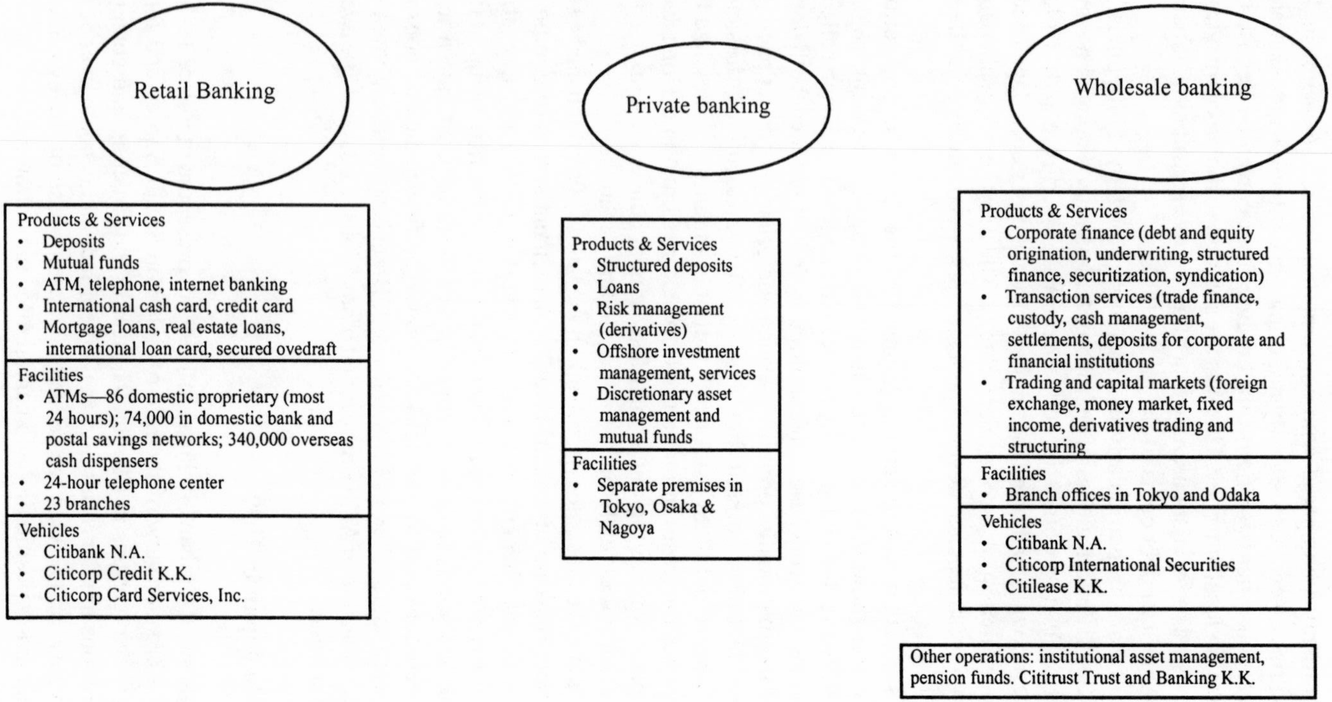

Retail Banking

Products & Services
- Deposits
- Mutual funds
- ATM, telephone, internet banking
- International cash card, credit card
- Mortgage loans, real estate loans, international loan card, secured ovedraft

Facilities
- ATMs—86 domestic proprietary (most 24 hours); 74,000 in domestic bank and postal savings networks; 340,000 overseas cash dispensers
- 24-hour telephone center
- 23 branches

Vehicles
- Citibank N.A.
- Citicorp Credit K.K.
- Citicorp Card Services, Inc.

Private banking

Products & Services
- Structured deposits
- Loans
- Risk management (derivatives)
- Offshore investment management, services
- Discretionary asset management and mutual funds

Facilities
- Separate premises in Tokyo, Osaka & Nagoya

Wholesale banking

Products & Services
- Corporate finance (debt and equity origination, underwriting, structured finance, securitization, syndication)
- Transaction services (trade finance, custody, cash management, settlements, deposits for corporate and financial institutions
- Trading and capital markets (foreign exchange, money market, fixed income, derivatives trading and structuring

Facilities
- Branch offices in Tokyo and Odaka

Vehicles
- Citibank N.A.
- Citicorp International Securities
- Citilease K.K.

Other operations: institutional asset management, pension funds. Cititrust Trust and Banking K.K.

Source: Citibank.

The operations can be divided into three business segments: retail banking, private banking, and wholesale banking. Each of the business segments offers distinct products and services to clearly defined market segments supported by specific facilities, and works through certain legal vehicles.

The Citibank Retail Bank

As of June 1999 Citibank operated or was in the process of opening twenty-three retail branches in Japan. These branches are designed and operated in accordance with Citibank's global retail banking operations formats and procedures. A Citibank retail consumer from the United States, walking into a Citibank retail branch in Japan, would probably find little difference. Products offered generally run the gamut of consumer deposits and loans. Part of Citibank's initial market positioning strategy was to specialize in foreign currency deposits. Traditionally, Japanese banks were not aggressive in offering foreign currency deposits, apparently fearing claims by unsophisticated customers who may have suffered an unexpected exchange loss. Citibank, which targeted sophisticated clients and specifically trained sales staff how to speak to customers about exchange risk, approached this market aggressively. Many Citibank clients began a relationship with the bank in order to make foreign currency deposits.

Services for Globalized Japan, At Home and Abroad

Citibank's retail service included many products specifically designed for Japanese traveling or living abroad. Services such as international cash cards, access to ATM machines internationally, toll-free telephone center service to callers from outside Japan, international student credit cards, and international Visa cards all position Citibank uniquely in this particular marketplace. In summer 1999 Citibank and Japan Airlines jointly issued a credit card that provides JAL mileage and discounts as well as access to cash in local currency at ATMs abroad.

A Consistent Innovator of Client-Oriented Services

At the same time, however, Citibank has been striving to enhance convenience for Japanese at home and to more clearly identify itself as a part of the domestic banking system. This is seen in Citibank's extensive links with domestic banks' ATM systems and, particularly, as of January 1999, online with the ATMs of the postal savings system. By repeatedly being the first bank to initiate services (including 24-hours-a-day, 365-days-a-year, fee-free

ATMs and toll-free telephone banking; free telephone banking from over-seas; and commission-free cash withdrawals from designated bank network ATMs), Citibank has gained a deserved reputation for being prepared—un-like Japanese banks—to confront regulators and to push through client-ori-ented innovations. It has, in other words, like minor players in many industries, been prepared to lead and create new areas of competition for customers, where existing dominant players prefer the status quo.

Of course, Citibank expects clients to pay for services, and it expects to make money from its innovations. It is usually able to do so without obviously charg-ing clients more than competitors; indeed, customers seem to be getting a lot of free service. Citibank achieves this by managing its business better than Japa-nese banks—specifically by setting high minimum fees and balance require-ments, which ensure that its customers are relatively big-ticket, active, and, therefore, profitable. Citibank makes money where the Japanese banks lose be-cause it does not see the need (in Japan or the United States) to subsidize a large number of small depositors. The financial results of Citibank's Japan branches in the years ending March 1998 and 1999 are shown in Figure 12.2.

Building Deposits, and Making Good Money, But Still Undevel-oped in Consumer Lending

For many years, the Citibank retail bank in Japan seemed and largely ap-pears to remain (not unlike the Japanese banks), liabilities-driven, meaning primarily in the business of gathering customer deposits. Figure 12.2 shows that this focus has been exceptionally successful since 1997. As Japanese banks grew shakier and the Japanese yen began to weaken against the U.S. dollar, Japanese depositors flocked to Citibank to open foreign currency de-posits. How has Citibank in Japan been using its ballooning deposit base, fully $14.6 billion (¥1,751.5 billion) at March 31, 1999, up $2.9 billion, or 24.8 percent from the previous year? The answer is not publicly available, but we believe that most of this money has gone to funding assets originated by the corporate and private banking departments. Citibank consumer bank-ing assets—loans and credit card receivables—are still relatively small and slow-growing. This stands to reason, given Citi's market targeting: affluent Japanese are not usually also borrowers of consumer credit.

Citibank began to place more emphasis on consumer lending, including mortgage lending, in 1999, when a highly borrower-friendly mortgage loan, with flexible repayment features, was rolled out. To achieve the returns it wants and to effectively relend its now massive liabilities, Citibank will con-tinue to emphasize the consumer lending market, especially mortgages.

Citicorp Credit K.K., Citicorp's initial foray into unsecured consumer lend-ing, is dormant. Consumer credit is now managed out of Citibank's branches.

Figure 12.2 **Performance of Citibank Japan Branches**

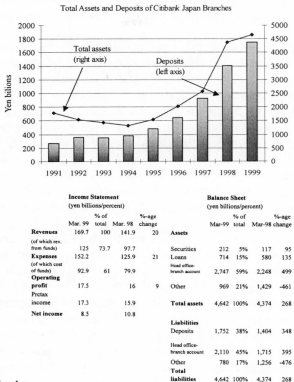

Total Assets and Deposits of Citibank Japan Branches

Income Statement (yen billions/percent)					Balance Sheet (yen billions/percent)				
	Mar. 99	% of total	Mar. 98	%-age change		Mar-99	% of total	Mar-98	%-age change
Revenues	169.7	100	141.9	20	**Assets**				
(of which rev. from funds)	125	73.7	97.7		Securities	212	5%	117	95
Expenses	152.2		125.9	21	Loans	714	15%	580	135
(of which cost of funds)	92.9	61	79.9		Head office-branch account	2,747	59%	2,248	499
Operating profit	17.5		16	9	Other	969	21%	1,429	-461
Pretax income	17.3		15.9		**Total assets**	4,642	100%	4,374	268
Net income	8.5		10.8						
					Liabilities				
					Deposits	1,752	38%	1,404	348
					Head office-branch account	2,110	45%	1,715	395
					Other	780	17%	1,256	-476
					Total liabilities	4,642	100%	4,374	268

Source: Citibank.

We would expect to see in the early 2000s a rededication to the nonmortgage consumer finance business, which would include credit cards. Citibank has for many years been the leading card issuer in many Asian countries. Citi's lack of commitment to Japan reflects not a lack of interest or knowhow, but rather an appreciation of the overcapacity and underpriced situation of the card market in general in Japan in the 1980s. In the shakeout that seems inevitable in the 2000s, there will be opportunities for Citibank to expand its card franchise, leveraging its other franchise assets in Japan.

Breaking New Ground in Co-Location and Coordinated Sales with Affiliate Nikko Securities

In December 1998—as soon as regulations permitted—Citibank began to offer retail clients its proprietary Citifunds family of mutual funds. The funds were sold by direct mail to depositors and by telemarketing. Very likely, with so much competition in the market (Chapter Seven), Citibank—like almost all other banks—found the growth of mutual funds assets under management disappointing.

This background could help to explain Citibank's decision, announced in mid-August 1999 (*Nihon Keizai Shimbun*, August 14, 1999), to experiment with operating joint sales offices with Nikko Securities. According to the announcement, Citibank and Nikko would combine in Citibank's original building location the operations of Citibank's Gotanda branch and Nikko's nearby Shinagawa office. Nikko would take the first two floors, and Citibank would occupy the third floor. Citibank's 24-hour ATM would be located on the first floor.

Under the agreement, Citibank and Nikko would carry out mutual customer introductions and joint marketing strategies, cross-selling regular deposits, foreign currency deposits, mutual funds, and stocks in their co-located offices.

This was a remarkable innovation for both Citibank and Nikko. To some degree, Fuji Bank and Yasuda Trust had already set the precedent of joint officers (Chapter Ten), and, of course, Citigroup is the largest shareholder of Nikko, and the two have a wholesale joint venture (Chapter Thirteen). But this was the first example of a co-location of marketing offices between Japanese and foreign companies. Clearly, the companies were, like Fuji and Yasuda, looking for some cost savings. But the real promise of the experiment would be that combining banking and securities services in one location, and backing Citibank's products like deposits and Citifunds with the sales power of Nikko brokers, would result in greatly increased sales and asset volumes. Like much else done by Citibank in Japan, it was a competitive innovation that market competitors would watch with great apprehension.

The Citibank Private Bank

Citibank's private banking business also operates with a globally managed business structure. But, like the business in the United States, it is a much more locally driven business. There are essentially two types of private banking: Swiss-style private banking and U.S.-style private banking. In the former, symbolized and practiced best by the Swiss banks, private money from individuals is held and managed by banks in locations offering tax-free status to nonresidents. For the wealthy non-Swiss who keep money in Swiss banks, earnings on this money are not taxed in Switzerland (or often, because the accounts are secret, in the countries where the owners are living). In U.S.-style private banking, banks provide specialized services to people who are building wealth, usually through operating their own businesses. U.S. private bankers can offer little in terms of confidentiality from tax authorities. What they do offer is business skills and the ability to provide credit to entrepreneurs who are often leveraging personal wealth to expand businesses or who need counsel and advice in business-related matters. U.S. private bankers also offer asset management products and services.

Backing Out of Swiss-Type and Moving Into U.S.-Type Private Banking Services

Citibank got started in private banking in Japan in the mid-1980s. Like many foreign banks, it began with an offshore Swiss-banking approach, since this was the model for private banking globally. Like some others, Citi learned that the market for Swiss-type private banking in Japan is exceptionally small, since few Japanese have assets outside the country. Over time, Citibank's private bankers changed their focus to domestic business owners. Naturally, they targeted first those with overseas interests and relative sophistication. Credit—to purchase a flat in Hawaii or New York, or to finance trade—was and is an important product.

As we noted in the preceding chapter, Japan's market is not the most congenial for independent entrepreneurs. Japanese owners of small- or medium-sized businesses are commonly part of business groups that have grown larger since World War II. Often, these owners are elderly and most in need of investment products. Citibank private banking is well-known for structuring deposit products for sophisticated investors using derivatives. Such deposit products usually have a minimum investment requirement of $1 million equivalent. They contain an element of exchange risk, but principal is guaranteed. Such products are targeted by private bankers at business owners, who may be investing personal or company funds.

Now the Undisputed Leader in Private Banking

Citibank is the undisputed leader among foreign banks in private banking in Japan. In terms of professionalism and depth and scope of products and services, it is probably the leader in the entire marketplace. Citibank has essentially transferred and localized U.S.-style private banking, a discipline—like consumer finance—that Japanese banks still have not learned. The success of Citibank's private banking business was impressively illustrated in December 1998, when its private banking organization in Tokyo moved to separate and highly distinctive premises. It was further evidenced by the opening of a separate office in Nagoya in May 1999 (bringing the number of offices to three, including Osaka). By late 2000 the Citibank private banking plans to have a sales force of some 300 private bankers, up from 200 in 1999 (*The Nikkei Financial Daily*, July 11, 1999).

The Wholesale Bank (Global Corporate Banking)

Citibank wholesale bank, what remains of the corporate and financial institutions banking business built up since the 1950s, operates from a head office in Tokyo and an office in Osaka. Japan's changed marketplace and Citibank's rigorous capital allocation strategy have combined to cause this segment's operations to become more specialized and customized. This is a continuation of the niche strategy of the 1980s, but the niche has gotten progressively narrower. There are now three product areas: corporate finance, transaction services, and trading and capital markets. Citibank, as one of the main bankers to the world's largest companies, still offers a variety of commercial banking services, but it will not compete on price with other banks to provide these services. It is prepared to see the business go elsewhere (in fact it would usually prefer it) rather than discount.

A good example of Citi's corporate focus is the $5 billion syndicated loan for Japan Tobacco funded in May 1999, for which Citibank Tokyo branch was arranger and lead underwriter. Citibank brought together 27 banks in this deal, the largest syndicated loan fundraising ever in Asia. Japan Tobacco (JT) is a AAA client and this size syndication would provide substantial fees for the lead underwriter and arranger. This transaction was referred to repeatedly by Sandy Weill and John Reed, co-chairmen and co-CEOs of Citigroup, as evidencing the synergies and value-added of Citigroup, since Saloman Smith Barney was advisor to JT on the underlying transaction, JT's acquisition of the overseas business operations of RJR Nabisco.

Citibank's wholesale banking strategy and structure are being integrated with the securities and investment banking strategy of Salomon Smith Barney under the Citigroup umbrella. Citicorp International Securities, the investment banking arm, that managed syndications fixed income securities and equity origination, and securitization, before the Citicorp-Travelers merger, will probably be integrated into Nikko Salomon Smith Barney. Another company whose operations may be restructured is Cititrust Trust and Banking. The company has been reasonably successful in winning mandates for public pension funds management (Chapter Six), but this market is changing. It will be necessary to integrate the trust business strategy with the larger asset management strategy of Citigroup, including again Nikko Salomon Smith Barney.

What the structure looks like in the future is less important than what it delivers. What is clear is that Citibank and Citigroup are and will remain at the forefront of financial services and innovation in Japan in the foreseeable future.

American Insurance Group

In the postwar period probably the only foreign financial company to rival Citibank as both a symbolic and actual player in the Japanese market is American Insurance Group. AIG is one of the United States's most global companies, with over half of revenues coming from outside the United States. The company is proud of its Asian roots. It was originally established in Shanghai in 1919 as American Asiatic Underwriters. In 1939 its headquarters was moved from Shanghai to New York.

AIG was the first foreign nonlife insurer to enter Japan after the war, establishing a branch of American International Underwriters (AIU) in 1946.

AIG Group Companies and Businesses

Figure 12.3 presents a summary of the major business of AIG in Japan. Let us examine each in turn.

AIU Insurance. AIU is the oldest and largest foreign nonlife insurer in Japan. It offers more than 200 products. Major lines are fire/property, automobile, personal accident, overseas travel, corporate executive liability and life (package), casualty, and marine cargo. AIU is a leader in automobile insurance, which it introduced in the 1960s. It pioneered overseas travel accident insurance. It has achieved a niche in providing comprehensive accident insurance for students and their schools. In recent years the company introduced such new products as directors and officers liability, environmental impairment liability, and employment practices liability. In the year ended March 31, 1999, the company booked $1.9 billion in gross premiums, with accident insurance accounting for 46 percent, automobile insurance for 29 percent, fire insurance 11 percent, and other types 14 percent.

AIU operates some 100 offices nationwide and employs about 1,800 people. At the same time, it relies predominantly on a network of more than 15,000 sales agents (1998). AIU presents itself as an "agency company" that invests in agents and nurtures long-term "partnerships."

Alico Japan. Alico Japan is a branch of American Life Insurance Company. It was established in Japan in 1973, the first foreign life company to commence business after World War II. The company, offering a range of life and special contract products, is the largest foreign full-line life insurer. It has been a pioneer with many "first in Japan" products, including nonpar level term and whole life insurance, full in-hospital coverage, living benefits

Figure 12.3 **Schematic of AIG Group in Japan**

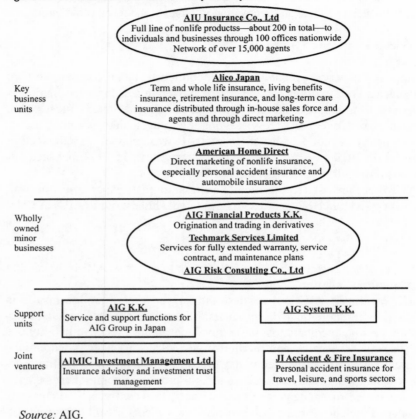

Source: AIG.

insurance, long-term care insurance, and interest sensitive whole life. In 1998 it introduced a discounted Club Nonsmoker life insurance and a no-qualification-necessary whole life product *Hairemasu*.

In the year ended March 31, 1998 revenues from new business were 29.8 percent from whole life insurance, 24.1 percent from group insurance, 15.0 percent from term insurance, 5.3 percent from medical insurance, 1.8 percent from endowment insurance, and 24.1 percent from other types.

Alico Japan has developed multiple distribution channels, including in-house salesman training in consultative selling and a nationwide network of agents, with nonlife agents trained to sell Alico products. Alico was the first company to offer products by direct marketing and to tie up with bank lenders to package product sales.

As of March 31, 1999, Alico Japan had $101 billion (¥12.12 trillion) in outstanding policies, of which $88.6 billion were individual policies. Premium revenue was $2.44 billion, up 17 percent from the previous year. Operating profit was $184 million.

American Home Direct is the Japanese branch of American Home Assurance Company (American Home Japan). It has been a pioneer and leader in direct marketing of nonlife insurance. The company started operations in 1960. It began focusing on direct marketing of personal accident insurance in 1982 when restrictive regulations were relaxed.

In 1996, when competition on rates and differentiated risk pricing were permitted, the company was the first to sell automobile insurance by direct marketing. In 1997 it introduced the first risk-differentiated product, offering up to 30 percent savings in premiums for drivers with good records and other qualifications. Sales are mainly via print and electronic advertisements, backed by a telephone center. A second channel is through market agents, including credit card companies, catalogue sales companies, and department stores.

In the year ended March 31, 1999, American Home's net premiums totaled $184 million (¥22.2 billion), up 41.5 percent over the previous year. Some 60 percent of gross premiums received were from accident insurance, 32 percent from automobile insurance, 7 percent from fire insurance, and 1 percent from other types (data from the Nonlife Insurers' Association).

AIMIC Investment Management is a joint venture with Mitsubishi Trust and Banking Ltd. in investment advisory and investment trust management that is 70 percent owned by AIG. It was established in 1997. In May 1999 it held $611 million in discretionary accounts.

JI Accident and Fire Insurance is a 50/50 joint venture between AIG and Japan Travel Bureau. Its primary focus is providing a variety of nonlife insurance products, particularly personal accident insurance, for the travel, leisure, and sports sectors. It was established in 1989.

Techmark Japan is the Japan branch of Techmark Services. The company provides and administers fully insured extended warranty, service contract, and maintenance plans covering new and used automobiles, home appliances, computers, and credit card purchases.

AIG K.K. and *AIG Systems K.K.* provide support services for the group. *AIG Risk Consulting* provides services both inhouse and for the general market. *AIG Financial Products Japan K.K.* is a derivatives trading boutique.

Looking for New Worlds to Conquer

AIG has established a leading position in the Japanese market, comparable to that of Citibank in banking. The question on the minds of AIG management today is: what next? In particular, how can AIG build on its strengths and achieve substantial new long-term growth in the new environment being created by the big bang?

The answer is undoubtedly in consumer-related financial services, both on the investment (mutual funds) side and also on the credit (consumer lending) side. On January 1, 1999, AIG acquired SunAmerica, based in Florida, whose main business is providing savings and investment products targeted at retired or soon-to-be-retired persons. SunAmerica offers fixed and variable annuities, mutual funds, investment counseling, trust services, and guaranteed investment contracts. Hank Greenberg, AIG chairman, indicated when the acquisition took place that AIG planned to expand SunAmerica's business into international markets, notably Japan.

Variable Annuities (Mutual Funds) Launched in 1999

With a legion of life and nonlife salesmen and agents, who are now permitted to sell mutual funds and other investment products, its large individual customer base, and its deep understanding of the market, AIG is in an ideal position to launch a consumer investment business selling products and services similar or identical to those offered by SunAmerica. A variable annuity product—similar to those offered by SunAmerica—was launched in August 1999. It was a U.S. dollar product, essentially a mutual fund.

To realize its potential, AIG will need to establish or acquire a securities license and/or a trust banking license. AIG is accustomed to looking far into the future. With such a perspective, it is possible to conceive of AIG purchasing a Japanese securities company or trust bank and targeting the buildup of a market presence comparable to the presence it holds today in the insurance sector.

Next: A Foray into Consumer Finance?

Another area of opportunity is in consumer lending. AIG Consumer Finance Group is developing consumer finance business in a number of emerging country markets, especially, according to the company, "where the AIG name lends strong support and market acceptance." This would certainly be the case in Japan. And we have seen that the consumer finance market has the kind of economics that are attractive to companies like AIG. GE's entry into the consumer finance market through acquisition of Lake supports the view that the image of consumer finance companies is no longer so disreputable as to be a barrier to foreign entrants with substantial brand equity to lose. AIG, one of the most successfully aggressive and opportunistic players in the Japanese market, should not be long in seizing the clear opportunities in consumer finance.

Chapter Thirteen

The Bold Innovators: Merrill Lynch and Citigroup

Merrill Lynch: Eternally Bullish on Japan?

Among all U.S. securities companies, the allure of the Japanese marketplace has always been strongest for Merrill Lynch. Merrill Lynch's two coequal business organizations—private client (retail) and the corporate and institutional client (wholesale)—have both seen opportunities in the Japanese market and perceived that in Japan, as nowhere else outside the United States, synergies could be achieved through a comprehensive market development approach. Also, Merrill Lynch has seen the Japanese marketplace evolve, deregulate, and globalize in ways that have continuously opened profitable business niches to a firm with advanced techniques and an aggressive, opportunistic management style.

Merrill opened a representative office in Tokyo in 1964. It established itself to do securities business and opened a Tokyo branch in 1972. An Osaka branch was opened in 1978. In the past twenty years the company's retail and institutional businesses have co-existed, sometimes sharing business licenses and entities, but their management and strategies have been distinct. We will examine each in turn.

In the 1980s, when Merrill in the United States was still more a retail broker and less an institutional heavyweight, Japan's sales-driven individual investor marketplace seemed to match its own. At the margin, the company saw itself taming the "churn-and-burn" passions of brokers hired from the big four Japanese brokerage houses, offering clients a more consultative approach. But the emphasis was still on sales and commissions, and not yet on asset gathering, and—in the second half of the bubble decade—commissions revenues continued to climb.

Rapid Expansion in the Late 1980s

As Merrill's private client business expanded globally in the 1980s, Asia, particularly Japan, was a high-growth region. Successful private client operations in the Tokyo and Osaka branches and the rising Japanese stock market encouraged Merrill to open strictly retail offices in Nagoya (1985), Yokohama (1988), Kyoto (1989), and Kobe (1990). In 1990, at the peak of the bubble period, the private client organization had some 250 staff, including 100 brokers, working out of six offices. By 1992, with the stock market averages at less than half their 1989 levels and average daily trading volumes of 268 million shares, compared with 893 million in 1989, the retail business was losing close to $30 million a year.

In late 1992 and early 1993 the senior management of Merrill's private client group in Japan—including this writer—undertook a multi-month strategic analysis of the retail business in Japan, employing the Gemini Group as consultants. The findings were sobering. Whatever had been the case in the 1980s, by the early 1990s what might be called "normal Japanese retail investors" had abandoned the market. The typical broker—whether at Merrill Lynch or Nomura—had a handful of active clients, most of whom viewed the stock market as a casino in which to place speculative bets. The brokers served as willing croupiers. Stocks, if bought, were quickly sold. Many brokers had induced their clients to trade options and futures. (With so few clients, brokers needed to ensure a high volume of trading—easily done in options and futures—in order to generate enough commissions to justify their salaries and to avoid getting fired.) Although Merrill was still a sales-oriented company, its management knew that speculators—like Las Vegas gamblers—always lose in the end. They understood that their brokers' handful of clients would one by one surely join the disillusioned multitudes. In the meantime, inevitably, claims of broker impropriety were mounting.

Withdrawal from the Retail Market in 1993

Another revelation of Merrill was that, by the early 1990s, there were little, if any, sales on non-yen products by Merrill Japan. If ever the company had, as initially envisioned, filled a market niche by offering non-yen, international products, it was no longer doing so. In the late 1980s the easy money to be made in the Japanese market was in selling Japanese stocks. Merrill had fallen in with the crowd and hired brokers from Japanese houses who knew only Japanese stocks. With such people came customers only interested in Japanese stocks. So the vision, if there was one, was lost.

And what of the future? Could the retail business be downsized and restructured? This was the toughest judgment, and it was negative. With hindsight, Merrill executives began to doubt that the Japanese market had ever been an "investment market" for individuals. The minuscule yields offered by Japanese stocks and the absence of any perceivable shareholder value mentality among corporate managements now seemed inimical to the interests of investors. Merrill executives now began to see the entry of large numbers of Japanese individuals into the market in the 1980s as an aberration for a nation of risk-averse savers. They sensed that it would be many years, and much would have to change, before such persons again entrusted funds to securities companies.

Against this negative assessment and the prospect of continuing losses for years to come, the decision was taken in 1993 to close down completely the private client business in Japan. During that year, the Kobe, Kyoto, and Yokohama branches were closed. Nagoya was converted into a small institutional office. Retail operations in Osaka and Tokyo were shut down. Clients were advised to close their accounts. The entire private client workforce of 250 people were transferred or terminated.

The Yamaichi Purchase and Re-Entering the Market in 1998

In 1997 Merrill Lynch private client senior management in New York could congratulate itself on having made a sensible decision four years earlier, since the decision had probably saved the company substantial money. There was, however, a worry that it had also foreclosed what seemed to be an emerging, and potentially big opportunity. Japan's financial system was in crisis. Its banks and, particularly, brokerages were weak and discredited by scandal. The domestic stock market was in a prolonged bearish cycle. Interest rates had fallen and were reducing yields on personal savings to the vanishing point. The Japanese yen appeared no longer on a permanent appreciation trend.

On the positive side, Merrill Lynch executives knew that the Hashimoto government had passed legislation promising to deliver a big bang-type reform in the Japanese financial marketplace in 1998. A long-term view suggested that the Japanese financial marketplace was at a cyclical bottom, with nowhere to go but up. This was particularly evident in the area of retail financial services, especially brokerage and asset management. With a growing sense of urgency, Merrill executives began to believe that Japanese individuals—planning for retirement, with a high level of savings earning close to zero yield—could be converted from savers to investors and brought back to the investment market *if offered a consultative, long-term relationship.*

In late 1997 Merrill was presented with what was the "opportunity of a lifetime" (*Institutional Investor* 1999) to return to the Japanese retail market as a significant player when Yamaichi Securities, then Japan's fourth largest brokerage, collapsed and was forced into liquidation. The collapse stunned the financial market, highlighting the weakness of the brokerage sector. The

Ministry of Finance (MOF), in charge of maintaining stability, approached other domestic brokers to take over Yamaichi's operations and staff. There were no takers.

Merrill Lynch Japan Securities is Born

After discussions with MOF, Merrill Lynch agreed to take over virtually the entire Yamaichi retail brokerage operation, including some thirty-three offices and 2,200 staff, of which some 1,100 were brokers. This was clearly a strategy reversal and a big bet for the private client group, whose key executives were John L. Steffens and Winthrop H. Smith. In February 1998 they set up a new company, Merrill Lynch Japan Securities, distinct from the existing institutional business operated as Merrill Lynch Japan Incorporated (Figure 13.1). In the first half of 1998 a new executive team, headed by Ronald Strauss, began to reorganize the resources of the former Yamaichi and to implement programs designed to realize the strategy of the new company. This was to build an individual investor franchise by offering long-term wealth management and investment services, using a consultative sales approach. Profitability would come, as increasingly in the United States from asset management fees, rather than brokerage commissions. Persistency and volume of assets under management would be the profit drivers, rather than brokered trading volume. To emphasize the point, the marketing slogan of the company would be, as in the United States, "The difference is Merrill Lynch."

Merrill Lynch Japan Securities (MLJS) officially began sales activity in July 1998. But, having had only a few months to train former Yamaichi brokers to be Merrill Lynch "financial consultants," management had little confidence that its sales force understood or could articulate to clients Merrill's new approach to the market. Orders were issued through the branch network that financial consultants (FCs) should refrain from trying to sell products, but rather should try to gather customer assets in money market accounts. One issue was that many of the products Merrill wanted to sell, essentially a variety of mutual funds, were still under development. But the larger issue, still with the company in 1999, was the quality and professionalism of its FCs.

Brilliant Move or Black Hole?

The challenge of reeducating the Yamaichi sales force was anticipated by Merrill management, though executives often complained that progress was slower than hoped. What came as a surprise was the narrowness and relatively poor quality of Yamaichi's client base. There turned out to be fewer

Figure 13.1 Schematic of Merrill Lynch Group Entities and Products in Japan

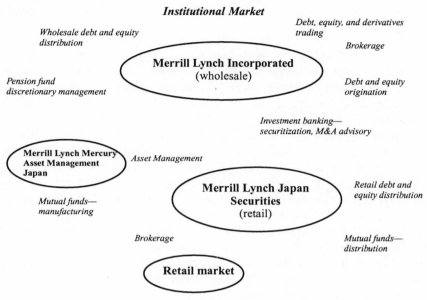

Institutional Market

Debt, equity, and derivatives trading

Wholesale debt and equity distribution

Brokerage

Merrill Lynch Incorporated
(wholesale)

Pension fund discretionary management

Debt and equity origination

Investment banking— securitization, M&A advisory

Merrill Lynch Mercury Asset Management Japan

Asset Management

Merrill Lynch Japan Securities
(retail)

Retail debt and equity distribution

Mutual funds— manufacturing

Brokerage

Mutual funds— distribution

Retail market

Source: Author.
Note: Italics indicate products and services.

active clients than expected and the kind of activity seen was not very different from that which had soured the company on the market in 1993. Thus in 1998 and 1999, the company found itself challenged to a degree greater than expected. Also, costs—always a potential problem in Japan—proved greater than planned.

In the 1998 accounts of Merrill Lynch & Co., Inc., the parent, the start-up of MLJS was posted at a pretax loss of $230 million, a very large number (Merrill Lynch & Co., Inc. 1998 Annual Report, p. 39). The lower section of Table 13.1 shows the Japanese regulatory reporting income statement for MLJS at the end of the Japanese financial year March 31, 1999. The operating loss was $215 million (¥ 25.9 billion). This was for some nine months of operations after July 1998. During this period revenues were $28.3 million (¥3.4 billion), and general operating expenses were $228.8 million (¥27.5 billion). Also, the company amortized some $15 million of a remaining $74 million of start-up costs carried as an asset on the balance sheet. The final net loss figure of $73.2 million (¥8.8 billion) results from an extraordinary profit of $93.4 million (¥11.2 billion) recorded from distributions from a silent partnership (a limited explanation of this partnership is provided in the MLJS 1999 Report). For our analysis, we ignore this item and focus on operating results.

Is the Strategy Right?

How are we to assess this performance and what is the outlook? Clearly Merrill got itself into a significant expense hole with the Yamaichi acquisition. The question is whether it can build revenues quickly enough to crawl out of the hole. The company is still maintaining that it can break even within three years, that is, in 2001.

The fundamental and still unanswered question is whether Merrill's asset gathering and long-term relationship approach can be made to make money in the Japanese market. One reason to be optimistic is that—with the deregulation of commissions in October 1999—it is almost certainly true that the traditional brokerage commission-driven model for the securities business in Japan is no longer viable. Asset management seems virtually the only alternative for a relationship-oriented company (the other model would be discount, perhaps online, brokerage, where relationship is not the main service). The challenge inherent in its market-leading strategy is that no one can say how quickly the market—meaning the mentality of a substantial number of individual investors—will catch up. Initial market feedback to Merrill's consultative selling approach—where clients were asked questions about their financial assets, risk tolerance, and plans, so that FCs could offer advice on asset allocation and recommend specific products—was mixed. Investors were unaccustomed to being questioned in this way (except by life insurance salesmen), and most were reluctant to tell the FCs much. Merrill has supported the consultative approach with media advertising and launched a highly information and advice-oriented web site in September 1999. The effectiveness of these actions will only slowly become clear. In the meantime, while it has been changed in the United States, the advertising slogan for MLJS in Japan will remain "The difference is Merrill Lynch."

Building the Retail Business: Day by Day, Account by Account

The first six months of 1999 were good for MLJS, as for every other Japanese broker, as the rising domestic market (driven by effectively zero interest rates) brought many Japanese individuals back to securities houses. Merrill was able to increase the number of accounts from some 40,000 in March to some 51,000 in July. Revenues were strongly above plan, though (contrary to Merrill's strategy) the main contributor was traditional brokerage com-

Table 13.1

Performance Indicators for Merrill Lynch Japan

Merrill Lynch Japan Incorporated (wholesale)
(Yen billions)

	Mar 97	Mar 98	Mar 99	Change 98/99
Sales revenues	62.8	74.5	98.2	32%
of which				
Commissions	32.9	54.1	58.2	8%
Financing	4.2	5.4	13.7	152%
Trading profit	25.8	15.0	26.4	76%
Operating profit		9.4	19.3	105%
Ordinary profit	6.8	9.4	11.7	25%
Net profit	−1.4	1.8	9.0	392%
Total staff	588	664	738	
Commissions breakdown				
1. Brokerage	14.2	24.7	22.5	
Stocks	12.4	22.2	20.2	
Bonds	1.7	2.4	2.3	
2. Underwriting	1.3	0.9	3.6	
Stocks	0.2	0.1	0.4	
Bonds	1.2	0.9	3.2	
3. Other	17.4	28.5	31.9	
Trading profit breakdown				
Stocks	10.5	2.5	2.2	
Bonds	15.2	12.8	23.8	

Merrill Lynch Japan Securities (retail)
(Yen billions)

	Mar 99
Sales revenues	3.4
of which	
Commissions	2.1
Trading profits	1.2
Ordinary profit (loss)	−25.9
Net profit (loss)	−8.8
Total staff	2,011
of which	
General office	857
Sales representatives	1,154

Sources: Annual reports. Merrill Lynch Japan Incorporated 1999. Merrill Lynch Japan Securities Co., Ltd. 1999.

missions as FCs found buyers again for individual stocks. Mutual fund sales—the strategic business focus—were also increasing, particularly sales of Japanese equity funds. MLJS was planning to increase its FC salesforce to 2,000 from some 1,150 over the next two years.

Thus the trends both in the market and in the company were positive. Some of the questions of strategy were also being answered in the highly encouraging form of imitation by competitors. This was the key development and Merrill's fundamental need—for the market to change. And change of the right kind was happening. Many observers have expressed doubt about Merrill's prospects. For the record, the writer believes that Merrill will ultimately succeed and prosper in the retail market, as it has in the wholesale market.

The Key Role of Merrill Lynch Mercury Asset Management

In both Merrill wholesale and retail strategy, but particularly in the latter, Merrill Lynch Mercury Asset Management (MLMAM) is playing a key role. In 1997 Merrill Lynch acquired the Mercury Asset Management Group, the leading independent U.K. asset management firm. This acquisition substantially increased Merrill's international assets under management, from both private individual and institutional sources. In Japan, MLMAM is the vehicle through which Merrill is manufacturing mutual funds (which are distributed through MLJS and other brokers, banks, and insurance companies) as well as offering discretionary investment advisory services to pension funds. As of May 1999 MLMAM had a total of $3.4 billion under management in investment trusts. As of March 1999 discretionary pension fund management mandates for domestic sponsors totaled $8.3 billion, which ranked MLMAM ninth among all investment advisors in the market.

In 1999 MLJS was offering twenty-four mutual funds. Seventeen were its proprietary funds, manufactured by MLMAM. In Merrill's strategy acquiring assets and managing them over time is the key business driver. MLMAM is central in this strategy.

Merrill's Wholesale Juggernaut: Merrill Lynch Japan Incorporated

Merrill Lynch's 1998 Annual Report made special mention of the excellent performance of its Japanese wholesale business, for which the vehicle is Merrill Lynch Japan Incorporated (MLJ). Executives at the wholesale company were carping that the losses in the retail business were giving the appearance of problems in Japan that could affect their bonuses.

The performance of MLJ in the three years ended March 1999, according to Japanese regulatory reporting, is presented in Table 13.1. Clearly, according to these numbers, MLJ is highly profitable and growing fast. Total revenues in the year ended March 1999 were $818 million (¥98.2 billion), up 32 percent over the preceding year. Operating profit was $160.8 million, and net profit after tax was $75 million (¥9 billion).

Breaking down the revenues, we can understand how MLJ is making its money. The largest revenue category is commissions, and within this category the overwhelming contributors are stock brokerage commissions of $168 million (¥20.2 billion) and "other" commissions $270 million (¥31.9 billion). In the Tokyo market in 1998, MLJ was one of the three leading foreign brokers (the others were Morgan Stanley Dean Witter and Goldman Sachs: see Chapter Fifteen) buying and selling securities for the accounts of institutional clients, like international equity mutual funds. Serving such clients, MLJ achieved about a 6 percent share of trading volume on the Tokyo Stock Exchange, making it a major player. The "other" category includes fees for such activities as mergers and acquisitions advisory. In 1998 and early 1999, MLJ's investment banking department was advisor on a number of large international M&A deals, involving such companies as Sony, Renault, and Japan Tobacco. Trading profit was another major contributor, at $220 million (¥26 billion), and here the action was all in fixed income securities. MLJ was active in both the primary and secondary markets. In the former, it was actively originating asset-backed securities. New products included packaged loan-backed securities. Trading profits in derivatives were also up substantially (Merrill Lynch Japan Incorporated 1999 Annual Report).

No Longer Just a Foreign Broker

Along with Morgan Stanley, Goldman Sachs, and Salomon Smith Barney, Merrill Lynch has clearly become far more than a niche "foreign" player in Japan's market. MLJ and its U.S. peers are now clearly on the mezzanine level, just below the Big Three and above the second tier local brokers. In terms of technology, knowhow, and professionalism, they are often the market leaders.

In the future MLJ hopes to move further and faster into this mainstream role by becoming a lead underwriter of securities—both bonds and stocks—for both Japanese and foreign companies. In 1998 the company achieved some successes in the domestic straight bond area, as we see in Table 13.1. But the numbers are still small. Key to MLJ's strategic vision is a broad-based retail as well as institutional distribution capability. MLJS, if successful, could provide this capability. One day not many years away, it is thus hoped, the retail business will help to earn bigger bonuses in the pockets of MLJ's wholesale brokers.

Citigroup: Sandy Weill's Marriage of Convenience with Nikko

In April 1999 Sanford Weill, co-CEO of Citigroup, told the *Nihon Keizai Shimbun* that Citigroup was expecting the Japanese market to become one of the largest contributors of corporate revenues within five years. Weill had come to Tokyo with co-CEO John Reed to officiate at a mammoth kickoff reception at the Hotel Okura for Nikko Salomon Smith Barney (NSSB), which had started business on March 1. At the reception, Weill found it hard to restrain his delight. A suddenly booming market in March and April was bringing foreign investors back to Japan, and NSSB had surpassed even the most optimistic expectations, achieving profitability in its first month of operation.

The alliance between Travelers Group and Nikko Securities, announced in June 1998, was Sandy Weill's creation. Weill followed this move in Japan with the merger with Citicorp to form Citigroup. In early 1998 Weill saw an opportunity in Japan's weakened securities sector to achieve a major positioning advance for Salomon Smith Barney. He knew the president of Nikko, and reportedly made the approach personally. Nikko, the weakest of the Big Three, which had recorded an operating loss of $318 million for the year ended March 31, 1998, accepted the advance (see Chapter Four for details). In 1998 Travelers invested $1.83 billion (¥220 billion) in Nikko and became the largest shareholder.

Nikko Salomon Smith Barney

From Travelers' and Weill's standpoint, the short-term benefit of the tie-up with Nikko was the agreement to create a new platform from which to launch an expansion by Salomon Smith Barney. The platform was Nikko Salomon Smith Barney, a joint venture owned 51 percent by Nikko and 49 percent by Salomon Smith Barney (SSB).

NSSB was constituted by bringing into the company Nikko's entire wholesale securities structure—its equity and bond trading departments, its underwriting and product development group, and Nikko Research Center (a subsidiary)—and all of Salomon Smith Barney's operations, including equity and fixed income trading, research, and investment banking. The company is operating with a dual-head structure in most departments.

It is difficult to conceive that Citicorp would ever have pursued the deal that Weill struck. Joint ventures are hard to manage, perhaps especially for U.S. companies, which tend to want control. Although Citigroup has majority ownership in a derivative sense, given its shareholding in Nikko, it is in a minority position in the JV itself. Thus, when problems and disagreements arise, as they inevitably will, Citicorp could be over-ruled at the JV level.

Looking beyond this point, to the actual operation and position of NSSB in the Japanese marketplace, we can see Weill's vision. With 1,100 employees (about 500 from Nikko and 600 from SSB) and equity capital of $920 million (¥110 billion) NSSB started as a major player, in both financial strength and trading power, and in state-of-the-art technology and products. Add to this "foreign" advantage the relationships of Nikko with major corporates and other institutions in the markets, and the combination looks exceptionally strong. Further add the potential to use Nikko's domestic retail network for distribution, as well as to use Nikko's relationship brokers to source corporate leads. The mixed parentage of NSSB allows the company to offer the local and international services for which, in many transactions, Japanese issuers need to hire co-lead managers, one local and one foreign. It should prove a powerful combination.

How has NSSB been doing? So far so good, and not just in the brokerage and trading area that helped boost revenues in the first month of operations. NSSB achieved a third-place position in the domestic bond underwriting business, capturing about 15 percent of the business. In investment banking, NSSB advised Nissan in its discussions with Renault (advised by Merrill Lynch). It was also opposite Merrill Lynch when it advised Japan Tobacco on its purchase of the overseas tobacco operations of RJR Nabisco. In the near future, NSSB is targeting growth in securing major privatization deals, like the IPO of NTT Docomo, an $18 billion transaction for which rival Goldman Sachs was global coordinator and Nikko won the domestic distribution mandate.

Weill's Unfinished Japan Agenda

Coming before the merger that created Citigroup, the alliance with Nikko was clearly a stand-alone SSB initiative. And while former Travelers Group companies and Citicorp entities are making progress in merging operations in many other markets, there are obvious obstacles to integrating NSSB and other Citigroup entities, most obviously Citicorp International Securities, Citigroup's 100 percent-owned investment bank. The policy of management now seems to be not to force issues, but rather to look for areas of natural cooperation. What seems to be an ancillary, but nonetheless promising result of the investment in Nikko Securities is cooperation with Citibank in approaching the retail market with a combination of banking and securities services. This was evidenced in mid-August 1999 with the announcement that co-located Citibank-Nikko Securities retail offices would begin operating on an experimental basis (see Chapter Twelve).

What really seems to be Weill's unfinished agenda in Japan, and part of his vision for making Japan a major profit contributor, is insurance. In his April 1999, interview with the *Nihon Keizai Shimbun*, Weill clearly stated his desire to enter the insurance market in Japan. He indicated that Citigroup was talking with Japanese insurance companies and looking for an acquisition. With Sandy Weill, where there is the will, there will certainly be found the way to make a major entry into insurance in Japan. For this entry we only need to wait.

Chapter Fourteen

GE Capital's Awesome Assault

The great potential of the Japanese marketplace in the twenty-first century, and a model of how to realize that potential, is nowhere more clearly seen than in the audacious assault on the market by GE Capital Services (GECS), the nonbank financial services arm of General Electric Corporation. A relative newcomer to Japan, whose first office was opened in Tokyo in June 1993, by 1999 GECS had completed acquisitions that made it the largest foreign financial group in the country.

Dennis Dammerman, GE Capital Services chairman and CEO, interviewed in the *Weekly Toyo Keizai* in July 1999 described GECS's vision as building a diversified financial service operation in Japan with a focus on life insurance, consumer finance, equipment leasing, and real estate. By 1999 operating assets in Japan totaled some $15 billion, indicating that the company was well on its way to realizing the vision. As impressive as what the company had already accomplished, however, particularly in the Japanese context, was *how* it had done so and planned to continue to do so. Unlike any other foreign company ever (and like very few Japanese companies), GECS was applying successfully in the Japanese market the same acquisition strategy and techniques it had applied in other markets. The blazing pace and mammoth (and increasing) scale of GECS's acquisitions were causing real disquiet among Japan's weakened and somewhat disoriented financial companies. It was as though a fox had entered the henhouse.

Building Acquisition Momentum in the 1990s

Figure 14.1 presents a schematic of GE Capital Services' businesses in Japan in 1999. The businesses fall under one of two GECS operational units, GE Capital Corporation (GECC) and GE Financial Assurance (GEFA). Let us review the history of how these businesses were acquired.

August 1994—Minebea Credit

GECC acquired three consumer finance subsidiaries of Minebea, a ball bearings maker, which was restructuring and withdrawing from credit loan ventures

Figure 14.1 **Schematic of GE Capital's Businesses in Japan in 1989**

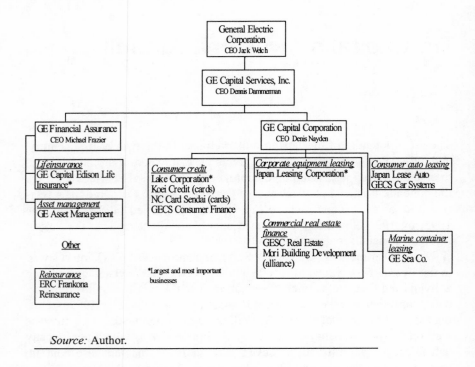

Source: Author.

---

entered into in the 1980s. The three subsidiaries, Minebea Credit, Nakama Shopping Service and NC Card Sendai, reportedly had assets of $1 billion, fourteen branches, 350 employees, and 360,000 accounts. The acquired businesses provided home improvement and education loans and credit card services. The transaction excluded some $500 million in real estate loans.

April 1995—Shin Kyoto Shinpan

GECC reportedly paid about $100 million for Shin Kyoto Shinpan's shopping credit and credit card operations. The acquired operations had twenty branches, 250,000 cardholders, and the installment credit accounts of 15,000 shops in the Kansai region.

September 1996—Marubeni Car System

GECC reportedly paid between $230 and 275 million for an 80-percent stake in Marubeni Car System's vehicle leasing subsidiary. MCS had 18,800 vehicles under lease, primarily to small businesses and individuals, and revenues of $160 million in the year ended March 1996. To acquire 80 percent of the equity it was necessary for GECC to negotiate with several shareholders. Sixty-seven percent of equity was acquired from Marubeni, while 6 percent was bought from Orient Corporation and the remaining 7 percent was acquired from Yasuda Fire & Marine and Dai-Tokyo Fire & Marine.

December 1997—Koei Credit

Koei Credit was a subsidiary of financially weak, Osaka-based Kofuku Bank, which ultimately failed in 1999. Koei Credit was a mid-size consumer finance company with some 450 employees, an outstanding loan balance of $433 million (160,000 loans), and fifty-four outlets primarily in the Tokyo area. Koei's operation were taken over by GECC's MCS Service unit.

February 1998—Toho Life

On February 18, 1998, Toho Mutual Life Insurance Company and GEFA announced agreement to establish a new life insurance company in Japan. The new company, GE Capital Edison Life Insurance, began operations on April 1 with a total of $1.2 billion in capital ($600 million from each party). GE obtained control of approximately 90 percent of the voting stock in the new company, which acquired Toho Life's business operations and sales network (approximately 7,000 agents). All new policies after April 1 were to be written by the new company. GE Financial Assurance reportedly paid over $580 million for Toho's business operations rights.

In 1998 Toho Life was the fifteenth largest life insurance company in Japan. Assets in March 1998 were some $25 billion (¥3 trillion). Its assets and premium revenues had been falling since 1994 as the company began to record operating losses due to loan defaults and negative spread on policies. In May 1999 the company was forced to close by regulators when it was found to be insolvent (see Chapter Five).

July 1998—Lake Corporation

In November 1998 GECC concluded the purchase of the consumer finance business of Lake Corporation, the fifth largest subprime consumer lender in Japan (the acquisition had been agreed to and announced in July). GECC acquired the Lake name, trademark, and consumer finance business infrastructure, including 564 branches and 2,700 employees. At the time of the deal, Lake had some $4.41 billion (¥529.5 billion) in loan receivables and 1,409,000 customers nationwide (see Chapter Eight).

GECC Capital did not purchase a part of Lake's assets, including loans, real estate and art.

March 1999—Japan Lease and Japan Lease Auto

GECC reportedly paid $4.6 billion (¥550 billion) to purchase the lease business of Japan Lease (*Nihon Keizai Shimbun*, March 10, 1999), the third largest leasing company in Japan. In late 1998 Japan Lease was seeking protection from creditors under the corporate rehabilitation law (i.e., it had filed the equivalent of a Chapter 11 bankruptcy petition) after its parent, Long Term Credit Bank (LTCB), was nationalized, and because of its large portfolio of bad real estate-based loan assets. Japan Lease's gross assets were about $6.2 billion (¥740 billion). GECC also purchased Japan Lease's auto leasing subsidiary, Japan Lease Auto, which had assets of about ¥130 billion. In total, GE Capital purchased the combined total of $7.3 billion (¥870 billion) in assets of Japan Lease and Japan Lease Auto. This was the largest acquisition ever in Japan.

Under the GECC umbrella, Japan Lease and Japan Lease Auto Services retained their entire 530-person staff and started operations from March 4.

GE's Scary Confidence and Efficiency

The speed, confidence, and efficiency of GECS's acquisitions has had a stunning effect on much of Japan's financial community. As GECS's executives are wont to say, having completed some 300 acquisitions around the world in the five years to 1999, the company has a well-defined and disciplined process for due diligence and execution of acquisitions which it applies to all situations, and Japan has been no exception.

There is also a post-acquisition process of bringing GE's "best practices" to the acquired company. Japanese managers in the acquired companies have found the thoroughness of GE's "six sigma" management technology something new. They also remark on the uncompromising discipline with which GE managers adhere to and apply the "six sigma" methodology.

A bit scary and new to Japan is GE's bias for speed and action. The comparatively rapid speed with which GE has managed to execute and achieve results is receiving anxious and amazed attention from Japanese competitors. It was noted, for example, in the case of Japan Lease Auto, which had been under court-supervised restructuring. After GECC decided to buy the company, it took only five months for GECC to settle all the company's debts and to receive approval from the court to buy and restart the company. This was lightning quick by Japanese standards (*Nihon Keizai Shimbun*, March 5, 1999).

Specific Strategies and Plans for Key Acquisitions

As noted above, GE Capital views Japan as a key growth market, and its plans are to develop a diversified financial services operation. Denis Nayden, CEO of GECC, stated in March 1999 that GECC hoped to increase the profit contribution coming from Japan from $300 million in 1998 to some $600 million in 2001. Nayden, like all other GE executives, emphasized that GE will continue to pursue its 20 percent ROE and 15 percent annual revenue growth objectives, leveraging both internal growth and, particularly, additional acquisitions potential (*Nihon Keizai Shimbun*, March 5, 1999).

Let us look at the strategies and plans for some of the key acquisitions.

Consumer Credit—Growing Lake and the Card Business

In consumer finance, GECC is most focused in areas where it already has substantial expertise in other parts of the world. It is targeting financial services subsectors with strong long-term growth potential and high margins, or the potential for margins to improve over time. The areas are unsecured consumer lending, the specialty of Lake, and credit cards, provided by Minebea and Koei Credit, as well as GE's own card company.

As we saw in Chapter Eight, Lake is one of top five industry players. Over 90 percent of its $4.4 billion in loans are unsecured, carrying a maximum interest rate of 29.2 percent. GECC is moving quickly to increase its share of market. In the first six months after the acquisition, Lake increased its number of outlets from 597 to 740. This was double the pace of industry leader Takefuji. In the few years before the acquisition, Lake's growth had been constrained by the difficulty of getting funding from Japanese banks, which, for many reasons, had stopped lending. This situation had allowed Aiful to overtake Lake in the industry rankings. Now, backed by the GE Capital Group's funding power, Lake has begun an aggressive loan expansion program. One first step could be to raise average loan levels, which, at some ¥340,000 in mid-1999, were somewhat below its peer group average (*Weekly Toyo Keizai*, July 10, 1999).

GE is well-known for seeking to be number one or number two in its industry sectors. But this is not actually a requirement. What is considered essential is that businesses achieve sufficient scale to be cost competitive and that the business sector promises to deliver continuously attractive growth and profitability. In the card area, we perceive GE still to be a small and relatively weak player. Here is where we should expect more acquisitions.

Residential mortgage financing is on the lips of many GECC executives as a new area of activity. With the big bang, it is possible to conceive of a variety of approaches to the market, including direct marketing. Here GE could either "build" or buy a vehicle.

Life Insurance—Making GE Capital Edison Life Pay

In Jack Welch's GE, not every acquisition is expected to be successful. In fact, failures are smiled upon as evidence that the company continues to take necessary business development risks. GEFA's purchase of the life insurance operations of Toho Life, and the consequent formation of GE Capital Edison Life, show how gutsy GE can be.

The deal itself, as described above, was brilliant. GEFA bought Toho's business franchise without taking on the liability of Toho's past lending and business strategy mistakes. As it happened, even after receiving a huge payment from GE, Toho collapsed under the weight of its bad assets and "negative carry" (see Chapter Five).

What about the new company and its prospects? The company started business in April 1998. The company was awarded a "double A" credit rating by S&P based on the strength of GE. Products offered included the existing products of Toho Life, notably the popular health insurance product, Pegasus. The company sought to differentiate itself by adopting a highly tailored and "special-packaging" approach to the market, providing numerous risk-differentiated rider options (including accident and health policies) to a nondividend-paying whole life policy. This created a relatively low-priced but also customized product. The company introduced a number of new products to the market, including a U.S. dollar fixed return annuity.

In June 1999 GE Capital Edison reported that it had sold $19.5 billion (¥2,333.5 billion) in personal life insurance policies and $55.6 billion (¥6,669.6) in group insurance policies in the year ended March 1999 (*Jiji Press*, June 10, 1999). On March 31, 1999, its assets were $2.7 billion (¥327.6 billion), up 41 percent from the previous year. Outstanding policies totaled $17.6 billion (¥2,116 billion), up from zero. Ordinary profit for the year was $5.8 million (¥700 million). By mid-1999 the company had a total of 2,033 inhouse employees and some 6,693 agents. It operated fifty-eight sub-branches and 487 sales locations.

This dramatic growth suggests that the company knows how to compete in the marketplace and will continue to succeed. The future course of the company, as described by its president, K. Ron Baldwin (*Weekly Toyo Keizai*, July 10, 1999) will be focused on achieving internal growth, rather than growth through acquisitions (where opportunities appear limited). The company will concentrate on increasing volume through existing sales channels by continuing to introduce new products and by increasing the effectiveness of salesmen through training in a consultative selling approach. A second priority is to open new markets by establishing new channels, including a new sales group whose representatives are financial planners. Other new channels would be selling products through banks and securities companies, direct marketing, and the internet.

Leasing and Commercial Finance

Typically, GECC is taking the long view in staking out such a major position in Japan's leasing market. As in other financial sectors, the leasing market in the late 1990s is in trouble. Competition has driven down net financing yields to levels below those needed to cover risks. Contract values have fallen due to declines in new equipment investment, and defaults are on the rise. Many firms are losing money, and consolidation—usually orchestrated by main banks—is prevalent. As noted above, Japan Lease—financially weak itself— was caught in the bankruptcy and nationalization of its parent, LTCB.

As in many sectors, the marketplace is fragmented, with over 300 players. Orix (Chapter Eleven) is the largest Japanese leasing company and the market leader. In Japan almost all leasing has been of the finance lease-type, which is basically collateralized lending. There has been relatively little operating lease-type financing, where the equipment belongs to the leasing company (although Orix is strong in this area). Finance leasing has been largely "plain vanilla" with little except rate to differentiate services. Consolidation has been taking place partly because banks have been increasingly unwilling to finance, or have raised pricing, for leasing companies whose price discounting strategies have caused them to be increasingly unprofitable.

As a GECC company with a AAA credit rating, Japan Lease hopes its low funding costs will help it compete successfully and profitably in the price-driven financial lease marketplace. Also, the company is hoping to build an operating lease business where structuring and service can be differentiators. For these businesses to really take off, changes in the tax laws to provide tax benefits for both lessors and lessees are needed—and are anticipated (*Weekly Toyo Keizai*, July 7, 1999).

In the marketplace for operating leases, Japan Lease is likely to face the toughest competition from Orix. The same applies to the auto leasing marketplace. In 1999 Orix led the market with a fleet of some 170,000 vehicles. Japan Lease Auto was second with about 120,000 vehicles. At these levels, 8.5 percent and 6 percent market shares, respectively, neither company held a dominant position in a highly fragmented market of 375 auto leasing companies. This industry segment will also see significant consolidation in the next few years, which will be an opportunity for further expansion through acquisition that we can expect both GECS and Orix to seize.

In the area of commercial finance, particularly in commercial real estate, we can expect to see more activity from GECS. In this business, vehicles are less important than deal-doing skills, which GECS has evidenced it has in abundance.

GE Capital's Long-Term Strategy

Although it appears broad, the market approach of GE has been in reality relatively narrow. Even with GECS's AAA rating and competitive funding capability, there are sections of Japan's financial marketplace—like commercial banking—where structural issues seem to militate against anyone but the most specialized boutique players making significant returns on capital. As suggested above, GECS has identified a number of market segments that hold the promise of meeting its growth and ROE requirements and has been willing to invest heavily in these segments. We can expect this disciplined but aggressive strategy to continue.

For good business reasons, GECS has a bias for bigness, as well as for action. We can therefore expect to see further acquisitions in existing business areas for the purpose of limiting competition, lower units costs, and creating market presence. In short, we can expect GE Capital to continue to be one of the biggest foreign financial players in Japan.

Chapter Fifteen

High-Tech *Zaitech*: Morgan Stanley Dean Witter and Goldman Sachs

In the late 1980s and early 1990s, partial deregulation and new financial instruments allowed financial firms to create new "financial technologies," called *zaitech* in abbreviated Japanese, which—in the heady atmosphere of the times—were aggressively offered to financial and nonfinancial firm customers. Inevitably, like the times themselves, the term *zaitech* later came to connote speculative and imprudent financial dabbling and quasilegal manipulation of financial books for the purpose of "window dressing."

But *zaitech* was not all bad, and, in the context of big bang deregulation, the concept is making a comeback. New financial technologies, like securitization, are playing an important role in resolving some of the Japanese system's post-bubble structural problems. And the leading sources of the new positive *zaitech* are firms like Morgan Stanley Dean Witter, Goldman Sachs, J.P. Morgan, Salomon Smith Barney, and Merrill Lynch.

In the previous chapter we examined the business of Merrill Lynch. Below we will look closely at the businesses of Morgan Stanley and Goldman Sachs. We will see that these firms are now firmly entrenched in Japan's marketplace, no longer just niche players, but market-moving trading and brokerage powerhouses second only to Japan's Big Three brokers. We will also see that these firms are in the forefront of bringing new *zaitech* solutions to problems and opportunities in the Japanese market, are increasingly winning lead underwriter positions for Japanese corporate bonds, and are—along with Merrill and Salomon—the preferred advisors in cross-border M&A transactions. We saw in Chapter Seven that Goldman has been exceptionally successful in providing asset management products to Japan's retail marketplace. In short, these companies have begun to realize the huge potential of the Japanese marketplace and are positioning themselves at the market's leading edge to grow rapidly in what will certainly be a changed marketplace going forward.

Table 15.1

March 1999 Results of Leading Foreign Securities Companies vs. Nomura

(In Yen billions)	Morgan Stanley Dean Witter	Merrill Lynch	Goldman Sachs	Nomura
Sales revenue	103.0	98.2	85.3	359.3
of which				
Brokerage commission	39.5	22.5	16.7	80.0
Other commission	20.2	31.9	20.8	68.6
Trading profits	25.4	26.4	29.7	97.6
Ordinary income	14.5	11.7	17.6	45.1
Net Income	16.2	9.0	15.9	−241.8
Value of equity trading	17,632	11,574	10,237	28,343
Total staff	838	739	734	9,802

Source: The Nikkei Financial Daily, July 6, 1999.

Morgan Stanley Dean Witter

In 1999 Morgan Stanley Dean Witter was operating in Japan through four principal vehicles. The largest and most important was Morgan Stanley Japan (MSJ) Limited, the securities vehicle established as a branch of a U.S. securities company. Morgan Stanley entered Japan in 1970. MSJ was established in March 1984. The company has a paid-in capital of $300 million and some 838 employees. For the twelve months ended March 31, 1999, this company registered sales revenues of $858 million (¥103 billion) and net income of $135 million (¥16.2 billion) (see Table 15.1).

MSJ is engaged in fund-raising and M&A advisory services for corporations and institutional investors, and equity and fixed income sales, trading, and research. MSJ was the first foreign member of the Tokyo Stock Exchange (TSE), admitted in 1986. MSJ is the largest of the foreign brokerages in Japan, both in terms of revenues and employees. Products include foreign and domestic equities, convertible bonds, warrant bonds, high yield bonds, commercial paper, medium-term notes, futures and options. Table 15.1 shows that in FY1998 the value of equities traded by Morgan Stanley in Japan was $147 billion (¥17.6 trillion), an amount more than half as large as Nomura Securities. In 1998 and 1999 the firm regularly achieved a 6 to 7 percent share of total TSE trading volume, an impressive display of the depth and power of MSJ's trading operations. MSJ serves clients by providing research.

In late 1998 the company had twenty-three analysts in Japan covering over 240 stocks.

Three other Morgan Stanley vehicles are Morgan Stanley Bank, Tokyo Branch, Morgan Stanley Asset & Investment Trust Management, and Morgan Stanley Realty. The bank branch (officially a branch of a bank domiciled in Germany) was established in 1991 as a vehicle through which to handle foreign exchange business and to book derivative (e.g., swaps) positions. Capital is some DM 200 million. In the year ended March 1998 recurring revenues were $383 million and recurring profits $28 million.

Morgan Stanley Asset & Investment Trust Management was established in February 1987 and is capitalized at $225 million. In 1995 the company was the first U.S. company to obtain a dual investment advisory and investment trust management license. The company has produced some twenty funds, including Japanese equities, foreign equities, bonds, and money market products. At the end of May 1999 the company was managing $1.8 billion in mutual funds assets (in investment trusts). At the end of October 1998 it was managing $2.3 billion in pension fund assets under discretionary mandates from mainly public pension funds.

Goldman Sachs

Goldman Sachs operates in Japan with a set of vehicles similar to that of Morgan Stanley. These include Goldman Sachs Securities, Goldman Sachs Bank, Goldman Sachs Investment Advisory Company, and Goldman Sachs Investment Trust Management Goldman opened an office in Tokyo in 1974 and established Goldman Sachs Securities as a branch in 1983. It became a member of the TSE in 1986. Table 15.1 shows the FY1998 performance of Goldman Sachs Securities (GSS). Overall sales revenue was $710 million (¥85.3 billion), ranking the company third among the foreign Big Three brokerages. In ordinary income, before nonrecurring items, however, GSS was the best of the three at $147 million (¥17.6 billion). This was a figure almost half that of Nomura Securities. Total GSS staff was 734 persons, compared with 9,802 for Nomura.

The relatively high profitability of GSS is due to a number of factors, among them strong trading profits, notably in the futures and options derivatives area. We would suggest, however, that the correct view of GSS is of a well-balanced company, with exceptionally strong competitiveness in all its major businesses: equity and debt trading, derivatives, corporate finance, and investment banking (we will highlight some of these areas below).

When the pension fund market was opened to foreign investment advisors in 1991, Goldman moved quickly to establish Goldman Sachs Investment Advisory Company. As of March 1999 this company held a position of fifteenth place among all investment advisors in Japan, with $5.6 billion under discretionary management from public and private sponsors (see Chapter Six for details). Goldman Sachs Investment Trust Management Company, established in 1996, clearly perceived the needs of Japanese distributors— securities companies like Nikko and Kokusai—for new products and active product support, and experienced explosive sales growth. At the end of May 1999 the company had achieved a leading position among foreign mutual funds companies, with assets under management topping $12.1 billion (see details in Chapter Seven).

Relationship Building in the 1990s

During the 1990s the leading foreign, especially U.S., securities firms took advantage of strong overseas, and especially U.S., debt and equity markets to help Japanese companies raise or refinance debt and equity capital. It was common for one of the big three U.S. firms to be chosen, along with one of the Big Three Japanese securities firms, as joint global coordinator for any large international issues. For example, Goldman Sachs was joint global coordinator for the international equity offering of Japan Tobacco (JT). In placements of Japanese Yankee bond debt in the U.S. markets, often a lead management role was within reach. Goldman Sachs won such a role for NTT in Japan's largest Yankee issue. The firms also began to make progress selling advisory services to Japanese companies engaging in acquisitions or divestitures in overseas markets, particularly the United States.

Goldman Sachs helped its traditional customers Sumitomo Trust, IBJ, and Fuji Bank raise funds through private equity placements in the United States in the first quarter of 1999.

Leading the Market in High-Profit Securitization and M&A

In 1998 and 1999 Morgan Stanley and Goldman Sachs (together with Merrill Lynch, Salomon Smith Barney, and, to a less extent, J.P. Morgan) originated transactions and captured deals that showed that they were now in a new marketplace category. For any doubters, it was now clear that these firms were no longer marginal niche players on the periphery of main business and deal trends. They were key players at the center of mainstream market trends— often, through their technical knowhow and delivery capability, the originators of the trends. These companies were now taking business that would five years before have been handed to Japanese relationship banks. Now, in many cases, the Japanese banks were not even competitors.

Purchase and Sale of Nonperforming Loan Assets

Table 15.2 shows a particular area of activity by foreign financial firms, in which Goldman Sachs and Merrill Lynch are particularly prominent. This is the purchase of nonperforming assets from Japanese financial institutions. In the fiscal year April 1998 to March 1999, the total book value of such purchases was some $66.7 billion (¥8 trillion). The main sellers were Japanese banks receiving injections of public funds. Investment banks like Goldman Sachs and Merrill Lynch, as well as vulture funds, like Lonestar of the United States, raised investor funds totaling over $1 billion and were actively buying distressed assets. In FY98 Goldman Sachs reportedly took the largest market share in purchase of unsecured loans (*The Nikkei Financial Daily*, March 23, 1999).

The assets also include real estate (Table 15.2). Here both Goldman and Morgan Stanley have been institutional buyers. In many cases, these assets have been securitized, that is, legally converted to collateral backing newly issued securities which, usually, have been placed with other institutional investors. The first public securitization of a Japanese commercial mortgages transaction, closed in March 1999, arose from the purchase by Morgan Stanley Real Estate Fund of condominium units from Daikyo, Inc., a leading property developer (Table 15.2). The ¥9.9 billion acquisition was financed by a loan from Morgan Guaranty Trust, for which repayment was arranged through issuance of ¥6.5 billion in three-year bonds. The bonds would be redeemed by sale of the condo units.

M&A and Privatization Advisory

In 1999 Japan's financial market was shaken by a number of major M&A transactions. The shock was not from the transactions themselves, but from the fact that the business of advising the principals had been taken exclusively by foreign firms. To Japanese banks and securities companies, this was chilling proof that the foreigners were now perceived as at least equal, if not superior in their ability to meet the needs of corporate customers in complex transactions in the Japanese marketplace.

Specifically, in the transaction in which Renault made a $5.4 billion investment in Nissan Motors, Renault retained Merrill Lynch, and Nissan retained Nikko Salomon Smith Barney. In March 1999 Sony Corporation undertook a $2.6 billion all-share acquisition of three affiliated companies. This was the first stock swap transaction in Japan, newly allowed under the amended Company Law. Sony retained Merrill Lynch as advisor; the affiliates retained Morgan Stanley. In the first quarter, JT acquired

Table 15.2

Bulk Purchases of Nonperforming Assets and Real Estate by Foreign Investors

Buyer	Seller	Book value (Yen billions)
Second half FY1997		
Goldman Sachs	Sumitomo Bank	40.0
Bankers Trust/Deutsche Bank	Crown Leasing	280.0
Goldman Sachs	Tokyo-Mitsubishi Bank	12.5
Lonestar	Tokyo-Mitsubishi Bank	20.0
Unknown	Sanwa Bank	150.0
Merrill Lynch/Lonestar	Sanwa Bank	400.0
Secured	Mitsui Trust	130.0
Unknown	Sumitomo Bank	100.0
Second half FY 1998		
J.P. Morgan/U.S. Daiwa Securities	Tokyo-Mitsubishi Bank	100.0
Merrill Lynch/Lonestar	Sanwa Bank	30.0
Merrill Lynch/Lonestar	Fuji Bank	50.0
Unknown	DKB	200.0
Unknown	Sumitomo Bank	60.0

Purchase of Real Estate by Foreign Investors

Sales date	Buyer	Seller	Property	Price (Yen billions)
Mar 98	Goldman Sachs	Yamato Life Insurance	Head office building	50.0
Mar 98	Morgan Stanley	Daikyo	1,184 Rental apartment units	9.9
Feb 99	AIG/Mitsui Real Estate	Japan Energy	Head office building	70.0
Mar 99	Goldman Sachs	Toho Life Insurance	Head office building	30.0

Source: The Nikkei Financial Daily, March 23, 1999.

the overseas tobacco operations of RJR Nabisco for $8.5 billion. JT retained Nikko Salomon Smith Barney as advisor; RJR Nabisco retained Morgan Stanley. NTT hired Goldman Sachs to advise on its intended acquisition of International Digital Communications (ultimately bought by Cable & Wireless). When Sumitomo Rubber negotiated a tie-up with Goodyear, Sumitomo retained Warburg Dillon Reed as advisor, and Goodyear retained Morgan Stanley.

Over the years, Goldman Sachs and Morgan Stanley had played large and small roles in many M&A transactions involving Japan and Japanese companies, but the scale and number of deals in 1999 seemed to indicate a quantitative and qualitative leap forward in these firms' tier position. In 1998 the number of M&A transactions involving Japanese companies reached a historic high of 834 (*Nihon Keizai Shimbun*, April 26, 1999). This was an indication of the restructuring going in the Japanese economy, the pace of which will certainly accelerate, creating more opportunities for foreign advisors, particularly when a principal is involved. Another reason foreign advisors will gain share was observed in the Sony deal (*Asian Wall Street Journal*, May 7–8, 1999). Some 40 percent of Sony stock is held by large foreign institutional investors. Fear that foreign shareholders might file lawsuits if M&A terms and conditions were perceived to be inimical to their interests was a reason for selecting foreign advisors, whose advice on these issues would surely be more reliable than that of Japanese companies. With foreign ownership of Japanese companies through public share purchases rising, foreign advisors are likely to find many more Japanese managements turning to foreign firms for M&A advice.

In the M&A area, Goldman Sachs has been particularly successful in privatization advisory, a highly prestigious and lucrative specialty. In 1999 Goldman advised the Japanese government on the sale of Long Term Credit Bank's $11 billion worth of U.S. assets and advised the Tokyo court on disposal of Japan Lease's operations. In 1998 Goldman was global coordinator, along with Nikko Securities, for the $18 billion global IPO for NTT DoCoMo (the mobile telephone company). Morgan Stanley expects to begin sharing with Nomura the privatization advisory field in an IPO transaction for Japan Railway East.

Underwriting of Domestic Bond Issues

On April 15, 1999, NTT—the Japanese telephone company—issued a ¥120 billion ten-year straight bond in the domestic market. NTT may be the most prestigious—as well as the largest—issuer in corporate Japan. Given its origins, NTT is considered a quasisovereign issuer, the virtual embodiment of "Japan, Inc." What was remarkable about this bond issue, and what caused a great stir in the marketplace, was that NTT selected as the administrative book-runner and lead manager for the issue a foreign securities company, Goldman Sachs. This was a first for NTT and a major achievement for Goldman. The co-lead underwriters for this transaction were Goldman Sachs, Morgan Stanley, and IBJ Securities. What shook the market was the realization that foreign houses, and particularly Goldman Sachs, had dominated this major bond issue and that the Big Three domestic houses had been ex-

Table 15.3

Lead Management of Domestic Straight Bonds by Foreign Firms

Lead manager	Issuer	Date	Amount (Yen billions)	Position
Goldman Sachs	NKK	June 88	10	Co-lead
	NTT	June 98	100	Co-lead
	Chubu Electric	July 98	30	Co-lead
	Toyota Motor	September 98	50	Co-lead
	Chubu Electric	January 99	30	Co-lead
	NTT	April 99	120	Sole lead
Morgan Stanley	Sumitomo Electric	May 98	10	Sole lead
	Mitsubishi Corp.	November 98	70	Sole lead
	Mitsubishi Corp.	January 99	15	Sole lead
	NTT	March 99	70	Co-lead
	ACOM	April 99	10	Sole lead
Merrill Lynch	Toyota Motor	February 98	50	Co-lead
	Toyota Motor	February 98	150	Co-lead
	New Nippon Steel	May 98	10	Sole lead
	Mitsubishi Corp.	May 98	50	Sole lead
	Toyota Motor	July 98	100	Co-lead

Source: The Nikkei Financial Daily, April 16, 1999.

cluded. NTT managers were quoted as saying that Goldman and Morgan Stanley were chosen because they had proven to be highly professional and adept at managing liquidity of NTT issues in the secondary market. Morgan Stanley had been involved in eight previous NTT issues (*The Nikkei Financial Daily*, April 16, 1999).

In recent years, Goldman, Morgan Stanley, and Merrill Lynch have built track record and tier position with large utility issuers (Table 15.3). In January 1999 Goldman Sachs was the first foreign firm to play a sole-lead underwriter role for another big straight bond issuer, Chubu Electric Power. In 1999 Goldman was named along with Merrill Lynch as a lead underwriter-designate by Tokyo Electric Power.

The Japanese domestic bond issue market, which is vastly larger than the international issue market, is a market where foreign securities firms are aggressively seeking to expand. In the year ended March 1999, foreign firms acted as co-lead or lead underwriters for $2.7 billion (¥318.3 billion) in domestic straight bond issues, a 3 percent share of the market. This compares with $375 million, or 0.5 percent of the market, in the previous fiscal year. Goldman Sachs, Morgan Stanley, and Merrill Lynch have been able to win an increasing number of mandates, based on their experience and, particularly, on their exceptionally strong market trading and placement capabilities. We can expect continued increases in market share and tier position from these companies, as well as from competitors like J.P. Morgan and Nikko Salomon Smith Barney.

No Stopping the Leaders

Is there any stopping the leading foreign firms, Goldman Sachs, Morgan Stanley, Merrill Lynch, and others, in Japan's new marketplace? It is hard to see how. After two decades of steady progress, these firms have developed experience, scale, management knowhow, and, increasingly, relationships, that seem unbeatable. In every transaction and sales pitch, it remains necessary for the companies to compete, including in "soft" areas like relationship. But now this competition is increasingly being conducted on the basis of "equality"—that is, objectively, without favoritism, on the merits—with local firms. After many years when this was not the case, veterans in the foreign financial industry are feeling good about themselves and their futures.

Chapter Sixteen

Aiming High and Low: American Express and Associates First Capital

The rich opportunities of the Japanese marketplace are well evidenced by the fortunes of two firms that have targeted customers on different ends of the socioeconomic ladder. American Express has established itself as the premier "status" card in the Japanese market through sedulous cultivation of both its "card members" and vendors. Associates First Capital has, on the other hand, built a business catering to a cash-strapped and impulse-driven clientele whose main priorities are convenience and confidentiality. In both cases, the companies have achieved highly profitable and defensible market positions which they continue to strengthen by employing a mixture of locally grown and imported skills, people, and knowhow. Let us take a closer look at these two companies and their businesses.

American Express

American Express (AMEX) traces its business origins in Japan to 1917, but the key year in the postwar history was 1954, when the company reentered Japan, establishing what would become the card company, American Express International, and the banking unit, American Express Bank. Through the 1980s and 1990s AMEX's objective in Japan was primarily building its card business. Other business lines—banking, travel, and, particularly, travelers' checks—were important contributors of revenues at certain times during this period. But by the late 1990s, primarily for market reasons, they had all declined to insignificance.

In 1999 the core of AMEX's business was the card company, run through the legal vehicle American Express International, Inc., a branch of the head office company with offices in the Ogikubo suburb of Tokyo and in Osaka. Organizationally within AMEX, the business was part of the global Travel Related Services (TRS) group. This business employed some 700 people and in the year ended March 31,1998, reported $42.3 million in pretax earnings (*The Consumer Credit Monthly*, November 1998), up 40 percent from the previous fiscal year. American Express Bank still maintained a 20-man branch in Tokyo, but its business was limited to correspondent banking and it was losing money.

In 1997, AMEX established in Tokyo a small office of American Express Asset Management International (AEAMI) and obtained an investment advisory license. With one portfolio manager, one trader, and a small analytical group, this office was charged with picking Japanese stocks to constitute the Japanese equity component of global equity portfolios (either mutual funds or assets managed for institutional clients, like pension funds) managed by American Express in either the United States or Europe. In August 1999 AEAMI announced that it would enter the Japanese pension fund market, that is, it would begin to seek pension fund management mandates from Japanese pension sponsors. A conservative five-year goal of $1 billion under management was indicated (*Nihon Keizai Shimbun*, August 4, 1999). In December 1998 AMEX established its retail financial services company, American Express Financial Advisors (Japan) in Tokyo (this writer was the first company representative). This company, with some twenty employees, registered as a securities company in January 1999 and began direct mail offerings of mutual funds to AMEX card members in March.

For most of the 1980s and 1990s, the strategy and the revenue-driver for AMEX in Japan was the card business. In 1980 the AMEX Gold Card was launched in Japan. In 1983 AMEX issued its standard Green Card in Japan. By 1990 the company had issued one million cards and was targeting growth to five million cards by the end of the decade. In 1991 the company launched the Optima revolving credit card. In 1993 it began offering Platinum Cards in Japan and introduced a membership incentive program, Membership Plus.

In November 1997 AMEX tied up with Credit Saison to launch a co-branded card. This tie-up was extended in February 1999 with a further tie-up with the Postal System (post offices) and the Postal Savings system (*Yucho*), making the card an AMEX, Saison, and *Yucho* joint card. The added value was access to the post offices' extensive cash dispenser system for cash advances.

The Privileges and Costs of AMEX Membership

The brand and image consciousness of Japanese society is something every foreigner finds unique. AMEX early on sought to exploit this cultural trait by positioning the AMEX card as the most prestigious card in the market, endeavoring to give the impression that AMEX "membership" proffers privileges not available from other card companies. Certainly the company's

Membership Plus program has been effective in this respect. The program offers one "point" for each ¥100 in spending. Accumulations of 5,000 points (from spending of about $4,200) permit redemptions of services, such as a dinner at a good restaurant or discounts at hotels. Points can be converted into mileage on a one-to-one basis and used in the frequent flyer programs of seven airlines, including Japan Airlines (JAL). Other privileges include an exclusive magazine (*Impressions*) with distinct editions for Green, Gold, and Platinum card members. AMEX has been unusually effective at cultivating and signing up merchants to accept the AMEX card. The company has some 500,000 merchant relationships in Japan. The ubiquity of AMEX merchants obviously is convenient for card members. It may also be reassuring for the many members who value prestige but desire to be associated with a major brand.

One of AMEX's unique market positioning features is its premier international and travel card. AMEX's "value proposition" for card members has been heavily weighted toward international travel and travel-related services, such as travel insurance. In the late 1990s the company in Japan obtained a nonlife insurance license and began selling Cigna travel insurance to members by mail. The AMEX travel service is also available to members.

One marketing technique has been to make the AMEX card relatively expensive. The standard Green Card carries an annual membership fee of $87.50 (¥10,500), the Gold Card charges $192.50 (¥23,100) and the Platinum Card charges a lofty $675 (¥81,000). For standard and Gold cards, AMEX's charge is at least double the fees charged by other firms. There is no card in the market with positioning or fees comparable to the Platinum Card.

How AMEX Makes Money

As explained in Chapter Eight, revenues of credit card companies in Japan come from four sources: financing of purchases (revolving sales credit); consumer lending (cash advances); vendors' commissions (called "interchange" in the business); and card member fees, principally annual membership fees. AMEX's traditional market positioning and strategy have meant that it has emphasized the last two revenue sources, doing little to develop the first two. (The Optima Card business was not actively developed initially and was later discontinued.) AMEX has been uniquely successful at building strong revenue streams on vendor commissions (at rates reportedly higher than other card companies) and membership fees. But current AMEX management is keen to find ways to break into the cash advance and revolving credit markets.

One new source of revenue has been sales commissions from the vendor (Cigna) for AMEX's sales of travel insurance to its card members. This reportedly has been a strong and growing revenue stream.

Some Challenges Ahead

Notwithstanding its unique and successful market position, AMEX has some problems. One is that its population of card members is too small (the company has dramatically failed to achieve its early five million member target) and the profile is increasingly problematic. While AMEX card members are typically above average in income and spending, they are older and more often male than is ideal. Another problem is that AMEX's revenue streams are too narrowly concentrated in the fees and merchant commissions areas.

These problems have been evident for years. In the mid-1990s AMEX hired a consultant, Bain & Company, to help devise a medium-term growth strategy. The conclusion was that AMEX should seek to expand in Japan through "strategic alliances" with large local companies. AMEX approached many companies and entered into many discussions. The one concrete result was the tie-up with Credit Saison. That arrangement has allowed Credit Saison—which has many young, particularly female, customers in Japan, but weak international affiliations—to offer a card that is convenient for overseas travel. AMEX has been given the opportunity to expand its customer base into a younger, more female market segment.

In hindsight, however, the strategy of tying up with local companies was probably a costly diversion. Alliances with local companies usually disappoint, and the Credit Saison deal seems no exception. Prior to 1999, the last significant new product launched by AMEX was its Platinum Card in 1993. As of 1999, the alliance strategy had been discarded and a number of new product programs were being put in place.

New Initiatives—Mutual Funds, Insurance, Credit Cards and Lending

In 1999 and 2000 we can expect AMEX to roll out a number of major new initiatives designed to increase the number of card members and its revenues per member. There will also be an expansion of products and services. As of mid-1999 AMEX had already integrated the marketing strategy of American Express Financial Advisors (Japan) (AEFAJ) with TRS's own strategy. The securities company was mailing its mutual funds offerings directly and exclusively to AMEX card members, offering card members preferred terms and the ability to earn Membership Plus points on balances in AEFAJ mutual funds accounts. It was planned that during 2000 AEFAJ would begin to offer some exclusive financial planning services to card members.

AMEX's highly successful experience in selling accident insurance to card members by mail is expected to encourage the company to expand this business to other nonlife or even to life insurance areas. TRS could use its agency license to this end. AEFAJ could also be licensed to sell insurance.

In August 1999 AMEX announced that it would soon begin offering revolving credit cards and secured lending services. AMEX was tying up with vendors to provide financing (shopping credit) using its cards. It was also sending out solicitations to corporate card holders, offering to provide lines of credit for such purposes as office equipment financing (*Nihon Keizai Shimbun*, August 7, 1999).

AMEX, with its well-recognized brand and prestige image, has a highly valuable and defensible franchise in Japan. In the future we should see AMEX do more to exploit this advantage.

Associates First Capital (AIC Japan)

Little known to most Americans, Associates First Capital is a NYSE-listed company and one of the biggest and most successful providers of subprime consumer loans, commercial finance, and leasing in the U.S. marketplace. The company was first listed in 1937 but was acquired by Gulf + Western in 1968, then sold to Ford Motor Company in 1989. In 1996 Ford offered 19.3 percent of the company to the public through a relisting on the NYSE. In 1998 the company was fully spun off by Ford and became independent.

The growth of Associates First Capital has been phenomenal. It has recorded increased revenues and profits for 24 consecutive years. In 1998 before-tax profits were $1.9 billion, up 18 percent, and after-tax profits were $1.2 billion, up 19 percent over 1997. The company had operating assets of $80.9 billion, including $71.3 billion in loans. It operated 2,522 offices and employed 28,662 people. In 1998 some 12 percent of Associates's loan volume and 16 percent of its gross revenues came from operations outside the United States. Almost all of this growth was from Japan, where Associates has operated since 1979 under the name of AIC Corporation.

Growing Internally and Through Acquisitions

In the 1980s, when Citibank was executing a highly demanding niche strategy in the overly competitive and low-return large corporate market, AIC was building a foundation and steadily growing its business in the exceptionally lucrative, high margin and underserved low tier, unsecured consumer lending market (see Chapter Eight). The nonbank consumer lending market was first opened to foreign companies in 1977. The leading U.S. companies in the field, including Household Finance, AVCO, and Beneficial, all entered the market (as did several foreign banks, including Citibank and Security Pacific), by establishing finance company subsidiaries. By 1987, Associates had bought out the operations of all the U.S. nonbank affiliates' competitors. (In 1999 Associates acquired the rest of AVCO's operations around the world.)

Associates has grown the business of AIC steadily. Like GE Capital, the company has pursued growth both internally and through acquisitions. In 1998 alone, the company made two major acquisitions. It bought from Daiei retail store chain, which was in financial trouble, DIC Finance, an Osaka-based company ranked fifteenth in the industry by pretax profits ($96.3 million in the year ended February 1998), reportedly paying $615 million. DIC had some $1.5 billion in loan assets, 208 branches and some 1,200 employees. AIC also bought out a small company based in Shizuoka, Nissen Company, with $198 million in loans (to some 65,000 customers), thirty-five branches, and 200 employees. After these acquisitions, by the end of 1998 AIC had achieved a sixth-ranked position in the market behind Lake (GE Capital) in terms of loan assets, with $4.2 billion on the books (see Table 8.1). In terms of profits, AIC was a clear number five behind the four leading Japanese companies, Takefuji, ACOM, Promise, and Aiful.

Unlimited Room for Expansion

Associates continues to look for acquisition opportunities in the consumer finance market. The field is wide open, with many companies focused on local markets and possessing small overall shares (see Chapter Eight). Also, many of the companies are going through generational transitions. Owners who founded the companies in the 1950s and 1960s are choosing between passing the business to heirs and selling out. In many cases, they are inclined to take a cash offer.

Unlike the industry leader, Takefuji, which offers only cash loans, AIC, as well as making cash loans, offers real estate loans, essentially home equity loans (about half of its portfolio is secured by real estate), and, through a subsidiary, issues credit cards and offers installment sales financing. AIC is expanding its ATM and cash dispenser service network. Understanding well the profit-building opportunities in credit card service delivery, the company has innovated such profit-generating ways as making revolving credit—that is, a loan—the "default" on its card.

This is one example of the management competence that has been the key factor in AIC's expansion. AIC has successfully transplanted from the United States and localized credit and operations management systems. Impressively, it has managed to achieve what many foreign companies aspire to but ultimately fail at: being a Japanese-style company—especially in the view of the marketplace—while maintaining U.S. standards of profitability, risk control, and accountability. Despite Japan's weak economy and an increasing trend in personal bankruptcies, AIC has managed to keep credit costs within standard limits and to increase business.

The Key Success Driver—Managing the Cultural Gap

What may be most remarkable about the achievements of American Express and Associates First Capital in Japan is how they have, through years of effort and selective localization, managed to bridge the cultural gap between Japan and the United States. We would offer the same comment about such other successful U.S. companies as Citibank and AIG. These companies, over many years, have consistently and mostly profitably applied the innovative approaches and proactive, opportunistic management philosophies of their U.S. parent companies to the often highly particular market and personnel situations in Japan. The challenge is evident in the case of Associates, whose customer base is 100 percent Japanese and largely blue-collar. This makes its accomplishment all the more impressive.

In short, the most successful U.S. companies, represented by AMEX and Associates, have shown that the substantial cultural differences between Japan and the United States are not real barriers to business prosperity in Japan. On the contrary, foreign perspectives and skills applied to the Japanese market often seem the recipe for industry-leading performance.

Chapter Seventeen

Proven (and Unproven) Winners: Fidelity, AFLAC, Prudential, DLJ Direct

Surveying Japan's financial marketplace, the observer is often surprised to find foreign, usually American, firms occupying large and profitable market positions, as well as smaller, but still highly profitable niches, in principal business segments. The observer may be further surprised to learn that a company has occupied its leading position for many years and that, outside of the United States, Japan is the largest and most profitable marketplace for the company's services. In the preceding chapter we examined the business operations of two companies, American Express and Associates First Capital. Below we will look at several more companies for which the Japanese market already is, or promises to be, their biggest and most lucrative market outside the United States.

Fidelity Investments

In the mid-1990s Fidelity Investment's management made a strategic decision to invest heavily and seek to establish a major position in the Japanese mutual funds market. From this decision followed a two-pronged approach to the marketplace: (1) *indirect selling of mutual funds through distributors* (until December 1999, securities companies; after December 1999, through securities companies, city and regional banks, and a few insurance companies, including Sony Life); and (2) *direct selling via advertising and telephone service centers.*

A Two-Pronged Approach to the Market

By 1999, only three years after starting in earnest, by virtue of its extensive newspaper advertising—intended to support both direct and indirect sales strategies—and of the stellar performance of most of its funds, Fidelity had succeeded in achieving a significant market position. For the U.S. head office, Fidelity Investments, Japan was now, along with Canada, the major overseas market and the largest growth opportunity in the world.

Not surprisingly, however, the results of the two-pronged approach varied. Selling through brokers turned out, as expected, to be fast and easy. In 1995 Fidelity began selling its Fidelity Japan Open fund through Nomura Securities, and in 1996 it offered Fidelity High Yield Bond Open through Nikko Securities. These Japanese brokerages were in need of attractive products and Fidelity was prepared to pay the distributors attractive commissions generally all of the 3 percent sales load and a "trail" of up to half of the 1 to 1.5 percent annual management fee. Sales were brisk.

The direct channel was more problematic. Without salesmen or a recognized brand, Fidelity made slow progress in attracting direct customers. At the end of 1998 its direct customer base numbered only some 6,000 clients, hardly a critical mass. Later the company began outbound telemarketing to try to increase new accounts and sales, but progress was still slow.

A key problem, or contradiction, in Fidelity's approach, was its dual channel. Inevitably, as long as distributors remain the major sales channel, Fidelity is forced to think first of the needs of its brokerage relationships and only second and indirectly about the market. For example, with respect to sales load, in 1999 Fidelity was charging 3 percent basic sales load for its equity funds, whether the funds were purchased through a broker like Nomura or directly from the company. The relationship with distributors—to whom it was necessary for Fidelity to surrender the entire sales load, plus an ongoing trailer—effectively foreclosed the option for Fidelity of discounting loads or ongoing fees for direct customers. Keeping direct channel sales loads at parity with distributors has stunted the development of this channel, while doing little to ensure that Nomura, Nikko, and other Japanese brokerages would not over time develop their own proprietary funds and decide to scale back their efforts to sell Fidelity's products.

Institutional and Individual Business Organization

In the United States, Fidelity is both a retail mutual funds company selling products directly to investors and a wholesale provider of asset management services to corporations and other institutions, for both institutional assets and employees' 401(k) plans. Having designated Japan (along with Canada) its second most important strategic market, the company is pursuing development of both its core businesses in the Japanese market.

Fidelity got its start in Japan as far back as 1969, when the company opened an office to begin analyzing Japanese stocks as part of its global investment business. In 1986 Fidelity joined with other foreign firms to be among the first to establish an investment advisory firm, targeting the institutional pension fund market. In 1987 this company was licensed to offer discretionary asset management services.

Fidelity formally entered the investment trust (mutual fund) business onshore when it obtained an investment trust management (ITM) license in 1995. This business was limited to selling to Japanese distributors, since an ITM company could not sell directly. Now, with the combined ability to offer investment advisory services and investment trusts, the company changed its name to Fidelity Investments Japan Limited (FIJL).

To execute its direct marketing retail strategy, Fidelity needed a securities company—the only company able to distribute mutual funds to retail investors until December 1998. Hence, in June 1997, Fidelity obtained a broker/dealer license and formally launched the Tokyo office of a new company, Fidelity Brokerage Services (Japan) Ltd.

Institutional and Retail Business Development

As an institutional and pension fund asset manager, Fidelity Investments was relatively inactive in the first years of its existence. The reasons were restricted access to and low profitability of the Japanese pension market. Until the mid-1990s the 5-3-3-2 rule (see Chapter Six) substantially restricted the proportion of funds which pension sponsors could place with firms like Fidelity, who were specialists in offshore markets, and many pension sponsors were prohibited by regulation from placing funds with other than trust banks and insurance companies. Liberalization in 1996 and 1997 provided greater access to public and private pension fund sponsors, but the reluctance of sponsors (especially public funds) to pay reasonable management fees cooled Fidelity's interest.

All this began to change in 1998 and 1999. In Japan's effectively zero interest rate environment and faced with severely declining investment results, private pension sponsors began actively to seek out the services of foreign asset managers. And they began to pay real management fees. In this more interesting market environment, Fidelity began to actively pursue pension fund mandates, particularly from private funds (public funds still declined to pay decent fees). As a consequence, in the period March to September 1998 Fidelity increased assets under management for private pension sponsors by 61 percent to $1.9 billion (public fund assets were still zero). By the end of March 1999 the amount was $2.36 billion, up 103 percent from the year before, again all from private sponsors (Nenkin Joho, July 5, 1999). This volume placed Fidelity in twenty-fifth place among all investment advisors.

Whatever its complications, Fidelity's retail mutual funds sales strategy has been successful. By the end of May 1999 funds in Fidelity's stock investment trusts totaled $2.9 billion, placing Fidelity in eighth position among all ITM companies and third among foreign competitors, behind Goldman Sachs, Alliance Capital, and Merrill Lynch Mercury. (In Chapter Seven we observed that Fidelity was ranked eighteenth in volume among all ITM companies. This is in terms of outstandings of both stock and bond investment trusts, the latter being heavily weighted in yen money market funds, which Fidelity did not offer at the time.)

In sum, in both institutional and retail markets, Fidelity has been remarkably focused and successful.

Fidelity's Product and Service Lineup

In April 1998 Fidelity began to offer a family of funds through both its direct brokerage and indirect distributor channels. As of mid-1999 the company was offering ten funds under its Japanese ITM license. These funds were Fidelity Japan Growth, Fidelity Japan Small-Company, Fidelity Global, Fidelity European Equity, Fidelity American Premium Equity, Fidelity Asia Equity, Fidelity Balanced, Fidelity U.S. High Yield, Fidelity Multi-Income, and Fidelity U.S. Short Term Government Securities.

In late 1998 and the first half of 1999 Fidelity scored major market advances, through both direct and indirect market channels and with both institutional and retail clients. The reason was the extraordinary performance of its Japanese equity funds. The Japan Growth Fund, established in April 1998, at the end of its first year had gained 12.7 percent in value, compared with 2.2 percent for the benchmark TOPIX (broad Japan stock market) index. The Japan Small-Company Fund had done even better, racking up growth of 64.7 percent in its first 12 months ending March 31, 1999, compared with the benchmark of 18.2 percent. The growth fund was managed by an American, Jay Talbott, who became something of a guru. The small-company fund was managed by an equally (or more) talented Japanese.

When, in the fourth quarter of 1998, the Japanese stock market began to recover after sinking to record post-bubble depths, Fidelity was well positioned to capture a surge of renewed individual and institutional, domestic and international interest in the Japanese market. The stock-picking skills of its research group, numbering some eighteen analysts covering some thousand companies, were also an important part of its marketing success. This group was managed in a separate legal vehicle, Fidelity Management and Research (Far East) Ltd., which was directly linked to Fidelity's global research organization.

Approaching the 401(k) Market

In late July 1999 Fidelity surprised the market by announcing that it would refrain from joining one of the three major groupings that were developing systems for record-keeping in advance of the introduction of 401(k)-type pension plans in fall 2000. Rather, Fidelity would separately approach the market offering its own system.

This was certainly a novel approach, but it reflected Fidelity's experience and capabilities developed in the United States. As a Fidelity executive explained it to the author, few record keepers in the United States make money from the service, and it is easy to lose money. This was a particular risk when offering record-keeping services to small companies, which are very likely to be a major part of the customer base of the three major groupings. Fidelity was unwilling to join a group of novices in Japan whose market strategy was unclear and whose development budget seemed to be open-ended.

Fidelity's gutsy decision was to convert its U.S.-origin 401(k) plan servicing technology to fit the Japanese market by developing a new "front end" system and then to target sponsor segments where profits could be expected. This was likely to be among a select tier of professional companies and associations, like those of doctors and lawyers.

Fidelity's logic seemed to make great sense. It was positioning itself to win (or not to lose) in two ways. Developing a profitable 401(k) plan administration business with its targeted approach, would certainly advance its position in the market. In any event, Fidelity would still be positioned to provide funds and manage assets (probably the only real way to make money) for all three of the system development groupings and to avoid associating with one to the exclusion of others. Fidelity was positioning itself to win in the new 401(k) plan market, no matter what. It was an opportunistic approach that had served the company well thus far and would probably continue to do so.

AFLAC–American Family Life Insurance

In fall 1999 American Family Life (AFLAC) marked its twenty-fifth year of doing business in Japan as a branch of the Georgia-based head office. The Japan branch mounted a publicity campaign to advertise this occasion, pointing with pride to its accomplishments. The company's pride is justified by its achievements. It has for many years been the largest foreign life insurance company in Japan (Alico has been number two) and in many ways the most distinguished.

For NYSE-listed AFLAC, which ranks twenty-third in the United States in total assets and twelfth in premium revenues, its Japanese business is not just an important division. Rather, with its Japanese business contributing some 90 percent of AFLAC's entire assets and some 80 percent of profits, it may be more accurate to call AFLAC a Japanese company.

A Record of Continuous Growth and Innovation in the "Third Sector"

As of March 31, 1999, the Japan company's total assets stood at $21.3 billion (¥2,550.4 billion), up 12.9 from the previous year. (Total AFLAC assets were $31.2 billion at December 31, 1998.) Premium income was up 7.2 percent. This was the twenty-fourth continuous year of double-digit asset growth. Ordinary profit before tax in Japan totaled $540 million (¥64.2 billion), up 16.6 percent from the previous year. (For the total corporation in 1998, net income was $486 million.)

A month after establishing its Japan office in October 1974, American Family began to offer cancer insurance, the first company in the market to do so. Subsequently, the company continued to focus on the "third sector" between life and nonlife products (see Chapter Five), being the first company to introduce nursing care and specialized medical care insurance for such conditions as dementia as a supplement to Japan's national health care system. In 1999 the company further broke new ground by offering an insurance policy for persons who had developed but subsequently recovered from cancer. By the late 1990s, American Family had an overwhelming 90 percent share of the cancer insurance market.

In the year ended March 1999 the company had 14.3 million policies outstanding, including 13.1 million cancer policies. New premium revenues from individual policies were up 28.5 percent to $3.5 billion, a performance better than that of any Japanese insurer. The company was also proud to announce that in the previous year it had paid out in claims for hospital expenses $1 billion, an average of $4 million a day. American Family's was the highest level of hospital claims paid in the industry, not just for this year, but in every year since 1995 (*Nihon Keizai Shimbun,* July 26, 1999).

Nurturing Agent Associates and Developing New Channels

From the beginning, American Family concentrated on selling through independent agents, called "associates." In 1998 these associates numbered over 20,000 persons in 5,200 offices nationwide. The company also operated directly some seventy-seven offices around the country in 1998. In-house employees numbered some 1,750 in 1999.

In January 1998, in response to competition, American Family set up a direct marketing department and in March established a sales call center.

Strong Head Office Support and Consistent Localized Management

What have been the keys to American Family's success? Getting into the market early was clearly important. Next was its focused and persistent development of specific Japanese market niches and continuing innovation, supported by head office technology transfer.

Also critical to the company's success was the continuity and market knowledge provided by a cadre of senior local managers. American Family Life has, since its beginning, presented itself as a "pure Japanese company." It is a model which other companies might profitably adopt.

Prudential Life Insurance

Prudential Insurance Company is the largest life insurer in the United States. In Japan, Prudential Life Insurance K.K., with total assets of $2.8 billion (¥333.1 billion) and outstanding policies of $89 billion, is number three in its category of foreign life companies (behind American Family and Alico). In the year ended March 31, 1999, the company expanded rapidly, increasing assets by 37.9 percent and policies-in-force by $14.3 billion or 18.9 percent. Ordinary pretax profits were low at $5 million, evidencing the company's heavy investments in people and in product and market development.

Early Entrant with New-to-Market "Consultative Selling" Approach

Prudential first entered the Japanese market in August 1979 by setting up a joint venture with Sony Corporation. In addition to capital, Prudential contributed to the joint venture a number of insurance products and management knowhow, introducing into the "hard sell," "product-driven" insurance marketplace the concept of "needs-based consultative selling."

Like several other life insurance joint ventures at the time (see Chapter Five), the Prudential-Sony marriage ended in divorce in July 1987. Prudential progressively sold its ownership in the joint venture to interests arranged by Sony. The majority Sony-owned company, Sony Life, continued to develop using many of the techniques learned from Prudential.

After deciding to break with Sony, Prudential established Prudential Life Insurance as a Japanese company in October 1987. Since its inception, Prudential Life has steadily pursued and refined its unique style of "needs-based consultative selling." It has hired and trained a sales force (like Alico Japan, males only) numbering some 1,600 persons, up from 500 in 1990. The sales force, called "life planners," are trained to make product recommendations only after understanding the client's overall financial situation and plans. They are required to be knowledgeable not only in insurance products, but also in key relevant tax and legal issues. Product recommendations are tailored to meet the specific needs and prospects of clients. Life planners try to build long-term relationships with clients, periodically reviewing clients' situations and amending plans and service prescriptions in light of changes. Planners promise to be available at any time to consult with clients.

Prudential has offered a range of term and whole life insurance policy options, old age and retirement income policies, and cancer and medical insurance riders. Life policies have been almost entirely the nondividend type, which has helped the company avoid the situation of high fixed-dividend rate policies and negative carrying costs prevalent among Japanese insurers. In 1999 the company was promoting a new product, the "Living Needs Special Contract." This product provided for the payment of the policy death benefit when it was determined that a policy-holder had only six months or less to live.

Entering a New Growth Phase: Leveraging Prudential Group Entities

Somewhat in the same way as AIG (Chapter Twelve), Prudential, having painstakingly built a solid business platform, is poised to launch aggressive new expansion plans in the post-big bang Japanese marketplace. Like AIG, the company had by 1999 created a high-potential product delivery platform in the form of its well-trained life planners, its existing client relationships, and its high-quality market reputation and name recognition. Prudential thus has the opportunity to push more product sales through this system. Big bang reforms have removed the regulatory barriers to doing this.

Prudential can be expected to begin aggressively to leverage the products and market positioning of its affiliates. These are a securities company subsidiary of the life company, Prudential Securities (Japan); an investment advisor, Prudential Investment Advisory Company; a primarily M&A-focused investment bank, Prudential Asset Management Asia (representative office); and a mutual funds JV with Mitsui Trust, Prudential-Mitsui Trust Investment Company. The most obvious cross-selling opportunities exist with selling asset management products, like mutual funds, delivered through the life planning system. As of June 1999 the Prudential-Mitsui investment trust management JV had been fairly unsuccessful in gathering assets, with only $160 million under management.

DLJ Direct—Setting the Online Discount Broker Standard

The competitive scramble for marketplace position unleashed by Japan's 1998-1999 big bang reforms is evident in no sector more than securities trading. In 1999 a host of new putative discount and internet brokers arrived on the scene, and virtually all major securities houses, including Merrill Lynch Japan Securities, introduced internet trading and at least partially discounted services. Of the three major foreign internet brokers (the other two being Charles Schwab and E-Trade), the one that reached the market first, clearly setting the standard for the others, if not for the entire market, was DLJ Direct.

DLJ Direct SFG Securities was formally established on March 24, 1999, as a joint venture between DLJ Direct in the United States and four Sumitomo Group companies—Sumitomo Bank, Sumitomo Marine & Fire Insurance, Sumitomo Corporation, and Sumitomo Trust and Banking. The company was capitalized at $12.5 million and began operations on June 11.

Abundant Online Information Services

The company is a purely internet provider, offering online services and discounted commissions. What appears potentially to set DLJ Direct SFG apart from the many competitors is its clear value proposition of high quality and abundant services at very low cost. Through its online delivery, DLJ Direct SFG provides discount brokerage, offering a range of Japanese equities, bonds, yen money market funds, onshore and offshore mutual funds, and foreign stocks and bonds. The company also offers online information of high value to customers, for a very reasonable price, and allows customers to select among information offerings to meet their specific information interests.

The information includes *real-time* stock prices for stocks on the Tokyo and Osaka stock exchanges, two securities news services, and a real-time stock index and foreign exchange rate service. The Tokyo Stock Exchange equity service alone can be purchased for a cheap ¥200 ($1.67) a month. The package of services is available for a total ¥1,100 ($9.17) a month. To entice new customers to sign up, all services were offered for free until September 1999. The menu of information services is certain to be expanded (and, we presume, the service fee raised) in the future.

Market-Grabbing, Low, Flat Rate Trading Fees

Of course, the main service offered by discounters is very cheap securities trading. DLJ Direct SFG entered the market with heavily discounted fees. It was one of two or three companies offering flat rates, rather than the ad valorem rates prevalent in the market. In 1999 its basic service tariff (for all trades up to $83,333) was, for internet trades, a flat ¥1,900 ($15.83) for trades at market and ¥2,500 ($20.83) for trades at specified prices, and, for telephone orders, ¥2,900 ($24.17) for trades at market, and ¥3,500 ($29.17) for trades at designated prices.

The scale of this discounting was dramatic. For example, at the fixed commission rates prevailing before October 1999, on a ¥5,000,000 ($41,667) trade the commission was $395.83. DLJ Direct SFG commission on the same trade in October was $15.83. Most other large securities companies were still charging about $125 (see Chapter Four for details of rate changes).

Only Well Capitalized Firms to Survive the Shakeout

The proliferation of discount and internet brokers in 1999 is certain to create severe competition for customers and volumes during a period that could last several years. This will be followed by an industry shakeout and consolidation, in which weak competitors close business or are acquired by others.

Clearly, with such dramatic discounting and low services charges, DLJ Direct SFG will need to build a lot of volume to cover fixed costs and make a profit. This process could take some time, during which it will suffer losses. However, its very large capitalization and strong backers suggests that the company will be a survivor. Its early entry and aggressive market-grabbing pricing strategy should also prove critical to its eventual success.

As of this writing, it is too early to tell how the low-end discount trading market will develop or who the most competitive and successful companies will be. We are intrigued by the possibility that, as in wholesale securities and investment banking, U.S. companies will emerge from the shakeout as the market leaders. To us, DLJ Direct SFG offers a persuasive model of how this will come to pass.

Part Five

How Foreign Financial Firms Can Win in Japan

Chapter Eighteen

Japan's Financial Marketplace in 2005

Thanks to the reforms of the big bang, it is highly likely that the development and change in Japan's financial marketplace over the next five years will be faster and deeper than at any time during the last fifty years. What, after the big bang has played out, will Japan's financial marketplace look like? More directly for our purposes, where will be the opportunities for foreign financial firms?

Below we review again the sectors surveyed in Part Two above. This time, we focus on the future. Our objective is to identify major market- and business-driving trends and to suggest likely scenarios for the interplay of competition. In the next chapter we will suggest strategies for firms seeking to participate in the growth of the post-big bang Japanese marketplace.

In the five years leading up to 2005, the combination of competitive pressures in the marketplace and unregulated ability to change is likely to evolve institutions substantially different from those that existed in 1999. Institutions will be compelled increasingly to seek and achieve specialization, differentiation, and optimization in respect of product lines, target market segments, geographic coverage, delivery systems and platforms, and level and kind of technology. To compete successfully with limited resources, institutions will increasingly focus resources and strategies, striving to seize profitable market opportunities. Thanks to the big bang, institutions will have a wide range of options in how they organize and staff their strategies. At the same time that institutional players change to meet the market's needs, the market will also change, to some degree in direct response.

Banking: A Rich Marketplace for Innovation and Specialization

The combination of IBJ, Fuji Bank, and DKB, announced in August 1999 and implemented over three years, by itself greatly transformed the competitive marketplace. Also, it set in train the further consolidation of the banking industry. By 2005 this process will be well advanced, with highly salubrious effects on the marketplace for financial services. The chronically overbanked and overcompetitive condition of the marketplace that prevailed for twenty years will be substantially ameliorated. Economics in the industry—in retail, wholesale, and investment banking—will improve.

We can confidently predict that in 2005 both the institutions in the banking services marketplace and consumers of banking services will think and behave very differently than they did in 1999. Compared with 1999, when most Japanese banks still offered an all-things-to-all-people approach and bank customers—whether wholesale or retail—were accustomed to receiving a full, fairly standardized set of products and services from their banks, 2005 will be a new world. Customers will be offered—and will expect to receive—differentiated services, from institutions that increasingly present themselves as specialized. Banking service providers will as never before be targeting markets, product and service segments and applying differential pricing, service, and platform strategies.

The situation in 1999 and prospective situation in 2005 for five broad market and product segments are presented in Table 18.1. What the prospective suggests is that the next five years will undoubtedly offer abundant opportunities for banks.

Wholesale Universal Banking: Rich Living for a Few Domestic and Foreign Players

Market demand for wholesale universal banking services will undoubtedly expand quickly in Japan's restructuring corporate marketplace. By 2005 it appears likely that a few domestic institutions will be as competitive as wholesale universal banks internationally, often through universal bank holding company structures. They will serve top tier corporate customers. Clearly in line to occupy this position are Mizuho Financial Group (through wholesale and investment banking entities under the holding company), Bank of Tokyo-Mitsubishi (BOTM), and Sumitomo Bank.

With significant barriers to entry, the select top tier universal banks will increase market share at the expense of other, lesser Japanese banks in services to large, global Japanese corporations and institutions. Competition will be with foreign investment banks and universal banks like Citigroup, and each other. Only the leading universal banks—and the two or three leading Japanese securities companies—are likely to be strongly competitive with U.S. investment banks in cross-border M&A advisory and fund arrangement transactions.

Table 18.1

Banking—A Rich Marketplace for Innovation and Specialization

Market/Product Segment	1999	2005
Large corporates, especially global players/Global universal wholesale banking	Significant and growing market need but no Japanese institutions providing world-class service, especially overseas.	Highly attractive segment served by a few domestic banks (BOTM, Mizuho Group, Sumitomo) and by foreign groups like Citigroup, Chase, and Deutsche Bank. Global corporates seeking services, including M&A advisory, globally
Large corporates, especially domestic/ corporate services (including lending)	Declining business. Banks losing money due to weak credit risk management and over-competition.	Economics improved. Nonbanks (finance companies, leasing companies) increasing market share. Main lending bank relationships remain along *keiretsu* lines.
Middle market corporate/banking services (including lending)	Underserved by banks offering only undifferentiated, inexpert service. Nonbanks in relatively strong market position.	Growing business. Regional or supra-regional banks (Asahi/Tokai) exploiting this segment. IBJ/Fuji/ DKB providing quality, differentiated service. Finance and leasing companies further expand position.
High net worth individuals and family-owned businesses/private banking	Not offered in earnest except by Citibank.	Rapidly growing market with increasingly sophisticated customers. Six to ten Japanese and foreign banks providing quality service and dominating the market.
Consumer/retail banking	Severe capital and resource drain for local banks. Products and services undifferentiated among banks. Underinvestment in new technonolgies and service platforms.	Transformed segment. Scaled down regionalized, and technology driven. BOTM, Mizuho Group, and Sanwa among few nationwide retail banks. Now profitable due to repricing and rationalization.

Source: Author.

Large and Middle Market Corporate Banking: Consolidation and Increasing Specialization

The corporate service sector, particularly for middle market companies, is certain to grow by 2005, and it is possible that its risk profile will improve. With the three top banks and foreign banks taking more of the top tier corporate business, Japan's second tier banks—especially the supraregionals—will seek to achieve a competitive position in serving small- and middle-sized corporations. We expect to see Asahi/Tokai achieve substantial success in their middle market corporate lending strategy, particularly in the Chubu and Kanto regions. Sanwa should also have success. Of course, the two universal megabanks, BOTM and Mizuho Financial Group, will also be targeting the middle market.

But increasing numbers of new businesses and spinoffs from restructuring in Japan's industrial and commercial sectors are likely to create a fast-growing market for financial services. Strong business growth can be expected for all players that take a targeted and differentiated approach to this market.

The corporate sector by 2005 will be the source of 401(k)-type corporate-sponsored individual retirement accounts. These and other corporate pension services will be big business. The business will be taken by trust banks, like the successor DKB-Fuji Trust Bank, that target this market segment, especially if they can leverage lending and other service offerings provided by affiliated corporate and retail banks.

High Net Worth Individuals/Private Banking

The private banking market in Japan was set to take off in 1999. By 2005 we can expect that it will be among the largest in the world. Increasing knowledge and sophistication and word of mouth will create a broader appreciation of the private banking services in the large prospective client base. More accessible markets for small business fund-raising and venture capital will help transform private banking from the Swiss ("old money") to the U.S. ("new money") models, increasing dramatically the opportunities for providers of professional private banking services (of the type only Citibank offered in Japan in 1999).

The market will certainly support a critical mass—say six to ten—significant nationwide private banking players. Growth will be constrained primarily by a lack of competent bankers and managers.

Making Money in Retail Banking

For most Japanese (and a few foreign) banks, the consumer business will be the key to their futures. It can hardly be doubted that by 2005 Japanese banks will have made much progress fixing their consumer banking businesses. This process began in 1999 with a new of sense determination and urgency in major banking groups like BOTM, Sumitomo Bank, and the new Mizuho Financial Group megabank. While smaller in scale than its rivals, Osaka-based Sanwa Bank could become the model of a retail-oriented bank, with highly

Table 18.2

Securities—A Larger Marketplace, Transformed by Technology

Market/Product Segment	1999	2005
Institutional/ wholesale securities	Strong, active market. Major foreign players entrenched and expanding.	Expanded, more sophisticated, profitable market. Universal banks (BOTM, Mizuho Group, Sumitomo) increasingly powerful players both domestically and internationally. Foreign houses continue to grow.
Retail/full service	Crowded field of Big Three and second tier Japanese brokers, plus bank-affiliated retail brokers. Also Merrill Lynch.	Expanded market served by narrowed field of players, including Big Four and Merrill Lynch. Technology and rationalization improve economics, while volume and asset management drive revenues. "Universal services" model (e.g., CMA-type account) key differentiator. Bank-affiliated brokers weak competitors (except New Japan) and IBJ/DKB/Fuji retail securities entity.
Retail/discount & limited service (internet)	Dozens of players entering new field. Price leaders incude well-capitalized DLJ Direct SFG and Nomura Fundnet (mutual funds).	Internet trading reaches high volume level but growth rates level off. Total market commissions insufficient to support many early entrants. Mergers and closings continue. A few market leaders continue to acquire share through acquisitions. Still over-competition in market.

Source: Author.

competitive retail securities, mutual funds, and banking services. Bank combinations and holding company structures will facilitate the investments in technology needed to create more efficient retail banking platforms.

Solving the retail banking profitability problem will entail doing a better job at seeing consumers as borrowers and not just depositors. The scope for consumer finance is broad. We are skeptical of the ability of most Japanese banks to succeed beyond mortgage-lending, however, even by 2005.

Securities: A Larger, Vibrant Marketplace, Transformed by Technology and Competition

Creative destruction on a massive scale was already evident in the securities industry in 1999 (Chapter Four). Competitive pressures and change, impacting most severely the traditional players, will only intensify in 2000 and beyond.

Three Market/Product Segments—In a Greatly Expanded Market

The Japanese securities market, in 1999 and 2005, is readily seen as three market/product segments (Table 18.2). In the sophisticated, *institutional/wholesale*, origination and distribution high segment, we can expect further increases in strength and market share from large U.S. and other foreign firms and the strongest Japanese group institutions. At the *retail/discount and limited service* low end, we can expect a shakeout and significant consolidation after a flurry of new entrants into the marketplace in 1999 and 2000. As in the United States after deregulation of commissions, brokerages will increasingly seek to manage assets and thus will necessarily compete with mutual funds and asset management companies, including life insurance companies, for individual and institutional assets. Firms like the Big Three (to become the Big Four in 2002 with the merger of New Japan and Kankaku) and Merrill Lynch in the middle, *retail/full service* segment are likely to be the most successful in this competition.

A major new competitive field will be the CMA-type brokerage account that provides transaction settlements and private asset management services. In the first few years, as many firms compete for market share, returns are likely to be driven down, even as costs—especially for systems development—remain high. This will be another factor driving consolidations.

On the other hand, the market itself should greatly expand. The post-big bang proliferation of products and services, as well as service providers, is almost certain to nurture participation in the securities market by new investors, institutional and individual, as well as create more type of securities. The relatively low level of securities, and, especially, mutual funds holdings by private individuals (Chapter One) will almost certainly rise, perhaps doubling or tripling. Defined contribution 401(k)-type private pension funds, as well as private and public institutional pension funds, will all grow enormously.

The Retail Market: Emergence of Three Types of Brokers

Very likely, in the Japanese context as in the U.S., on the retail level the securities industry will become dominated by three types of companies: (1) a few large companies offering "universal" financial services, with a heavy emphasis on financial advice and asset management, as well as full transactional services; (2) bank group-affiliated brokers, often operating under bank holding companies, offering more limited services; and (3) specialized, niche players like discounters and internet brokers.

In the universal brokerage service category, we can clearly see Nomura. Daiwa certainly will also qualify. Merrill Lynch Japan Securities can be expected to have built a successful universal financial business, including introduction of a CMA-type account. In the likely event that Citigroup takes an even larger share of Nikko, this company could become a second major foreign player in the market.

The bank-affiliated retail brokers were presented in Chapters Four and Nine. The most important of these will be the merged entity of New Japan and Kankaku Securities, which will become one of the new Big Four Japanese brokerages.

Perhaps the most interesting segment of the market will be the specialized, niche players. Very likely most new entrants will not survive or remain independent. By 2005, all market participants will be offering internet trading and account services. Internet and discount brokerage will often turn out to be the approach taken by nonbank and nonbrokerage financial institutions (e.g., by life and nonlife insurance companies), as a low-cost, low-infrastructure method of offering new products, and by nonfinancial institutions (like Softbank or H.I.S. Travel) just beginning to offer financial products.

Insurance: Wide Open for Innovators

Compared with the situation in 1999, the Japanese insurance marketplace could be possibly the most changed in 2005. The most important change will be the elimination of barriers between life and nonlife business entry in 2001, permitting insurance companies to take a comprehensive approach to the market (Table 18.3).

Corporatization, Competition, and Consolidation

Among the important changes expected is the conversion of most or all of the life insurance industry from mutuals to shareholder corporations. This conversion could well put in motion an industry consolidation with second and third tier companies combining to challenge the leader Nippon Life (Nissay). Also likely is equity investment in insurance companies by domestic bank holding companies such as the new IBJ/Fuji/DKB holding company and, very likely, by aggressive American and European insurance giants like Travelers (Citigroup), Prudential, AIG, American Express, ING and Allianz.

The Japanese life insurance industry has shown its vulnerability to competition from new (especially foreign) companies taking sophisticated, highly targeted and customized approaches to the market. In 1999 it was already

Table 18.3

Insurance—Wide Open for Innovators

Market/Product Segment	1999	2005
Individual/ life	Market saturated with traditional savings-type products. New policies slowing. Policies in force declining. Companies weakening. Foreign firms expanding with innovative products.	Japanese companies corporatized, some integrated into bank groups or under bank holding companies. Mergers and mutual investment among life and nonlife companies. Slow growth in market due to product competition from banks, securities companies, etc.
Individual/ nonlife	Slow volume growth and declining profits for most high-cost Japanese insurers. Beginning of consolidation of nonlife sector.	Complete cross-selling of nonlife and third sector products as life-nonlife restictions removed. Still seeking to streamline cost structures. Foreign companies continue to grow, finding additional product and service niches.
Individual/ third sector	Foreign companies lead competition under U.S.-Japan Agreement.	

Source: Author.

clear that the life insurance industry is also vulnerable to price competition from direct marketers. (This had been the case in the nonlife industry for some years.) We can expect intensified price competition, which will increase the need for product innovation and management efficiency. These trends will further promote foreign entry into the industry.

The driving force for change in the marketplace in 2005 is likely to be a substantial cooling in the Japanese consumers' love affair with savings-type insurance products. As mutual fund, banking, and brokerage competitors offer consumers an increased variety of attractive long-term investment products, insurers will have to respond with similar offerings. Insurance companies will all need to offer a larger menu of products.

Increasing Integration in Financial Service Groups

Whether through equity ownership under holding companies or alliances, insurance providers—both life and nonlife—will increasingly become integrated into financial service groups. The objective for the insurers will be to increase the productivity of their sales forces and client bases by sourcing more products. The tie-up between IBJ and Dai-Ichi Life to promote sales of each other's products is a harbinger of sales alliances between banks, mutual funds companies, and insurers. Competition in the asset management area will also drive closer group associations. An example is the 1999 tie-up between Daido Life, Sanwa Bank, and Toyo Trust to market pension fund management and mutual funds products (Chapter Nine).

Foreign Firms Thrive as Life-Nonlife Barriers Drop

By 2005 the many tie-ups formed in 1998 and 1999 between foreign firms and Japanese insurers in asset management, mutual funds development, and insurance itself will have evolved. Some of these tie-ups may be seen as the Trojan horses through which the foreign companies gained entry in order to take over the company. Others will have been learning platforms, from which both parties decided to pursue independent courses. Most will not have remained unchanged for five years.

Whether the competitive field is marketing channels, products, or client-focused marketing, we can expect foreign firms to continue to distinguish themselves, gaining additional market share and profitability by 2005. U.S. firms will be familiar with the open insurance market to exist from 2001 and will take full advantage of their relative experience and product development expertise.

The foreign industry leaders of 1999, AIG, American Family, GE Edison Life, Alico, Prudential, Cigna, AXA, and Zurich, will have strengthened and expanded their market positions. As indicated above, we would also expect to see some large new foreign players that have entered the market through acquisitions.

Asset Management

The problems facing Japan's public and private pension systems (Chapter Six) are so pressing and the need for resolution is so urgent, it is certain that the system will be vastly changed by 2005. What seems likely is that the system will be much more "privatized," with defined contribution pension plans constituting a significant part of pension assets. Also, the amount of funds in the system will be huge, and growing.

Reform of the government's Fiscal Investment and Loan Program—funded partially by pension insurance premiums—could result in a large increase in pension funds being mandated to asset managers. Defined contribution—401(k)-type—plans, introduced in fall 2000, will create a large new market for record-keeping services and for mutual funds (Table 18.4).

Table 18.4

Asset Management and Mutual Funds—A Shakeout Coming

Market/Product Segment	1999	2005
Institutional/ pension fund management	Market shared among life insurers, trust banks, and investment advisors. Market is large and growing. Investment advisors' share increasing as sponsors are dissatisfied with performance and products of traditional managers.	Market continuing rapid growth. Institutional and individual interest in mutual funds stimulated by introduction of 401(k)-type defined contribution plans in 2000. Reforms in public pension management providing more management opportunities. Many specialist managers targeting segments and offering tailored services. Most asset management JVs formed in 1998-1999 have dissolved.
Retail/mutual funds	Low level of mutual funds holdings began to rise after opening new channels in 1998 and with stock market recovery. Many entrants offered a plethora of new products. Many tie-ups between Japanese companies needing products and foreign manufacturers needing distribution.	Market greatly larger than in 1999 with mutual funds now in the range of 5 to 10 percent of personal financial assets. Consolidation in industry through mergers, acqusitions, and closings, but also growth. Pure manufacturers being disintermediated by distributors' own funds. Access to 401(k) market complicated by relationships of record-keeping groups.

Source: Author.

Post-Big Bang Consolidation of Traditional Players

By 2005 we would expect that the consolidation started in 1999 among many of the redundant asset management and investment trust companies within financial groups would be completed. Also, with mergers and consolidation going on in the insurance industry and in trust banking, we would thus expect to see fewer, but larger players within these groups.

With asset management a part of bank group strategies against clear market segments—for example, small corporates in the case of Sanwa and Asahi/Tokai—we can expect a more targeted and focused approach to private market segments. New pension fund marketing and services alliances formed in 1999 and 2000 (for example, DKB-Fuji Trust and Banking, and Daido Life,

Sanwa Bank, and Toyo Trust) are likely to have carved out secure and defensible market positions in the small- and medium-sized corporate market.

We expect record keeping for the corporate 401(k) market to be provided primarily by the three groupings of companies (Chapter Six) as a utility. However, some specialist companies, like Fidelity, will successfully offer tailored services to certain market segments.

Still a Wide Open and Growing Field

With the market growing and changing, we can expect to see many opportunities for new players, perhaps particularly foreign players, who offer differentiated strategies and technologies. Boutique firms will find it relatively easy to offer services as subadvisors to funds managers maintaining relationships with the pension sponsors. The marketplace trend seen in the 1990s of awarding mandates for performance, rather than relationship, and being prepared to change managers is certain to continue.

Mutual Funds

As in the United States in the 1980s and 1990s, the advent of a 401(k)-type defined contribution pension system will be one of the key drivers in the demand for mutual funds products and in assets under management by mutual funds companies. Another driver will be the growing interest and appetite for risk-bearing investment products by an increasingly knowledgeable and investment-minded population of all ages, wishing to reallocate funds held in savings (Table 18.4).

Market Shakeout and Winners and Losers in Distribution

There will almost certainly be a significant shakeout in the mutual fund industry, as in asset management, along with financial industry consolidation. As in the United States, it is likely that clear winners and losers emerge in distribution. And, as in the United States, it is likely that banks and insurance companies prove relatively weak and unsuccessful in distributing mutual funds.

By 2005 the dominant players in distribution of mutual funds are likely to be securities companies, trust banks, and the mutual funds companies themselves through direct marketing. We expect substantial success for companies like Nomura Fundnet (Chapter Ten) that target a broad but distinct market segment (for Fundnet, young people) and offer an easy-to-use service at reasonable cost.

Manufacturers like Goldman Sachs will always be challenged by the desire of distributors (e.g., securities companies) to keep control of investor assets by offering proprietary funds. To ensure continued growth, we would expect the major manufacturers to establish direct distribution channels (as Fidelity did in the late 1990s) parallel to their distributor-directed channels. We can expect most of these to be internet- or direct marketing-based and to offer distinct new products.

Acquisitions as Foreign-Japanese Tie-Ups Evolve

As in the insurance industry, we can expect to see the many tie-ups between foreign mutual fund companies and Japanese companies evolve into buy-outs by one party or selling out to a third party. Indeed, with the proliferation of tie-ups, whose purpose is usually a short-term offer of market access or technology transfer, such an industry restructuring seems predestined. This will offer opportunities to long-term growth oriented players, including foreign companies.

Consumer Finance

We expect that in 2005 the Japanese consumer finance marketplace will be much bigger and more competitive than it was in 1999. It will continue to be highly profitable, with strong growth. The main drivers are likely to be foreign companies like Citibank, GE Capital, Associates First Capital, and AIG (Table 18.5)

In mortgage finance, personal loans, and credit cards, we can expect key new players in the market like GE Capital, as well as established firms like AIC and Citibank, to introduce the market segmentation and marketing technology that has been successful elsewhere, gaining significant market advantage. This competition will drive an industry restructuring, particularly in the credit card business. Increasingly, credit cards will need to offer perceptible value-added. This will lead to an industry shakeout and the withdrawal of many companies, particularly banks.

Subprime Lending Still a Rich Market

In the fairly specialized segment of subprime lending, we can expect attractive conditions and a relatively limited number of major service providers. In particular, we do not expect Japanese banks to be able to become serious competitors to the traditional market leaders like Takefuji, ACOM, Aiful, and Promise or to the foreign specialists Lake (GE Capital) and AIC (Associates First Capital).

Table 18.5

Consumer Finance—Still a Rich Market

Market/Product Segment	1999	2005
Individual/ Unsecured cash loans	Subprime market highly lucrative specialty. Increasingly ATM/CD-delivered. Market growing with innovations like ACOM card. Japanese banks inactive. New entrants like Orix.	Still a large and lucrative market. New players reduced through acquisition. Banks largely not players. Foreign leaders AIC and GE Capital larger through acquisitions.
Individual/Secured lending-mortgage finance	Growing market with government involvement. Subspecialty of equity loans (AIC). Citibank innovating features.	Substantially enlarged market. Growth driven by innovations and strong promotion by banks and nonbanks (GE Capital). Citibank leading in innovation and marketing.
Individual/Credit cards	Crowded market with little differentiation.	Consolidated market. Many banks withdrawn. Major brands stronger.

Source: Author.

There will be considerable consolidation among providers in this marketplace, which was highly fragmented among local players in 1999. We can expect some new foreign entrants to the market via acquisition of local companies. We can also expect further acquisitions by companies like GE Capital and AIC in order to achieve increasingly important economies of scale in product delivery and service.

Such is the financial services marketplace that we foresee in Japan's near term future. It is clearly one of unlimited opportunities, and risks. The key question for foreign financial firms is how to take advantage of the opportunities and to gain rewards commensurate with the risks. It is to this question that we now turn.

Chapter Nineteen

Winning Strategies in Japan's Post-Big Bang Financial Marketplace

In the last chapter we viewed the likely changes in store for the Japanese financial marketplace in the years following the big bang reforms. We also suggested the market and product areas that will offer the most interesting business opportunities. Below we consider the approaches that foreign companies, new entrants as well as more established players, can take to realize these opportunities.

Alliances or Going It Alone?

The broad, industry-wide new market and product openings brought about by the 1998–2001 big bang reforms can be viewed as the expansion and culmination of more limited, sector-specific reforms in Japan over the previous twenty years. In the 1998–2001 period, as in previous liberalizations, many foreign companies are entering the market for the first time or executing new, more ambitious growth strategies. In each of the previous liberalizations, we saw two approaches taken by foreign entrants: joint ventures or alliances with local companies and go-it-alone, independent approaches. Today we are seeing a similar phenomenon, with most new entrants opting for the joint venture or alliance approach.

Doleful Lessons in Life Insurance

Not surprisingly, perhaps, the record of joint ventures and alliances is generally one of disappointment and, most often, dissolution. The life insurance industry is a good example. Newcomers in the life insurance industry in the late 1970s, Prudential and Allstate, and in the 1980s and 1990s, Equitable and Mutual of Omaha, began in joint ventures with firms like Sony, Credit

Saison, Orix, and Nihon Shimpan. In every one of these cases, the JVs ended with buy-outs by the Japanese partner. In only one case, Prudential, was the foreign partner willing and able subsequently to approach the market alone.

These cases illustrate well the dilemma of market entry. The large, successful Japanese players with whom joint ventures could conceivably have created dynamic synergies for the foreign entrants were not interested in tying up on terms attractive to the foreigners. The most critical business component, what the foreigners wanted and needed most—access to a broad customer base—was what the domestic players owned. What foreigners had to offer—new products and management technology, but limited investment capital—was, for the domestic players, hardly worth the price of sharing their hard-won, and still highly defensible, customer bases. Further, given time and some money, the large domestic players felt that they could obtain new products and technology on their own.

The companies whose interests were in parallel with the foreigners were Japanese companies seeking to enter the life insurance market, but whose main businesses were in another area. These companies needed the products and management knowhow that only foreigners were willing and able to offer. But what happened next? After absorbing the technology and learning the business from the foreign investors, the Japanese companies (we think the impetus for the break came from the Japanese side) had little compelling long-term interest in remaining in partnership. So they bought out the foreigners.

This situation of fundamentally conflicting long-term interests is the rule, rather than the exception, in joint ventures everywhere, which is why few last more than a few years. The proliferation of JVs and tie-ups in the Japanese financial market is largely a transient phenomenon, driven—as in the earlier case of insurance—by the temporary congruence of interests of new cross-sectoral domestic entrants and willing foreign entrants. We can expect most of the foreign-Japanese financial JVs formed in the frenzy of 1998 to 2001 to unwind and dissolve. These tie-ups have been particularly prevalent in the asset management and mutual funds areas, where foreigners have brought overseas investment expertise and technology to the table, and in insurance.

New Ways to Go It Alone

The way to success in the Japanese marketplace is easy to see: going it alone in a wholly-owned venture. We see the success and potential of this approach in virtually every financial service sector—banking (Citibank), securities (Merrill Lynch), insurance (AIG), asset management (Morgan Stanley), mutual funds (Goldman Sachs and Fidelity), and consumer finance (GE Capital and Associates). Of course, understanding the strategy and successfully executing it are two different matters. But the cases we have examined in previous chapters provide many important and useful lessons.

New Scope for Acquisitions

As evidenced by GE Capital in credit cards, consumer finance, insurance, and leasing (Chapter Fourteen), and by Associates in consumer finance (Chapter Sixteen), the foreign investor who decides to go it alone in Japan is no longer required to "build the business from scratch" as the only approach. Indeed, the cases we have reviewed are proof that, in the Japanese market, growth through acquisitions can now be posited as both the preferred and most feasible business development strategy.

Of course, executing such a strategy takes vision and confidence in one's ability to manage the business, as well as considerable capital. GE Capital is dealing with the management challenges by introducing its globally tested "Six Sigma" process. But other, more flexible and localized approaches are certainly also workable.

Changes in Japanese laws and regulatory practices as well as in the mentality of market players facilitate the process of acquisition. Each case seems to break new ground and to broaden the scope for innovation. We expect banking, until now for various reasons not a target for foreign acquisitions, to become one, as some foreign banks seek to join in the market success of Citibank. We see abundant opportunities also in the securities industry as the shakeout among new and old players, full and limited service providers, discounters and internet companies, unfolds.

Consolidation Among Foreign Entrants

Another promising market entry and development approach will be the one executed in the 1980s by Associates, that is, acquiring the businesses of foreign firms that have decided for one reason or another to withdraw. Targets are likely to be wholly owned. (JVs will not generally be attractive targets. The local partner would have an effective veto and would likely exercise it or, more probably, offer to buy out the foreign partner—but on terms highly disadvantageous to the foreigner. This is another potential eventuality arguing against formation of foreign-Japanese JVs.)

A variant on the above approach would be combinations, essentially JVs, between foreign companies specifically to develop a Japanese market niche. This sounds the same, but is fundamentally different from the foreign-Japanese JV situations discussed above. Here the foreign parties would be in the same position vis-à-vis themselves and the marketplace, and thus more likely to realize a continuity of interests as the venture developed. The main reason for this kind of combination would be to share the substantial costs and risks of business development in Japan's expensive and changing market environment.

Using Technology and Globalization to Drive Market Development

One critical enabling factor in market development in Japan, as elsewhere, today, that did not exist ten or twenty years ago, is technology. Whether it is the internet or systems that can be applied in Japan after the addition of a localized "front end," as in Fidelity's approach in 401(k) record keeping, there are clearly opportunities for many companies to enter market niches or to achieve critical mass of product and market coverage quickly by importing and adapting already developed technologies.

The same opportunities exist, and have been exploited by Citibank (Chapter Twelve) and American Express (Chapter Sixteen), to connect Japan and Japanese customers to proprietary global product and service systems, thereby achieving a highly defensible market position with a specific and growing market segment. This clearly is the strategy of Paribas in offering its global equities trading system.

Product and Service Opportunities in the Japanese Market

To repeat the view expressed previously by a Japanese insurance company executive, the post-big bang competition will essentially be a contest for consumer business. What do we see as the most promising product and service areas in this competition? And what marketing approaches are likely to lead to success?

Consumer Banking

Sitting on a consumer deposit base of some $2.3 trillion (of which foreign currency accounts for only 0.3 percent), Japanese banks are awash in the raw material used in their business. Still, most banks do not make money on their consumer businesses. The reason, as described in Chapter Three, is the structural mismatch between the high-cost sourcing of liabilities through their branch systems and the low-margin, high-risk placing of funds as loans to corporations. To restructure themselves and their marketplace, Japanese banks have begun to think of consumer and corporate businesses as separate "profit centers" and to manage and allocate resources accordingly. With the adjustment and differentiation by service of commissions for consumer remittances seen in 1999, the first industry-wide adjustment in eighteen years, we can see that a sea-change is occurring.

In the new world of competition for consumers and profit-driven service differentiation, foreign banks have abundant and highly applicable knowhow that is directly transferable to the Japanese market. Combined with a strategy of acquisition, U.S. consumer banks have opportunities to introduce new consumer products and services in both liabilities-gathering and account services, but also on the asset side, in consumer lending. As noted in the preceding chapter, we expect Citibank greatly to expand its consumer lending business in Japan. We are fairly pessimistic about how successful Japanese banks will be in consumer lending, apart, perhaps, from mortgages. But we can see much scope for other foreign banks to enter the market.

Specialized Consumer Lending

As we have seen in the case of Japan's subprime lenders, it is not necessary to locate or build consumer lending around a branch banking system. For a certain segment of the population, the anonymity and convenience of ATMs and cash dispensers is the preferred mode of receiving services. Other types of consumer lending, including mortgage lending, delivered through nontraditional channels, are likely to be an attractive new business area. By broadening the financing sources for finance companies (including the ability to issue debentures), big bang reforms have widened the scope for specialized consumer and commercial lenders. Mortgage lending—already targeted by GE Capital—delivered efficiently through direct marketing channels, is likely to be a highly attractive new growth area.

Private Banking

Private banking, of the U.S.-type and the type practiced successfully in Japan by Citibank (Chapter Twelve), will be a lucrative and high-growth business for a limited number of U.S. and European providers with the market knowledge and product delivery skills to compete against the market leader. The market certainly will support three or four additional U.S. players, most obviously Chase and Bank of America, and one or two European banks, most likely Deutsche Bank and Hong Kong and Shanghai Bank. The service approach must cover clients' business and personal credit and investment needs. It must offer customized financial advice—including tax, estate, and business management—and structuring and delivery of solutions onshore and offshore in multi-currencies.

Securities

In the retail securities area, with the Japanese Big Three securities firms operating extensive branch networks, plus offering internet trading; with a host of second tier brokers, often affiliated with banking groups, also approaching the market; and with a proliferation of discount and purely internet and direct marketers, the opportunities for foreign entrants will be limited.

Market entry is most likely to be through one of two approaches. The first, taken by Merrill Lynch (Chapter Thirteen), is to challenge the Big Three by offering a higher quality, more client-oriented and sophisticated "full service" relationship. The second, taken by DLJ Direct, is join the multitude of boutique and niche players trying to differentiate themselves both on price and service offering. While both approaches hold promise, we greatly favor Merrill's frontal approach against a relatively limited number of direct competitors. At the same time, given the expense and management challenges, we would be surprised if another U.S. firm tried to join Merrill in pursuing a full service approach, at least until Merrill's success is more evident.

As noted in the previous chapter, we can expect much consolidation in the lower, small end of the securities market. A smart strategy for a serious foreign player would be to acquire over time specialist brokers, eventually building a brokerage with multiple product and service offerings, each with a definite market niche or focus.

Insurance

The greatest post-big bang opportunities in the insurance area will be to offer well performing investment products, particularly mutual funds, as an alternative to traditional savings-type products, as well as to offer new products and product combinations and to exploit vast new distribution channels.

The opportunities for introducing new or additional products (e.g., mutual funds) will obviously be greater for players like American Family, Alico Japan, GE Edison, Prudential, AIG, American Home, and Cigna, which have already developed effective distribution channels and customer bases. Opening of the insurance sales and underwriting sector, however, will also permit new entrants from the securities and banking industries or even from such companies as American Express.

Companies like AIG and Prudential, with strong mutual fund and asset management capabilities, will obviously seize the opportunity to introduce new investment products. By 2001, the putative barriers between first, second, and third sector products offerings (Chapter Five) will be a memory (and even in 1999 were increasingly ineffective). The ability to offer tailored solutions through bundled product offerings will give a market sales advantage to companies able to marshal a sophisticated consultative sales force, either of agents or in-house salesmen. Alico and Prudential are likely to set the standard.

A firm like Travelers will need to make a major acquisition or form a large strategic joint venture in the insurance field, in order to gain the market presence it desires. This will position it to leverage all the resources of Citigroup and to serve both corporate and individual markets, offering across insurance, banking, securities, and asset management.

Asset Management and Mutual Funds

Asset management services, including mutual funds products both for retail and institutional markets, are likely to attract new and old entrants who can deliver differential features and, ultimately, performance (admittedly not an easy task over the long term). In a crowded field, differentiation will be key.

Approaching the Market from Offshore

Big bang reforms significantly relaxed market access restrictions on offshore mutual funds and on such mutual funds structures as "funds of funds." The liberalization allowed foreign mutual funds companies the choice of entering the market by setting up a domestic investment trust management (ITM) company (previously the inevitable route) or by simply reaching distributors or clients directly from offshore domiciled investment trust companies (Chapter Seven).

In order to improve profitability, we perceive that many asset managers will opt not to establish an ITM presence in Japan, but rather to deliver asset management and mutual funds services to institutional clients directly from offshore. To reach individual clients, they will use the relatively low-cost alternative of setting up a securities company as the selling vehicle.

Both Manufacturing and Distribution

The bargaining power in the marketplace is likely to remain weighted toward distributors, rather than manufacturers, of funds. For this reason, manufacturers like Goldman Sachs (Chapter Seven) should take the opportunity to establish direct sales channels, probably in the same way as Fidelity (both a manufacturer and distributor), through direct marketing. For this they will need to have a domestically licensed vehicle.

Dealing with 401(k) Market Gatekeepers

In the 401(k) market, only Fidelity appears to see profit opportunities in the record-keeping area. The key opportunities will be in successfully approaching corporations as they put together menus of investment options available to individual 401(k) plans. The three large combinations of institutions developing record-keeping services—(IBJ/Nomura, Mitsubishi/Sumitomo, and Nippon Life (see Chapter Six)—are certain to play a gatekeeping role or more in determining which firms can offer investment services. This is why some firms like Goldman Sachs have opted to participate in the groupings. Fidelity is set to approach the corporate and individual small business market directly with a customized product.

Winning Strategies in Japan's New Marketplace

To win in Japan's new wide-open financial marketplace, a firm will need to have the right strategy and to execute it effectively. Our analysis shows that the firms that have achieved success in both these respects have a strong commitment to the marketplace and a healthy mix of Japanese and foreign management talent. The firms have also flexibly applied strategies that have been successful in other markets to the market realities of Japan.

What this approach means in practice is intense training and coaching for Japanese managers, provided in most cases by expatriate managers who both know and can effectively transfer head office technologies and culture. Over many years, companies like AIG, Prudential, Goldman Sachs, AFLAC, Citibank, American Express, and Associates First Capital have learned how to combine the energies and talents of foreign managers with Japanese, in most cases transferring management of execution (and often, also, formulation of strategy) to local management.

Unlike a decade or two ago, the market in Japan today is filled with highly skilled and trained Japanese managers. The successful foreign firm in Japan will pay the price to retain and, most importantly, to gain the loyalty of such managers. It will also support these managers with expatriate staff who can bring needed perspectives, handle annoying head office information and reporting requirements, and effectively manage the flow of technology and communications between head office and the local company.

Needless to say, winning strategies will be long-term. Also, strategy planners must be prepared to see the model changed by new market realities or by the appearance of preexisting realities that planners ignored. In general, experience suggests that it takes longer and costs more than planned to execute strategies in Japan. (It remains to be seen whether GE Capital can continue its record of lightning-quick execution.) This means that cost consciousness and cost control should be an important element of strategies.

Should Japan Be the Next Major Market Initiative for Your Firm?

Should your firm, if it has not already done so, put Japan on the agenda as a new market initiative? Of course, the answer to this question depends upon your firm. There can be no doubt that if your firm is or aspires to be a global financial services firm, presence in some form in the Japanese market is required.

Our sense is that the Japanese marketplace in the early twenty-first century will provide indispensable opportunities for growth and competitive development for almost any important financial firm. As globalization progresses and world markets grow more intertwined, developments and trends in the Japanese marketplace will come to have added relevance within the global strategies of all important financial players.

In short, if your firm is or aspires to be a global financial service provider, or if your firm is looking for a second market in which to grow, it is almost certain that your next market opportunity, indeed your next market development imperative, is Japan.

Epilogue

The revolution in Japan's financial marketplace continues. Indeed, the pace is quickening. In the period between mid-August—when Japan's financial market was shaken by the announcement of plans of IBJ, Fuji, and DKB to create the world's largest bank holding company—and early November 1999 saw the following developments:

- Sumitomo Bank and Sakura Bank announced plans to merge on April 1, 2002. This combination will create Japan's—and the world's—second largest bank. The combined assets of the two banks are nearly $825 billion (¥99 trillion). Together they account for about 21 percent of lending in the Japanese market, against some 27.3 percent share of IBJ, DKB, and Fuji Bank (Table 3.5). The decision to merge the banks—rather than to form a combination under a holding company—will require a drastic consolidation of operations over a short time. Combined workforce cuts of 30 percent (9,300 positions) are planned by March 2000. This can also be seen as an acceleration and expansion of the individual restructuring plans of the two banks submitted to the Financial Restructuring Agency in March 1999, which called for combined staff reductions of 5,500 positions by March 2003. Faster and deeper—these words describe the pace and scope of restructuring in the banking sector.
- What excited much interest and speculation about this prospective merger, apart from its gargantuan scale, was that it will be between the financial cores of two *keiretsu* groups, Sumitomo and Mitsui. Such a cross-*keiretsu* merger would have struck most Japanese, including the

experts, as unthinkable only years ago. The announcement stunned the market, more for its implications for the nonfinancial companies of the groups than for the financial companies. The merger of their main banks will create pressures for consolidation of the nonfinancial companies. We touched on *keiretsu* relationships in Chapter Nine above. Our view remains that *keiretsu* relationships—even within a new hybrid *keiretsu*—will remain an elemental feature of business in Japan in the years ahead.

- On September 13, the Bank of Tokyo-Mitsubishi finally announced plans for its restructuring. According to a news release, all BOTM's domestic and overseas businesses will be affected. Domestically, the bank will overhaul its branch network by converting 135 of its over 300 branches to retail-only branches. Corporate business will be centralized in about 140 branches, of which twenty will offer specialized services and facilities such as a funding desk. Seventy to eighty branches will set up personal financial advisory service desks manned by specialists in asset management, financial planning, and mortgage lending. On the day of the announcement, the bank launched new telephone banking and internet banking services. In asset management, the number of branches selling mutual funds are to be increased from 48 to 180 over the following two years. Spending on new systems and technology in the four years through fiscal year 2002 is to reach $3.3 to $3.8 billion (¥400 to 450 billion), about a 30 percent increase over previous levels. The bank announced financial targets for the fiscal year 2002 of ¥340 billion in net income and 11 percent or higher return on equity.
- In the securities sector, Japan's reviving stock market lifted the interim profit performance of all major securities companies. For the first half of FY99 (six-month period ended September 31), operating revenue of Nomura Securities increased 46.8 percent to $2.24 billion (¥268.7 billion), yielding an after-tax profit of $612 million (¥73.2 billion). Nikko Securities saw half year operating profit increase 39.5 percent to $1.15 billion (¥138 billion) and net profit rise to $490 million (¥$58.6 billion).
- This was, however, the last period of fixed commissions. Full deregulation of brokerage commissions—the main revenue source of all Japan's brokers—arrived on schedule on October 1. The new world of free competition has finally arrived.
- The expected consolidation in the insurance industry, driven by the end of mandated premium rates, was heralded by the announcement on October 16 that three major nonlife companies—Mitsui Marine and Fire, Nippon Fire and Marine, and Koa Fire and Marine—will form a joint

holding company by April 2002. The combination will create Japan's biggest casualty and property insurance group, with assets of $50.8 billion (¥6.1 trillion), compared with $45 billion (¥5.4 trillion) for the current nonlife leader, Tokio Marine and Fire. The aim of the alliance is to allow the three firms to achieve operational economies of scale and to diversify sources of earnings.   Other combinations, in which the restructuring strategies of key shareholder banks will greatly influence outcomes, are sure to follow.

Within the recovery and restructuring of the Japanese financial services sector, foreign (particularly American) firms continued to move decisively to seize opportunities.

- Citigroup Inc. reportedly agreed to pay as much as $382 million to acquire 100 percent of Diners Club of Japan Inc. The deal was expected to be completed in November 1999. Citigroup acquired the 60 percent of ownership in Diners Japan held by Fuji Bank group, as well as 40 percent held by JTB. The acquisition will allow Citigroup to combine Diners Japan's 840,000 cardholders, with Citibank Japan's existing card customer base. The acquisition of Diners Club of Japan places Citigroup in close competition with American Express in the premier credit card market segment. The two companies begin with roughly equal numbers of customers. The rivalry between these marketing heavyweights will be fascinating to watch.
- Citigroup also announced in early November that it had purchased a 19 percent stake in the new internet brokerage firm of Nikko Securities, Nikko Beans. The price of the acquisition for Citigroup, which becomes the second largest shareholder, was some $18 million. This acquisition extends Citigroup's expanding relationships with Nikko Securities, the most important of which is the joint venture Nikko Salomon Smith Barney.
- It was announced by the Japan Life Insurance Association that a buyer for Aoba Life Insurance had been found. It is France's Artemis SA. The price is reportedly $208 million (¥25 billion).
- The Japan Life Insurance Association and government-appointed administrators are likely to agree with GE Capital Edison Life Insurance Co. on take-over by GE Capital Edison of the policies of failed Toho Mutual Life.
- The fate of Long Term Credit Bank was decided. It will be purchased by a foreign investor group led by Ripplewood Holdings LLC of the United States. The Ripplewood group will inject $1 billion (¥120 billion) to

revive the bank. Investors are reported to include Citigroup, GE Capital, and ABN Amro Bank. The new chief executive will be Masamoto Yashiro, formerly head of Citibank's operations in Japan.

And this is just a partial list. In the months and years ahead, there will be many more announcements of mergers, acquisitions, tie-ups, and, in due course, dissolutions and withdrawals in Japan's rapidly changing marketplace. One certainty is that with its massive capital stock, technological prowess, and newly reformed regulatory structure, the Japanese market will prove to be richly rewarding for many domestic and foreign firms. It is a prospect with important implications for the firms involved, and also for the global financial marketplace, indeed for the global financial system. It is a fitting and exciting start to the new millennium.

References

Books and Articles

1999 Trade White Paper. Tokyo: American Chamber of Commerce in Japan.

"ACCJ Viewpoint: Expanded Market Presence in the Non-Life Third Sector," Insurance Committee Views. Tokyo., October 15, 1998. American Chamber of Commerce in Japan. ACCJ.

Asamoto, Yuichi. 1999. *Za Seiho: Daraku no Kozo*. Toyo Keizai Shinhosha. Tokyo.

Carlili, Lonny E., and Mark C. Tilton, eds. 1998. *Is Japan Really Changing Its Ways?* Washington, D.C.: Brookings Institution Press.

Bank of Japan. *Financial and Economic Statistics Monthly*. various issues.

Daiwa Institute of Research Ltd. March 1999. *Strategy for the Financial Industry*. Daiwa Institute of Research Ltd. Tokyo.

DKB Research Institute, ed. 1998. *Nenkin no Shikumi*. Tokyo: Toyo Keizai Shimposha.

Financial Reconstruction Commission. March 25, 1999. Plans for Fuji Bank, Sumitomo Bank, Dai-Ichi Kangyo Bank, Industrial Bank of Japan, Sanwa Bank. Tokyo.

Furuse, Masatoshi. 1997. *Seimei Hoken Big Bang*. Tokyo: Toyo Keizai Shimposha.

Hall, Maximilian J.B. 1998. *Financial Reform in Japan: Causes and Consequences*. London: Edward Elgar Publishing Limited.

Ishi, H. "The Fiscal Investment and Loan Program and Public Entrerprises," in *Japan's Public Sector*, pp. 82-102.

Kaneko, Hirokazu, ed. 1999. *Seiho Anzendo Ranking*. Tokyo: Daimond K.K.

Koyama, Shozo. 1998. *Securities Market in Japan 1998*. Tokyo: Japan Securities Research Institute.

Imai, Morio. 1997. *Citibank vs. Nihon no Ginko*. Tokyo: Asuka Shinsh.

Ministry of Health and Welfare. 1997. *Health and Welfare White Paper*.

Ministry of Health and Welfare. 1998. "Report of the Study Commission on In-House Pension Fund Management."

Ministry of Health and Welfare, Pension Bureau, eds. 1998. *Nenkin to Zaisei*. Tokyo: Hoken K.K.

Ministry of Health and Welfare, Pension Bureau, eds. 1998. *Nenkin Hakusho: Nijuisseiki no Nenkin o Sentaku suru*. Tokyo: Shakai Hoken Kenkyusho.

Ministry of Finance. 1997. *Fiscal Investment and Loan Program Report.*

Mitaka, Mariko. 1999. "Nihon-Ban 401(k) Donyu o Hikaeru Kigyo Nenkin" (Corporate Pensions and the Introduction of Japan-Style 401[k]). Tokyo: *Sakura Research Institute Report*, Vol. 3, July 1999.

Shibata, Tokue, ed. 1993. *Japan's Public Sector: How the Government is Financed.* Tokyo: University of Tokyo Press.

Shimano, Kiyoshi. 1998. *Kinyu Gyokai Saihen Chizu.* Tokyo: Paru Press.

Suefuji, Takehiro. "Kuredito Kado Nyumon." *The Consumer Credit Monthly*, March 1999, pp. 70-71.

Takehiko, Nishio. 1998. *Numon Gaishikei Shoken Gaisha to Torihiki-suru Ho.* Tokyo: Ashita Kaori Press.

Tokyo Career Development Center (eds.) 1998. *Kigyo Gurupu to Gyokai Chizu.* Tokyo: Takahashi Shoten.

Weekly Toyo Keizai. Articles on GE Capital entry into Japan. July 10, 1999.

Weinberg, Neil. 1999. "Master of the Internet." *Forbes*, July 5.

Wood, Christopher. 1992. *The Bubble Economy.* New York: The Atlantic Monthly Press.

Zaikai Quarterly, ed. 1998. *Gaishikei Kinyu Kikan no Katsuyoho.* Zaikai Kenkyusho. Tokyo.

Periodicals, Newspapers

Asahi Shimbun
The Financial Times
Institutional Investor
Jiji Press
Kinyu Business
Moody's Investors Service
Nihon Keizai Shimbun
The Nikkei Financial Daily (*Nikkei Kinyu Shimbun*)
Weekly Toyo Keizai (*Shukan Toyo Keizai*)
Weekly Economist (*Shukan Economisto*)
The Asian Wall Street Journal
Yomiuri Shimbun

Trade and Industry Association Publications and Releases, Analysts Reports

Altherr, Walter. 1998. "Consumer Finance." *Jardine Fleming Research*, December 22.

Bank of Tokyo-Mitsubishi. News Release. 1999. "Bank of Tokyo-Mitsubishi Announces New Business Strategy." September 13.

Garone, Robert, et al. 1999. "IBJ Creating a Retail Securities Franchise." *Dresdner Kleinwort Benson Research*, April 1.

Gekkan Shohisha Shinyo (*The Consumer Credit Monthly*), various issues.

Japan Bankers Association. 1997. *Ginko Kinyu Nenkan.*

Japan Nonlife Insurance Association. various releases.

Japan Securities Dealers' Association. 1998. Membership Survey. November 18.

Nenkin Joho (*Newsletter on Pensions and Investment*). Tokyo: Japan Credit Rating and Investment Information Center K.K., various issues 1998-1999.

"Nihon no Ginko Joho: Peioffu dei Kieru Ginko." July 30, 1999. Toyko: *Seikatsu to Keizai.*

"Nihon no Ginko Joho: Peioffu dei Kieru Ginko." July 30, 1999. Toyko: *Seikatsu to Keizai*.

Ohara, Yukiko. 1999. "Japan Banks: Limited Effect on Earnings from Restructuring Plans." *Morgan Stanley Dean Witter Japan Investment Research*, March 26.

Perry, Dean, CFA. 1999. "Credit Cards." WestLB Panmure *Japan Equity Research*, March 16.

Report on Investment Trusts (Toshi Shintaku), Tokyo: The Investment Trusts Association. various issues.

Richards, David and David Atkinson. 1999. "Specialty Finance." *Goldman Sachs Investment Research*, December.

Tokyo Stock Exchange. 1998. *Annual Securities Stastistics*.

Toyo Keizai Shimposha, eds. 1999. *Kaisha Shikio* No. 308. 3rd ed. Tokyo: Toyo Keizai Shimposha.

Company Annual Reports

American Express. 1998.
American Express Japan. 1999.
Associates First Capital Corporation. 1998.
Bank of Tokyo-Mitsubishi. 1998.
Fidelity Investments. 1998.
Merrill Lynch & Co., Inc. 1998.
Merrill Lynch Japan Incorporated. 1999.
Merrill Lynch Japan Securities Co. Ltd. 1999.
Orix Corporation. 1998.
Sony Life Insurance. 1998.

Index

About the Author

Stephen M. Harner has lived and worked in Japan and China as banker, consultant, and diplomat for over twenty years. He is president of S.M. Harner & Company, Ltd., a consultancy providing strategic positioning services to financial services companies in the Japanese and Chinese markets (email: smharner@sh163b.sta.net.cn).

From 1975 to 1981 Mr. Harner was a Foreign Service Officer with the U.S. Department of State, serving in Hong Kong, Beijing, Tokyo, and Washington, D.C. He worked for Citibank in Japan for seven years during the 1980s and was chief representative of Merrill Lynch International Bank in Tokyo from 1991 to 1993. He was chief representative of Deutsche Bank in Shanghai in the mid-1990s. In 1999 he helped establish American Express Financial Advisors (Japan) in Tokyo.

Mr. Harner is an authority on business and economics in China, as well as Japan. He is coauthor of *China's New Political Economy, Revised Edition* and translator of *China's New Political Economy: The Giant Awakes,* by S. Yabuki. He earned a Master of Arts degree in international affairs from The Johns Hopkins University Nitze School of Advanced International Studies (SAIS) in 1975. Mr. Harner is fluent in Japanese and Mandarin Chinese, in addition to his native English.